SCREW

SCREW

The Truth About Walpole State Prison By the Guard Who Lived It

Michael McLaughlin
Russell S. Dynda
Warren Jamison

NEW HORIZON PRESS
Far Hills, New Jersey

Library of Congress Catalog Card Number 89-061207

McLaughlin, Michael
Dynda, Russell S.
Jamison, Warren
Screw

ISBN: 0-88282-048-6
New Horizon Press

Acknowledgements

Many people had a part in encouraging my interest in the corrections field. Among these, I owe a great debt of gratitude to my deceased friend and mentor, John A. Gavin. He was an instructor at Northeastern University and is the last correction officer to rise through the ranks to the position of Commissioner of Correction.

The 3-11 shift at Walpole State Prison from 1977 to 1979 supported my election as union local president and were my source of strength during the strained labor/management relations that followed. I want to thank the local's entire membership for their unity and support of majority opinion. And I'd like to acknowledge the majority of inmates who, in their own way, helped shield me from violence directed at me by their peers.

I'd like to thank Chet Curtis for building my confidence during our first news conference, and the Boston Herald for giving us permission to quote them.

To my first wife, Karen Parker, and my parents, Bernie and Rose, thank you for understanding my need to achieve my goals and for not pressuring me to leave Walpole for safer pursuits before that happened.

To my best friend, Ed Morandi, thank you for being there when I needed peace and quiet. And Bob Furtado, thank you for an enduring friendship that survived the wars of Walpole and remains strong to the present day.

I also want to recognize Martha Phillips, Nathan Hagen, and Elliott Stone, who allowed me time off to pursue this project. My thanks to Tom Hopkins for paving the way to my coauthor, Warren Jamison, who found Russ Dynda.

Special thanks to Sebastian Ortega, my stepson, who listened intently to my stories; to Claudia Chuber, my wife, friend and lover, who encouraged and advised me to collaborate and who helped me overcome a very tempting offer; and to my daughter, Camila, whose love has given me the lifetime goal of making her justifiably proud of her father.

Finally I'd like to thank Father Bob Doherty, who provided spiritual guidance, and above all, God, for watching over me all my life.

—Michael McLaughlin

Dedication

To my brother and sister corrections officers for the thankless jobs they perform, and to my wife, Claudia Chuber, without whose encouragement and support this book would still be a dream.

—Michael McLaughlin

To my sister, Marilyn, whose courage in meeting the trials of everyday life rivals any portrayed in these pages.

—Russell S. Dynda

For my wife, Kitty, who never stopped believing.

—Warren Jamison

Disclaimer

This is a true story, told without malice. We believe the public not only has the right to know what really goes on in the prisons that hold half a million Americans today, it has a pressing need to know.

The dialogues are reported to the best of recollection and, while the content is accurate, we can't claim to have quoted every conversation word for word. Time has passed since these many discussions took place. Where possible, we have checked them against documents written at the time.

We have endeavored to render the truth McLaughlin lived through as accurately and vividly as those turbulent years could be put on paper. Yet this is not only Mike McLaughlin's story. Other real people, sometimes dozens or hundreds of them, played roles in many of these events. Telling Mike's story of necessity involved telling part of theirs. Calling attention to actions that appear questionable can't be avoided if this book is to throw light into penology's dark corners.

Except for Mike's family, the other people fall into three groups: officials, guards, and inmates.

There seemed no point in changing the names of public figures. Even had these people been given fictitious names and physical descriptions, they would have been readily identifiable from their positions.

Many of McLaughlin's former comrades among Walpole's guards were contacted to ascertain whether they wanted their real names used. A failure to respond was considered an instruction to use a fictitious name. In every case their wishes have been followed.

Names of inmates in quoted newspaper stories are real. All the other inmates' names were changed on the theory that these individuals already have enough trouble in their lives.

Contents

1 | Busted 000

2 | Rat 000

3 | Death Valley Days 000

4 | Merry Christmas 000

5 | Mike, Get Yourself a Sponsor 000

6 | Meet the Press 000

7 | Pushing on a String 000

8 | McLaughlin, You're Under Arrest 000

9 | Your Goon vs. My Goon 000

10 | Shoot 'im, Steve! 000

11 | Tear The Place Down 000

12 | Just Another Day At The Office 000

13 | Dump The Duke 000

14 | A Perfect Ten 000

15 | A Man Called Peter 000

16 | Back From The Edge 000

Epilogue 000

1 BUSTED: $1 million-a-year prison drug ring

This headline leapt at me off the Boston Herald's front page. It was Sunday morning, August 17, 1986. Before I even read the lead paragraph, I knew it had to be about Walpole. Stark images from my days there flashed before me. The newspaper story began:

> Inmates at Walpole State Prison—including four killers—masterminded a $1 million-a-year drug ring that financed rental cars and apartments and paid salaries to outside accomplices, prosecutors charged yesterday.
>
> "The scheme was smashed by investigators who tapped cell-block pay phones the cons used to set up deals for cocaine and pills," said Norfolk County District Attorney William Delahunt.

Delahunt! Just the mention of the man's name triggered my anger. The picture that accompanied the article almost turned my stomach. It showed Delahunt sitting before a microphone, piously recounting the drug bust's details. In my opinion, he'd helped to foster the very conditions that allowed the drug ring to flourish.

I remember Delahunt as the inmates' advocate. He blamed the guards at Walpole for everything, and launched numerous investigations of our activities. Now he was in the limelight, prosecuting the cons instead of blaming the guards, claiming credit for this bust without a word of apology to the officers he'd tried so often to discredit.

Serious problems are nothing new to Walpole. It has been a maelstrom of violence from the day it opened. Governor Michael Dukakis' administration has, if anything, exacerbated the situation. Walpole has no claim to being a model prison. The drug bust proves that.

Recently I talked with some of my fellow guards who still work there. They told me that the reforms our union won under my leadership had gradually slipped away. Lax policy administered by bureaucratic managers again reigned. The ramifications have remained hidden from the public because the media has been kept in the dark.

No such news blackout existed during my tenure as president of the guards' union. I drove the publicity-shy Department of Corrections crazy by calling frequent news conferences on the steps of the prison's administration building to report on the appalling conditions inside. The D.O.C. had a lot to hide then, and they have a lot to hide now.

> The inmates devised a scheme where they would work from pay phones to use their contacts to distribute drugs within the walls and, at the same time, outside the walls.
>
> Assistant District Attorney Dennis Mahoney said officials are unsure how long the drug ring existed or how much cash the members stowed away before they were caught.

Walpole's inmates are getting more practical. When I worked there they'd use the phone for cute little things like calling my first wife, Karen, to threaten her life or to burn her ears with obscenities. Now they're using the phones to make money. It's called rehabilitation. Clearly our permissiveness is bearing fruit. I only hope we don't choke on it.

Assistant DA Dennis Mahoney says they don't know how long the drug ring operated. But the guards had reported the drug traffic way back in 1978. It could have been stopped then.

In that year I went on public record explaining how the drugs were coming in; I asked for a halt to contact visits; I pleaded for them to give us a drug-sniffing dog; I urged the DA's office to prosecute inmates caught dealing in drugs or committing other violent acts. But nothing was done.

Even after state commissions exonerated the guards of brutality charges, Delahunt would send in his own people to continue his investigations. My claim that inmate violence occurred in direct proportion to the level of drug traffic was never taken seriously. Why should important elected officials listen to a punk kid who was obviously in over his head as guard union president? They had patronage and position to worry about, and many things that wouldn't stand close scrutiny.

> But he (Assistant DA Mahoney) said the type and amount of drugs seized—including an uncut kilogram of cocaine—and the transactions overheard on the phone suggested 'a major distribution network involving thousands of dollars each week.'
>
> Six inmates were accused of running the syndicate, along with seven others outside the walls who were arrested in raids Friday night. Among those charged were convicted killers Robert E. Smith, 36, and Robert S. Wilson, 37, who authorities say worked as partners.
>
> The duo are already serving three life terms for the gruesome 1975 New Year's Eve slayings of a Tewksbury doctor, his wife and teen-age son.

Robert Smith and Robert Wilson—I remember them. Big fish now, they were just tough guys with no connections when they came to Walpole in 1977. Both were placed in the Maximum Security Section.

I saw Smith and Wilson regularly. A couple of times I wrote them up for minor infractions, but mostly they behaved themselves. Eventually management considered them sufficicently rehabilitated to be moved into Minimum Security.

Obviously, Minimum's freedom of movement had allowed them to make contacts and organize a gang of their own. The old gang leaders, Lyle Kramer, Connie Mancuso and others, had been moved out. That must have left a power vacuum for Smith and Wilson to fill.

Why should anyone be surprised that this drug gang within Walpole was being run by killers? The place is crawling with convicted murderers. It was designed to confine the state's most dangerous criminals. The newspaper's account of Smith and Wilson wiping out a doctor and his family is only one of the many blood-curdling tales, some even more gruesome, that you could read if you had access to the records of those incarcerated there. Smith and Wilson are bad news all right, but I've met worse at Walpole. I'd rather confront the two of them together than Peter DiLauro by himself. Vividly do I remember Peter, the ex-longshoreman, ex-boxer, and convicted cop killer, trying to reach me through the bars and tear me limb from limb with his gorilla-like arms.

> Also implicated were John Campbell Jr., 33, serving a life term for the 1980 strangling of another con, Robert Perrotta; Frederick Pidge, 32, doing life for the 1984 slashing murder of a Sudbury man; James E. Connors, 33, serving 40–50 years for armed assault on a dwelling; and Paul Decolargero, 27, of Somerville, serving 10–12 years for cocaine trafficking.
>
> Corrections officials said the six were moved to segregated cells away from the rest of the population at Walpole, known as Cedar Junction, and the lockup at nearby Norfolk Prison.

Wow, there's a revelation—they finally nailed John Campbell for Perrotta's murder! Speaking of gruesome, of the sixteen inmate murders I was exposed to, Perrotta's execution most deserves that description.

The reporter had the date wrong in the article: Perrotta was killed on Thanksgiving Day 1976. I remember the vicious crime as if it were yesterday—because I tried to prevent it.

Two other inmates took part in the killing. We knew who all three were but couldn't get management to move against them. In fact, during the four years I worked at Walpole, I never saw a conviction in any of the inmate murders, and few indictments.

Something doesn't make sense here. Why in hell wasn't Campbell kept in a Block Ten isolation cell after being convicted of killing Perrotta? During my tenure, regulations demanded that any inmate proved dangerous to others be kept there away from the population. Once in Block Ten, Campbell's contact with Smith and Wilson would have been severed. What was this, another management snafu? How did Campbell convince the Superintendent he was sufficiently rehabilitated to have the run of the place?

This brings me to James Connors. For him finally to be implicated in a drug smuggling ring at this late date makes my blood boil. Eight years ago my fellow officers and I knew a girlfriend of his was bringing as many as two hundred Talwin tablets a day into Walpole. We informed then Superintendent Fred Butterworth about the situation and of our intention to bust her.

Butterworth told us that under no circumstances were we to interfere with her. An undercover operation was in progress.

Some undercover operation. If it ever accomplished anything, we guards never knew about it. Month after month this woman continued to smuggle her deadly cargo in unchallenged. And now, after eight long years, they finally nail James Connors. Will the real reason for this incredibly long delay ever come out?

Inmates under the influence of drugs injured dozens of guards during those eight years. Every one of those guards should file suit against the state for criminal negligence. Let's turn up the heat and see what kind of bread we can bake.

> Investigators say most of the drugs were brought into the prison by women friends and relatives of inmates. The visitors hid the drugs in their bodies and delivered them at visits when physical contact was allowed.

On reading this I had to put the paper down and take a brisk walk around the room to cool down. They are finally acknowledging this now? Are they trying to say they just discovered it?

On November 20, 1978 I spoke before a Joint Committee on Human Services and Elderly Affairs at the State Capitol in Boston. Senator Jack H. Backman and Representative David J. Mofenson were cochairmen; five other senators and fourteen representatives made up the rest of the committee. The topic was "Violence in Prisons." My speech on that occasion is in the public record.

The first point I made was: "The single, most serious, threat to safe operation at Walpole is drugs." Further on I stated, "Let me give you a brief account of how most of it gets in. The woman puts the pills into a plastic baggie and secures the end. She then puts the baggie into a balloon and secures the end. She then puts the balloon into her vagina and enters Walpole. When she is safely inside she goes to the ladies room, removes the balloon from her vagina, and either puts it into her pocket or mouth. She then goes back to the visiting room where she passes it to the inmate either by hand or mouth."

No one wanted to hear this, least of all Senator Backman, another inmate sympathizer. He and other committee members attacked me verbally. Spectators booed and jeered me.

Now this old information pops up in Delahunt's investigation as if his brilliant department has made a startling new discovery. I can only guess at the amount of drugs carried into Walpole this way while

Delahunt stubbornly kept pointing his finger at the guards. How much pain and suffering resulted?

> The inmate dealers then sold the drugs to other prisoners, at extremely high prices. The cons were instructed to have money sent to an outside address, usually the seller's girlfriend.
>
> The friend on the outside served as the banker, and once she confirmed the payment, the drugs would be delivered.

I must admit, the inmates have become more sophisticated. During my time there I wasn't aware of any complicated banking transactions. Money or its equivalent changed hands directly. It was either pay up or die, often right on the spot. I knew of one case where an inmate was killed because he owed for three Talwin, pills that cost $5 each. Yes, high finance has finally reached Walpole. Isn't progress wonderful? This is rehabilitation on a grand scale, though not what the public thinks its tax money is buying.

> Mike Maloney, superintendent at the state prison in Walpole, said drug trafficking remains a major problem inside the prison, but said the arrests would put "a serious dent" on pushing inside the walls.

Who is he trying to kid? No way will this bust seriously dent drug trafficking inside his prison—not for very long anyway.

It'll set off a murderous power struggle. The Minimum end of Walpole is crowded with vicious inmates eager to seize the money and power that heading a drug ring brought Smith and Wilson. They won't hesitate to wade through blood to get it.

As long as contact visits continue, drugs will enter Walpole; as long as the inmates have access to pay phones, they'll traffic in drugs on the outside.

Since I left, anti-drug measures have actually slipped backward. Even in isolated Block Ten, where the worst of the worst are locked up, contact visits are allowed. The screen that once separated inmate from visitor has been removed. Will Maloney have it replaced? Will he restrict phone privileges to the outside?

Don't hold your breath while you wait.

Ten years ago they knew how the drugs were getting into the prison. They didn't stop it then; why should we believe they'll stop it now?

The article goes on to report about the raids and arrests on the outside and concludes:

> Delahunt said the ring was uncovered last spring by prison officials who suspected foul play and called in the drug task force.

A companion article by the same reporter, John Birtwell, also caught my eye. This one was headlined:

> INMATE COKE GANG HEADED BY
> MURDERERS, POLICE CHARGE
>
> Two cold-blooded killers who shot a Tewksbury doctor in the head as he pleaded for his life, and a con who castrated and strangled another prisoner are among the inmate gang accused of peddling drugs inside the walls of Walpole State Prison, say officials.
>
> "The six inmates were moved to isolated cells—they were already behind bars—after police cracked a major distribution ring suspected of pushing drugs inside and outside the prison."

I'm sure some of the Herald's readers wondered how this could happen in a maximum security prison. It takes millions of tax dollars to maintain such a facility. Why should the taxpayers continue to pay that huge upkeep? The way things are mishandled, all that money doesn't prevent these animals from reaching out into society at large. Many readers might well be reflecting on the state's decision to strike down capital punishment. Can we really rehabilitate such men once they've fallen to a certain level? How much of their outrageous behavior must we endure before we stop trying?

Unfortunately, most of the information the public gets about the prison system comes from suave politicians like Delahunt, Senator Backman and Governor Dukakis. Yet these people haven't worked among convicts for thousands of hours like I have. Their only exposure to the realities of prison life comes on an occasional guided tour that, you can be sure, is cleverly staged to give whatever impression the inmates or the administration wishes to impart.

How could these politicians begin to grasp the psychological motivations of men facing decades of imprisonment? Most public figures have no feel for the strange prison world where our normal standards of behavior have no meaning. Still, they smugly set policy, ignoring the recommendations of those with firsthand experience and insight.

So what makes me an expert?

I am a degreed penologist who has spent four years working with some of the worst inmates in captivity. When I was recruited by former Massachusetts State Commissioner of Corrections Frank Hall, he and I agreed on a positive program of inmate rehabilitation.

I still believe in that program. It was never implemented properly. Hall undermined the program because he could not accept one basic axiom of human behavior: if you reward bad behavior you will get more bad behavior.

That's what was happening at Walpole then, and I suspect it's still happening now. This is the philosophy that allowed killers like Smith and Wilson to move to a minimum cellblock where they had the freedom to orchestrate new crimes against society.

The Walpole administration feared that if they punished violent activity the perpetrators would act even more violently. They felt it safer to supplicate with privileges and possessions. "Keep the inmates calm at all costs" is their motto. "Promise then they will move on through the system if they control themselves."

The first thing criminals learn is how to spot and exploit weakness among potential victims. They quickly turned the administration's policies around and made their captors prisoners of their own psychology. The inmates in effect said, "If you don't give us what we want, we'll throw a tantrum. Not only might somebody get hurt, but we'll make sure the public hears about it."

The possibility that the public might become aware scares the hell out of the administrators. Since most of them are bureaucrats, their primary motivation is career advancement, not running a prison that provides security to the public and a positive penological experience for the inmates. The administrators therefore concentrate on maintaining a low profile for the prison so it can't embarrass them.

Ultimately, who suffers the consequences of this scheme to enhance public image at the expense of sound corrections practice? You need look no further than the recent drug bust for your answer.

If Walpole's present Superintendent, Mike Maloney, keeps on playing the permissive game, if Corrections Commissioner Fair persists in allowing contact visits in Block Ten, if Governor Dukakis continues to support corrections officials of proven incompetence, drug-driven violence will explode again within the prison. Don't doubt for a moment that it will spill over the walls upon those of us outside.

And don't think the painful lessons being taught at Walpole pertain only to Massachusetts. Permissive prison practices have strong advocates nearly everywhere; a mere shift in geography will not prevent the consequences of those permissive practices. To put it plainly, if you aren't vigilant of those who represent you, predators like Smith and Wilson could reach out into your community too.

Twelve years have passed since I first reported to the prison, a green young officer with idealistic views of penology. I actually looked forward with great eagerness to my first day on the job.

2 Rat

Sixteen murders! Five suicides! Countless guard and inmate injuries! That was Walpole's legacy for the preceding five years only.

The prison confined Massachusetts's most dangerous convicts. In the twenty-one years since its opening, Walpole had earned its reputation as one of the country's most violent prisons.

As I got out of my car, I paused to stare at the spacious complex. Beyond the landscaped parking lot, rectangular buildings in neat rows peered over a lofty circumvallating wall that supported evenly spaced watchtowers.

The view reminded me of a medieval city. Painted a chalky white, the prison stood out against the rural backdrop of green trees on gently rolling hills. I could've appreciated the scene's pictorial qualities had I not suspected the grim reality awaiting me inside.

This was to be my first day on the job at the Massachusetts Correctional Institute in Walpole. While feeling some anxiety, eagerness predominated. After all, I had requested my transfer here. Maybe it wouldn't be easy inside, but the experience should prove invaluable to my future aspirations as a penology professional. A year at Walpole should be enough to qualify me for a management position in the state's Department of Corrections.

I already had Commissioner Hall's ear. Hall had brought me into the Department just over a year before. He'd opposed my transfer to

Walpole at first, but I'd been persuasive. At twenty-six I had all my youthful confidence and exuberance. Challenges turned me on. With two years of solid experience and a degree in penology from Northeastern University behind me, I felt ready to be turned loose, actually looking on this transfer as my first step to the governorship.

Hall finally okayed the move.

Walpole's administration building sat just outside the wall, its rear butted up against the twenty-foot high barrier. I entered the lobby, arranged like a train station with rows of benches in the center. Vending machines and display tables stood against the walls; the tables were covered with craft items—jewelry, leather goods, lamps—made by the inmates and priced for sale.

A glass-enclosed control room manned by two officers occupied the lobby's rear wall. At an open window a big, heavy guy in slacks and sportshirt talked casually with one of the uniformed guards. Seeing no one else, I walked over to them.

"I'm here to see Ralph Bosley," I said.

"You must be Mike McLaughlin," the heavy guy in slacks replied after glancing at my green guard's uniform.

"That's right."

"Bosley's busy right now. My name's Regalado." After we shook hands Regalado said, "Come with me."

His sloppy appearance struck me as unusual. Granted, his physique would make it hard to be a snappy dresser, but at least he could have worn a dress shirt, tie and pressed trousers.

Regalado sauntered into an office a few feet down a hall, sat behind the desk, and motioned me to a chair opposite. He pulled out a file, plopped it on the desk, and studied it.

"I see you live in Arlington. Married four years to Karen. No children. Bachelor's degree in Penology, working on your Master's in Public Administration. Middlesex County House of Correction from March to December of 1974, Training Academy January '75, then assigned to the Security Management Team—"

Regalado looked at me. "That's the special new group Commissioner Hall put together, isn't it?"

"That's right."

"I hear it's only for hotshots." He gave me a smirk. "What happened, couldn't you cut it?"

I decided to overlook his crack. "It didn't go like I expected. Hall painted the job as investigation work. Once trained we'd be shifted from one facility to another to troubleshoot difficult problems.

"But after my academy training they sent me to Shattuck State Hospital, theoretically to take charge of security. In reality I performed the duties of an ordinary security guard—I might as well have been a watchman somewhere.

"I'm a corrections professional, so, after a year, I asked Hall for a transfer."

"To Walpole?"

"Why not? I want to make a career in corrections. I figure this is the best experience I can get."

To my surprise, Regalado laughed loudly. "You got any idea what's going on inside?"

"I think so. Besides what I've read, I've talked to a lot of Walpole guards who brought inmates to Shattuck for treatment. I know it's no picnic."

"You got that right." He thumbed through a few more papers in the file. "How'd you come to know Hall?"

"Met him at a college seminar he spoke at. We talked afterwards and he liked my ideas. I was really lucky; he offered me a job on the spot."

Doubt flickered in Regalado's eyes. "Yeah, you were lucky all right, him taking a liking to you that fast."

After listening to Regalado rattle off all those facts about my background, the poor impression created in my mind by his sloppy appearance shifted. Walpole's administration had to be on the ball after all, I decided. They had done their homework and knew all about me. That's the way it should be, I thought. Before working in an institution like this, a new employee should be thoroughly investigated.

At this point another man, this one wearing a coat and tie, appeared in the doorway. "You McLaughlin, by any chance?"

"That's right."

"I'm Ralph Bosley. What're you doing in here with him?"

"I was told you weren't available. Mr. Regalado was orienting me, I guess." I looked to Regalado to explain but he remained silent, his face suddenly plastered with a cherubic expression that told me I'd been had.

For a moment Bosley seemed unable to do anything but shake his head disapprovingly. Then he gestured for me to follow him.

"Johnny," he said to Regalado, "Stay away from the help."

Regalado, responding with a gesture I would see often at Walpole, raised his hands above his shoulders as if someone had the drop on him.

"Just trying to be of service, Mr. Bosley."

As we walked away, Bosley said, "Keep away from that guy unless you have prison business with him."

"Who is he?"

"That's Johnny Regalado! He's doing life for murder. He's also Raymond Patriarca's number three man. You've heard of Patriarca?"

"Yeah, he's the kingpin of New England crime. What's Regalado doing trotting around out here? Shouldn't he be in a cell?"

"He runs the Avocation Department, so he's responsible for selling the stuff in the lobby to visitors. Johnny's all right. He cooperates, stays out of trouble. Just keep away from him."

"How'd he get my personnel file?"

"He doesn't have your personnel file. I do."

"He's got a file. How did he get all that information about me?"

Bosley shrugged. "Who knows?"

That ended the conversation about Regalado. Later I learned that Johnny was known as "the maitre d' of Walpole." He owned a number of restaurants in the Walpole area. Word had it that Johnny fed the administration well for allowing him the run of the place. No one was afraid he'd try to escape. Why should he put himself through the hassle when he could run his lucrative businesses from his comfortable quarters at Walpole?

Generally Johnny and I would get along well. He only threatened to have me killed once.

After we got through the new-employee paperwork, Bosley had a guard give me a quick tour of the prison.

The usual route into Walpole is through the visitor's trap, a long, narrow room with electronically controlled sliding steel doors at each end. Only one of those doors can open at a time. From directly overhead a tower guard peers through an opening in the ceiling. The dimly lighted, cheerless room contains a metal detector and space for body searches.

The trap led us through the wall into the prison yard. We crossed "no man's land," a wide strip of blacktop along the wall. Well-kept lawns and landscaping covered the rest of the space between buildings. As we walked along a sidewalk toward the inner complex, I had to admit the place exuded a little charm.

We entered another lobby, this one just off the minimum security visiting room. At the lobby's far end stood another trap barring entry to the prison's living areas. Once through this inner trap I found myself standing just outside Inner Control, the prison's nerve center.

This secure room, enclosed by bulletproof glass, visually commands the prison's entire main corridor that extends in both directions. Only officers assigned to Inner Control are allowed inside. Extra keys, helmets, mace, and occasionally shotguns are kept here.

The main corridor runs nearly four hundred feet in a straight line. It provides the main access to every cellblock and support facility. At strategic points along the corridor, grilles of heavy bars extend wall to wall and floor to ceiling. Wide gates through these grilles can be swung shut to seal off sections of the corridor. Even with their gates closed, the grilles afford good vision, allowing one to see from one end of the corridor to the other. Just as important, they pose no obstruction to the telltale sounds of trouble.

All the cellblocks are set at right angles to the corridor. From the yard they look like separate buildings, from the inside like residential wings of a hotel. Only blocks Nine and Ten are two-tiered; all others have three levels.

Walpole is organized into two divisions: Maximum and Minimum Security. Cellblocks for each division are located at opposite ends of the main corridor, with the mess hall, auditorium, counseling rooms, law library, hospital and other service facilities in between. In theory at least, this arrangement separates the more outwardly perverse inmates from those trying to work their way through the system.

Blocks Nine and Ten, located at opposite ends of the corridor, house inmates posing extreme security problems. Nine, the Protective Custody Block, holds prisoners judged to be in mortal danger from other inmates; Ten, also known as the Departmental Segregation Unit (DSU), confines men who have shown themselves to be extra dangerous by attacking guards or other inmates. Ten is an alien world where the normal standards of human behavior have lost all meaning.

The Minimum Security Section has three cellblocks. Each cellblock houses seventy-two inmates in twelve cells on either side of three tiers. All these cells have a sink, toilet, window and cot. Since only a small peephole in their solid steel doors gives a view inside, these cells provide much greater privacy than the open bars used in Maximum.

The seven cellblocks in Maximum each hold forty-five inmates in three tiers of fifteen cells facing a solid wall. No windows to the outside here. Open bars instead of a solid door rob these cells of any privacy at all.

Access to the corridor from all cellblocks is controlled by grilled gates. Just inside these gates are the desks from which officers monitor activity in the blocks. Normal procedure calls for two officers to each block in Minimum; one officer to each block in Maximum.

Block A-6 held inmates who had applied for Protective Custody status but, in management's opinion, faced less danger than the prisoners trying to stay alive in Block Nine. While the supervision in A-6 was as close as in B-9, the physical layout could not offer as much security.

One last distinct feature of the Max-end is its gallery. This network of narrow passageways is on the same level as the third tier of cells but runs along the walls opposite the cells. From these vantage points, officers can look into all of Maximum's cells and observe everything going on. The gallery holds the panels controlling the individual cell doors. Unless a gallery officer turns the proper switch, a cell door can't be opened.

The next day I reported for work on the 3–11 shift. I soon learned the officers called it the action shift because most of the violence took place between 3 and 11 p.m.

Standing in the outer lobby during roll call I felt charged, eager to make a good first impression. The other officers seemed cool toward me but I didn't let that bother me.

Instead I focused my attention on Shift Commander Roger Lahoud. In his forties then, the cigar-puffing Lahoud stood about 5′ 10″ and looked in top shape. His uniform had been meticulously attended to: trousers with knife-edge seams, his badge and bars freshly polished, his boots so shiny I could see reflections in them. As he assigned work stations he spoke in soft but authoritative tones, his formal manner occasionally tinged with sarcasm.

Lahoud assigned a senior corrections officer named Jerry to orient me that first evening. As Jerry led me toward the Max-end, he said, "I hear you just transferred in from the Security Management Team."

I smiled. "Word sure gets around fast."

"Yeah, ain't it the truth." He stopped walking and gave me an intense look. "Any experience you had elsewhere isn't worth much here. This place is nothing like Norfolk or Concord. The worst of the worst are here, making Walpole a little Vietnam. There's danger all around you all the time. No matter whether they're classified Max or Minimum, these guys are dangerous."

"There must be some difference between Maximum and Minimum inmates."

"Sure there is. The guys in Minimum are cuter about covering the crap they pull. That makes them more treacherous, especially with their greater freedom of movement."

I grunted in disbelief.

Jerry said, "More murders are committed in Minimum's A-2 Block than anywhere else. We call it Death Valley."

"Then what's the point of dividing inmates into two sections?"

"The theory is that the guys who behave should get more privileges. The way it works out is that the clever guys—those who can break rules without getting caught—get into Minimum. The guys who stay in Max are the hard cases who're more concerned with keeping their tough-guy image than with gaining a few privileges. But don't ever forget they're all killers, rapists, bank robbers, what have you."

"Okay," I said tentatively.

Jerry went on, "Most of them act cooperative, but they wouldn't hesitate to stick a shank in you for the slightest reason—or just for the hell of it. Don't ever forget that."

"I won't. But, believe it or not, I'm still looking forward to working with them. They're the type I came here to learn about."

Jerry cocked an eye at me. "I hope you don't have to learn the hard way."

We stopped outside the first pair of Max cellblocks, Blocks One and Five. As always at the Max-end, the cellblock gates were locked. I glanced into Block One and saw the officer walking the second tier making his count. The inmates were locked in their cells.

"We make two counts," Jerry explained, "One when the shift begins and another at 10 o'clock, right before we get off. Except during the counts, Max-inmates are free to roam around inside the cellblock. So the officer stays down here at his desk. You don't want to be wandering around the tiers with the inmates free."

I noticed that towels and blankets draped over the bars of many cells made it impossible to see into them from the first level.

"At the academy they told us we're supposed to walk the tiers and observe the inmates."

Jerry looked at me like I was simpleminded. "Did they also tell you at the academy that most of these guys are armed? Shanks, pipes—we've even found homemade bombs in this place. You're armed with a pencil and a notebook."

"But how do you know what they're doing up there if you don't check on them?"

Jerry snorted. "They can stab you, or beat you over the head. Your only recourse is to write a Disciplinary Report that might get them Isolation Time or, at worst, sent to Block Ten."

"Doesn't that deter them?"

Jerry gave me a derisive grin. "Not much. They know they can probably beat the rap at the D-Board hearing."

I began to see Jerry's point. "How can they remain armed? Don't you shake the place down for weapons?"

"Sure, and we always collect all kinds of shit. Big deal—they just make 'em again. It's a fact of life here. That's why you stay off the tiers and near the door so you can get out if there's trouble."

I wasn't convinced. How could an officer do his job if he refused to confront the inmates? I had no intention of letting Jerry frighten me.

"How do I signal if there's trouble?"

"You get to the cellblock door, unlock it, step out into the corridor, and slam the door hard three times. Then you lock it again," Jerry said. "The noise will carry from one end of the corridor to the other and officers will respond."

I was incredulous. "That's it? No alarm button or anything?"

"I know it seems crazy. But everybody knows what three slams mean. Whenever you hear those slams, drop everything and run like hell to help whoever's in trouble."

"But what if you're in trouble and can't get to the door to give the signal?"

"Yell like a fiend. You gotta yell loud to get the attention of the officers in the corridor. That's why I tell you to stay near your desk by the door."

Jerry gave me a hard look. "Don't even go out on the flats." He meant the cement floor of the block outside the cells. "And when you're making your counts or moving around for any reason, stay under the tier overhead so nobody can drop shit on you. These bastards smuggle chunks of iron in from the metal shop so they can play 'bombs away' on your head."

Jerry made Walpole sound like the Colosseum when the Romans turned the lions loose. Already I was beginning to sense that many of the guards here weren't as tough as they'd made themselves out to be when I'd met them at Shattuck. It dawned on me that on the outside, with two officers controlling one inmate, looking tough came easy.

As we moved on, Jerry asked, "You met the brass yet? Superintendent Butterworth and his assistants, Larker, Tinker and McCoy?"

"Not yet."

"Fred Butterworth is an old screw," Jerry told me. "Worked his way up through the ranks. Fred had Larker's job before he took over the top spot."

Up from the ranks! Even before meeting Fred Butterworth I had respect for him.

"Now Larker," Jerry continued, "is a guy with exaggerated ideas about his abilities. He's had a lot of experience but he likes to throw his weight around too much. Tinker's just an old biddy. Poor guy's so high-strung he'll have a heart attack on the job one of these days. He makes a lot of noise but he doesn't have the guts to make a decision. McCoy's just a typical bureaucrat."

"You don't sound too impressed with them."

"Why should I be? They don't give a shit about the officers. When we get stabbed or beat up they take the inmates' side. You'd think Butterworth would be with us, but he's strictly in management's pocket now. Got too much at stake to back us." Jerry looked away and mused, "If only the union had more clout—"

I had tower assignments twice during my first three days. Easy duty. You sat up there with a radio going and watched the yard to make sure nothing unusual happened. With most inmates confined to their living areas during much of the 3–11 shift, the chances of something happening dropped considerably. Someone would bring you dinner, afterwards you'd just sit there trying to stay awake.

It took seniority to get a permanent tower assignment. Relief tower assignments usually went to new guys like me to give us a little more experience. Everyone wanted tower postings to escape from the mayhem inside. That is, everyone but me. I found tower duty crushingly boring. I resented it because it kept me from doing what I wanted most—to work with the inmates and become familiar with how they lived and moved.

When I didn't work a tower, I helped other officers make formal counts, did strip searches of inmates returning from visits, ran messages in the corridor, worked in the visiting room and, to my outrage, swept cellblocks. It flabbergasted me to learn that corrections officers were required to clean the cellblocks as part of their normal duties.

Not only did I find the task degrading (I saw it as being a maid to a bunch of bastards) but the inmates would subject you to scathing ridicule, and many of them tossed debris on the floor right after you passed by with the broom.

On my fifth day Lahoud assigned me to strip searches outside Inner Control. I'd wait for the click telling me the trap's inner door had been unlocked. Then I'd open the door and have the inmate strip down. This too was a degrading job: checking inmates' clothes for contraband. Often I'd find underwear still soaked with semen and a penis still oozing the last remnants of what must have been a brief and awkward ecstasy somehow contrived during the visit. However, many officers did like this duty because it kept them out of the blocks.

Once I had determined the inmate wasn't concealing contraband, I'd allow him to pass into the corridor. This routine went on without incident for a couple of hours.

I had just opened the door for perhaps the tenth time when I heard a loud metallic noise in the corridor. Not yet attuned to abnormal sounds in the prison, I glanced over at Inner Control and saw an officer waving his arms and pointing toward the Max-end. It still didn't register.

Then several officers raced past control, running from Minimum to Maximum. Officers began evacuating the control room, heading in the same direction. I knew then that the sound had been a door slam, and I bolted after the other officers. My heart was racing as fast as my legs. I recall thinking, I'm running into danger but I won't know what to do when I get there.

Trouble had exploded in Block Four, near the far end of the corridor. As I approached on the run I heard yelling and screaming. Sharp reports like firecrackers exploded. Three figures walked slowly toward me, two officers supporting another between them. The man in the middle dragged his feet, barely able to walk even with assistance. He was holding a bloody cloth to his neck.

The nearly thirty officers were gathered by Block Four's gate, grumbling angrily.

"What happened," I asked one of them.

"One of the fuckers stabbed an officer. Now they're busting their toilets and sinks and throwing porcelain."

The sharp reports of shattering sinks and toilets continued to echo out into the corridor along with the splintering sounds of porcelain striking concrete. Large white fragments sailed through the barred opening. Dangerous projectiles. Stopping one would be like getting hit by a heavy chunk of sharp glass.

The inmates were yelling things like, "I hope that son of a bitch we stabbed dies," and "We'll stick the rest of you motherfuckers."

Shift Commander Lahoud took charge, supported by Supervisor O'Rourke and Senior Officer Grove. They ordered several officers to Inner Control for helmets, night sticks, gas and two shotguns.

Spotting me in the group, Grove handed me a set of keys, singling out one. "Post yourself by the security grille near Block One. If anything happens we can't handle, seal the corridor. Stay on the other side of the grille and secure the gate."

I was disappointed, sensing that they didn't trust me enough to let me take part in the action. Nevertheless, I obeyed without protest. While waiting nervously at the grille gate, I practiced inserting the key in the lock, making sure I could perform that simple but important task quickly. If I failed to secure the Maximum end and the inmates overpowered us, we could lose the whole prison. My post was the gateway to the entire corridor.

Moments later officers in riot gear ran past and formed outside of Block Four. When two senior officers arrived carrying shotguns, Lahoud ordered a block assault. The pandemonium intensified and stayed at fever pitch while the mutinous inmates were dragged out of the block one by one. As they were dragged or carried they could only kick, spit and scream, which they did every inch of the way down the three hundred feet of corridor to Block Ten.

Even though less than ten inmates took part in the uprising, it still took a couple of hours to finish the transfer and restore order. If it had to be done forcibly, regulations limited us to moving only one inmate at a time through the corridor.

I felt relieved to see the riot put down without hearing shotgun blasts or smelling tear gas. At first glance the situation had seemed tense enough to require those measures. Later I learned that such disturbances had become almost routine to the veteran guards. Having experienced much tougher situations, they could put down most mini-riots without gas or firearms.

That evening the privilege of making the 10 p.m. count in Block Four fell to me. Only dim light filtered in, so I had to use a flashlight to see into many of the cells. Even with all the inmates locked in, I felt terrified knowing that an officer had been stabbed here only a few hours before. At one point I heard a noise behind me and terror buckled my legs. I had to grab the railing to maintain my balance.

The stabbing had shaken me so deeply that I'd lost the confidence it would take to face down someone who posed a physical threat. This sudden feeling of insecurity was totally new to me. My aggressive nature had led me into many fights in the past. I'd taken my share of beatings, but I'd never been terrorized, and I'd never backed down. But I'd never had to face such extreme circumstances.

Holding onto the railing on that dim cellblock tier, I realized that working at Walpole could not be compared to street confrontations. There the fights would end and you'd go home and forget them. At Walpole I would be in close contact with the same men day after day. Any who wanted to attack would have frequent opportunity. Revenge could be plotted over days, weeks—even months! At that moment it sank in that I'd be faced with potentially deadly violence eight hours of every work day at Walpole.

I recognized then that to survive, both physically and mentally, I must put myself into a special frame of mind, and maintain that heightened awareness every moment inside the walls. I must operate like a soldier in combat who knows that at any second someone might try to take his life.

I could accept this grim outlook only because I figured on being at Walpole just a short time. I could now see why Jerry had called the place "little Vietnam."

By the next afternoon I had pulled myself back together and had committed myself to facing my fear. During roll call Lahoud asked for volunteers to bid into Block Four on a permanent basis. The officer who had been stabbed there would recover, but he would need several weeks to recuperate.

Lahoud's request met with a silence that surprised me. After he dismissed us I approached him.

"Mr. Lahoud, I'd like to bid on Block Four. I know I'm new here, but I've got a couple of years' experience elsewhere and some good training behind me. I think I could do a good job in Four."

A puzzled frown appeared on Lahoud's face. He gave me a long look before putting his hands on his hips.

"You're right, Officer McLaughlin, you are new. That's why you'll work where I tell you to work. Understand? Now report to your tower."

He'd done it to me again. Another goddamn tower assignment.

I didn't let Lahoud's refusal discourage me and kept on volunteering for the toughest assignments. On occasion I'd get one, but usually Lahoud assigned me to something else.

One of my most stressful assignments turned out to be my first experience working the main visiting room. With three weeks' experience behind me I was beginning to feel some confidence. Working the visiting room looked like a breeze. It wasn't a block assignment but it sure beat sitting in a tower.

Assigned with me was another new officer, Dave, who had come to Walpole only a month before I had. Procedure had us logging the visitors in and out, enforcing the visiting rules, and watching for the passing of contraband. Even though visitors were searched before entering the prison, many things—drugs in particular—always seemed to slip through.

Regulations allowed inmates to see their visitors outside on the lawn and, on nice days, this was preferable to the hard wooden benches inside. I didn't realize just how preferable until about an hour after my shift started.

I watched three couples stroll outside. They got cozy but nothing in the regulations forbade that. When the couples sat down and started necking I got self-conscious and turned away.

After a time I looked out to check on them and my lower jaw dropped. All three couples had stretched out, the man supine, the woman sprawled on top rocking back and forth in an age-old rhythm. Dresses covering the major point of contact provided the only concession to modesty; the guys were pawing their partners' upper bodies and emitting groans of sexual delight.

I couldn't believe my eyes. Not only were they in full view of the visiting room, but anyone going to or from the administration building had to pass right by.

The regulations were silent on the matter but, even so, I knew this couldn't be acceptable behavior. But how was I to handle it? No one had briefed me about something like this. Why should they? This was something out of the ordinary, wasn't it? Yet this being Walpole, I couldn't be sure. I finally decided to let the couples finish and then tell them not to do it anymore.

Only one thing wrong with that strategy: they weren't finishing. They just kept going and going. And going.

Then the phone rang, interrupting my mental search for a dignified way out of this mess. I answered the phone and found myself talking to one of the tower guards.

"McLaughlin, can't you see what's going on in the yard?"

"Er, yeah."

"Well you better see it's stopped or I'm reporting it to the control room."

"Okay." I sighed heavily. I had no choice now; I had to confront the couples. Taking a deep breath, I hitched up my pants and walked outside, desperately wanting to avoid embarrassing anyone—myself included. I walked up to the nearest couple and spoke in a quiet, hesitating voice.

"Look you're going to have to be more discreet."

They paused, and glanced up at me. "Oh, yeah. Thanks, officer."

I made the same overture to the second couple and got a similar reply. When I got to the third couple, I even got a little cute. I bent down and picked a few dandelions I found poking out of the grass before again repeating my "order." This couple also politely voiced their understanding.

I straightened up, squared my shoulders, and marched back to the visiting room, proud that I had dealt with a difficult situation.

Reaching the door I turned back to give them one more glance. My stomach sank. They hadn't stopped! The three women were still sittin' and rockin' as if I'd said nothing.

I went inside and pointed the problem out to my fellow officer.

"All right, Mike," Dave said. "You take the desk. I'll handle this."

"You will? Great. I want to see how this is done."

I figured I was there to learn. Obviously I hadn't applied the right technique. Even though Dave was new too, maybe he could teach me something.

Dave walked outside, found an inmate who wasn't enjoying a woman's favors, and spoke to the man. This inmate, in turn, walked out on the lawn and said something to each couple. Then he returned to Dave, nodded his head and went on his way. Dave came back inside.

"Okay, Mike, you can go back out there. I handled it."

I said to myself, By having another inmate talk to them he handled it? Wow, there are subtleties I'm not aware of around here.

But when I walked back outside I found the three couples as before. They hadn't stopped at all!

Now I started to do a slow burn. I sat down on the stairs to think this thing out. Obviously Dave was useless. At what point should I get tough with these people? I knew what being deprived of sex could mean to a man. But this—out in the open—it had to be stopped. Somebody with experience should come out here and show me how to do it.

Just then I heard the faint ring of a phone in the control room. A moment later the trap door opened and out stomped Lahoud, puffing on his ever-present cigar like a locomotive going up a steep grade.

He took one look at me and I knew he was pissed. I thought that, in his next breath, he'd tell me to leave the institution, that I didn't have what it takes, that I was through.

Instead he didn't say a word. He took another quick look at the couples on the lawn, gave me one more withering stare, and then walked back inside.

There went the Shift Commander, the guy I'd been trying my damnedest to impress. I figured I'd just shown him I was incapable of doing my job.

I looked at those couples and started getting really angry. "An inmate's feelings are not worth losing my job over, goddamn it!" I muttered aloud.

I got up, walked over to the first couple, and in a firm, sharp voice said, "If you don't stop what you're doing this instant, I'll terminate this visit!"

Suddenly everything changed. She got off him and together they headed for the visiting room. The other two couples heard, but they all waited for me to give them a direct order before stopping. Then they followed the first couple. Within seconds the lawn was empty.

I knew then that I'd never again allow embarrassment to affect me when faced with similar situations. If inmates weren't embarrassed to screw in public, why should I feel embarrassed to make them stop?

Time and again the inmates tested my mettle in this area. Many of them had totally abandoned normal sexual mores in the attempt to satisfy their appetites. More than once I observed mothers having sex with their sons, or sisters masturbating their brothers. I also knew of situations where a sister paid off her brother's debts by signing up for a visit with the creditor and sexually servicing him. When we detected this kind of thing we'd stop it. But as long as contact visits were allowed, inmates would find ways to turn them into sexual encounters.

When the shift ended and we turned in our paperwork to the control room, Lahoud was waiting. He called me inside, the only time I was allowed into the control room during my first year. Lahoud's supervisor, the assistant deputy, was standing there too, along with three other senior officers. All waited to see how Lahoud would deal with me.

Lahoud took this time. He surveyed me closely, his arms folded, his cigar spuming. When he finally spoke his tone was matter of fact.

"Officer McLaughlin, tell me something. How can you with a Bachelor's degree in Penology, almost a Master's degree, and three years of correction experience, allow six people to fuck on our front lawn? Would you explain that to me please?"

My heart sank, and for a moment my mind groped for excuses. At last I gulped and said, "Mr. Lahoud, you're absolutely right. You can be sure it will *never* happen again."

Before another word could be spoken, I turned and left, determined never to back down from another inmate situation.

I had come to Walpole with a few specific ideas of my own on how to deal with inmates. Some of these ideas came from the classroom, some from my experiences at Middlesex and Shattuck. My most important insights, however, had been pounded into me during the lock-up simulation part of my Academy training.

In this exercise a group of us guard-trainees were taken to a jail and treated like inmates for about forty hours. They subjected us to extreme harassment so we'd gain a quick understanding of how men's perspectives could shift when thrown behind bars.

It worked, certainly on me. Within a few hours I became so rebellious and abusive that the officers described me as "the toughest inmate they'd ever had to deal with in that exercise."

While I learned things about myself, I learned even more about the emotional stress facing those behind bars. In that short period I drew three conclusions about dealing with inmates: first, always tell them the truth; second, keep your word when you promise something they want or threaten to punish; third, treat all inmates equally.

In the lockup exercise I experienced the frustration of having those rules broken. I felt the rage that results, saw it overwhelm my self-control, and went through the frightening, but fortunately temporary, personality change it caused. All this happened to me after only forty hours—I could only guess at the distress, the rage, the personality change that would afflict a man who, after being confined for forty days—or forty weeks—still faced years of imprisonment.

Another lesson I learned is that dignity enhances your authority. I determined immediately to avoid using the foul language prevalent among inmates and guards. Only in certain situations did it serve a purpose. Holding foul language to a minimum would improve my image and make me appear less threatening. Anytime you make an inmate feel threatened and back him into a corner, even verbally, you ask to be attacked. I reasoned that speaking softly and carrying a big notebook would be more effective than an aggressive way of talking.

From the beginning I'd seen these principles violated at Walpole. Had the inmates shown reasonable deportment, I might have reevaluated my ideas, figuring I lacked experience. But the fiasco on the lawn outside the visiting room fortified my views and further convinced me to apply my own brand of psychology.

My attitude didn't sit well with the other officers. I asked many questions of them, often in a pointed, accusative way, as if I suspected someone wasn't doing his job properly. I sensed that they didn't like this but I still pressed them defiantly. I didn't realize how deeply I was mistrusted until Lahoud pulled me aside one evening after the 10 o'clock count.

"Officer McLaughlin, I haven't quite figured you out. Everybody knows you're friends with Hall. Everybody knows you were on the Security Management Team. It's everyone's impression that you're a rat for the administration. Frankly I don't care if you are or not because I don't think you can hurt me. But if you are a rat, I suggest you be careful in here. And if you're not, I'd suggest that you stop asking so many questions."

This came as a blow: branded a rat—and by everyone!

"But, Mr. Lahoud, asking questions is how I learn."

Over time I learned that Lahoud had a gift for sizing up men. I felt that he believed me.

"If that's your purpose," he responded, "remember that the knowledge will come in time. Don't be so impatient to grasp everything right away. Knowledge comes from the experience of working with inmates over a period of months. Keep in mind that you have to depend on your fellow officers. Don't turn them against you."

I saw his point. After that I cut down on the questions, and those I did ask, I phrased diplomatically. Soon I found a number of the officers warming to me. I feel sure that Lahoud had something to do with that.

3 Death Valley Days

Slowly Lahoud increased the frequency of my block assignments. Through those first months I remained a relief officer, working a block only when its regular officer was sick or had a day off. No matter how volatile the block might be, I relished these opportunities. I'd stand at roll call listening to Lahoud recap happenings on the 7–3 shift that might affect us. Lahoud pulled no punches. On occasion he stated that an officer working a certain block might be stabbed that evening.

The other relief officers would fidget nervously, worrying that they'd be assigned to potential trouble spots. I shared some of their anxiety but remained determined to quickly establish a reputation for competency. After I heard my name called, assigning me to one of these tense areas, I'd smile with pride all the way to my post. Not only had I been given the opportunity to work with inmates, but Lahoud had acknowledged me before my peers. The other officers would look at me strangely, as if they thought me crazy. How could I walk into a lion's den with a smile on my face?

Once on my own inside the block I ignored prior warnings and did as I'd been trained to do at the Academy: walk the tiers. I saw this not only as proper procedure, but as essential to establishing my authority. How could I expect the inmates to respond to my orders if I cowered behind my desk whenever the cells were unlocked?

Most inmates were bigger than me. At 5′ 7″ and 155 pounds, I wasn't exactly a menacing figure. I was also aware that from the third tier I faced a fifteen foot drop to the concrete flat below. More than once an inmate stepped out to block my way on one of the upper tiers.

"Hey man," they'd say, "what do you think you're doing up here?"

"I work here, that's what," I'd respond firmly.

"Yeah, well we live here."

"Yeah, maybe, but it's my job to know what you're doing."

Often in the beginning, upon returning to my desk I'd find the Senior Officer in the corridor waiting for me.

"McLaughlin, stay off the tiers. Haven't you been told not to go up there?"

I'd restrain myself from telling them that I perceived this policy of avoiding the tiers as fear of doing the job. Most of the officers thought it was a joke that I'd even consider going up on a tier while the inmates roamed free. To actually see me up there must have convinced them I was nuts. Despite their warnings, however, I never had a serious problem while patrolling the tiers.

The inmates soon learned that when I entered the block they could expect a day or evening of enforced discipline. An officer could not impose extended isolation time (done in their cells) or remove privileges from an inmate unless ordered to do so by the Disciplinary Board (the D-Board). The officer could, however, on his own initiative lock up an individual or the entire block for the duration of his shift. This I did without hesitation whenever I faced flagrant disobedience.

My appetite for block assignments did not subside, but I had trouble satisfying it under Lahoud. Even after six weeks, he continued to treat me like a new man, usually assigning me to strip searches and towers. I overcame this problem after learning I could work as much overtime as I wanted. I immediately began requesting it.

The 7–3 Shift Commander loved to see 3–11 officers so he could put them to work in the tougher blocks. Whenever I worked for him I'd step forward without hesitation and volunteer.

"That block's open today? I'll take it."

"You got it, buddy," he'd always say.

No resistance, no lecture, no warnings. All I'd hear would be sighs of relief from the regular 7–3 officers. It seemed they liked me better than the guys on my own shift.

Routinely I'd work a tense block all day and then appear at roll call for my regular shift. I suffered through several weeks of this before Lahoud realized I had enough experience to justify my eagerness to work tough blocks on successive shifts.

During a block assignment you could expect inmates to put constant pressure on you, probing to see just how much they could get away with. Most of their antics seemed innocuous, but if they saw they could get you to bend the rules a little, they'd keep pushing until you gave all the way. Many of the guards did give in and, once that happened, were constantly walked on. I kept my guard up and did a fairly decent job of enforcing the rules. But first I had to learn a lot the hard way.

The inmates could turn a routine like receiving milk for breakfast into a major crisis. Unlike the Minimum inmates who ate in the mess hall, Maximum inmates ate all their meals in the block. After the morning, afternoon, and evening counts, food came rolling in on carts and was then served cafeteria style by the officers.

The cells would open, the occupants would emerge, form a line, and file by to receive carefully allotted portions. Most of the inmates would then eat on benches on the flats.

The amount of food delivered had been measured so that all forty-five men could be fed with a minimum of waste. Naturally, everyone was to receive equal portions. In the case of milk, this amounted to two small cups, or about 12 ounces.

The chow line always reflected the pecking order in the block—the toughest inmates and those with the most influence always came first. Most of these guys had big forty-ounce marshmallow containers with them. After getting their eggs, bacon and whatever, they'd stop to get their milk. Usually two large drums of milk came with the cart.

The first time I had this detail I got into trouble right away. The first guy in line—big, burly, threatening-looking—stopped in front of me and held out his marshmallow container.

Since there's no regulation designating a specific container in which an inmate must receive milk, I put what I thought was two cups in his jar. I should have realized before I started that these guys hadn't brought big containers along to settle for 12 ounces of milk. The size of their jars made 12 ounces look paltry. That was part of the game.

"Gimme some more," the big inmate grumbled, still subdued.

"That's about two cups. It's all you get."

"C'mon, gimme a bit more." He was getting a little annoyed.

I thought, all right; I've got plenty here. No use having a scene. So I gave him a little more.

The next guy came along and we went through the same routine, except I had already given him as much as the first guy.

"Gimme more," he growled.

Most of these guys probably switched to something stronger than milk by the time they were ten years old. But in prison you try to get as much of whatever's available as you can.

"I already gave you more than I should've. You're only supposed to get two cups."

"Hey man, what's your problem? You got plenty here. Gimme some more."

The bastard had seen me back down with the first guy, and he wanted to see how much further he could push me. Still trying to avoid a confrontation, I gave him a little more.

Now the third guy wanted even more than the second. When I tried to draw the line, he and those right behind him started raising their voices and getting disorderly.

"Hey, it's not your fuckin' milk. Give him some more."

"There's only so much. I won't have enough for the guys at the end of the line."

They yelled at me, "That's not our problem! You should make sure you have enough! We want more milk!"

Being new I didn't want to start a riot over a few ounces of milk. I could just see trying to explain to my superiors afterwards that guards had gotten injured or maybe even killed over milk. So I figured, to hell with it. I started filling everyone's container.

Sure enough, I ran out of milk with several inmates still to serve. These, of course, were not the most violent, but, nevertheless, they complained loudly. A moment later the senior arrived and I got chewed out. Before he said a word I knew what I'd done wrong.

Never again did I bend the rules for an inmate over food. They'd want to choose the piece of meat they were getting, or reject an egg because the yoke was broken. If they didn't like what I was about to give them, I would say, "This is your portion. If you don't want it, move along." Often they'd stand there glaring, trying to back me down, but I wouldn't budge.

I felt sorry for the weaker inmates. No one would give them anything. You'd see them scrounging around on the floor for cigarette butts. If I did see a better piece of meat, I'd try to save it for one of them. Usually, though, the next piece up went to the next in line.

Sometimes the tough guys would swear and empty their full trays into the trash can. They had their image to maintain. And besides, in their cells they had plenty of food they'd bought at the canteen.

Sometimes an inmate would throw his tray on the floor or against the wall. One time a guy turned the food cart over, setting off a mini-riot. But I never let the fear of that change my approach.

If my resolve was going to be shaken, it probably would have happened the day I was assigned to clean out a murdered inmate's cell. It was the first murder since I'd started at Walpole.

It had happened in A-6, the overflow Protective Custody Block. Obviously this guy should have had the Maximum Protective custody of Block Nine. Somebody had gone into his cell and caved in his head with a mop wringer. Motive? Anyone's guess—as was the murderer's identity.

When I went into the cell I found half an inch of blood on the floor, blotches of it on the walls and large gobs all over his belongings. That day I found out just how strong my stomach was.

Not long afterwards, another inmate was stabbed several times and thrown off a third tier. He landed right in front of an officer sitting at the block desk. It was dark. From his position beneath the overhang the officer had seen nothing until the body's startling arrival on the concrete six feet from him. I've always wondered how I would have reacted had I been sitting there. Nevertheless, I continued to walk the tiers.

No one ever seemed to be convicted for these inmate murders. I knew the inmates were good at covering their tracks, but it seemed strange that, after so many killings, no one had been caught and punished. Officers always seemed to be nearby. One night I saw why this didn't necessarily make a difference.

Shortly before the 10 p.m. lockup, I relaxed at my desk, in a Minimum block. The flats were empty, everything was quiet. Most of the inmates had returned to their cells; the others were visiting. The main lights were out. Individual lamps provided some illumination, and a few cells were lit by the glow of TV tubes. Everything seemed normal.

Suddenly I heard a commotion up on the second tier. Stepping out onto the flats to get a better look, I saw the shadowy outlines of several inmates crowded into a darkened cell. I could just make them out holding inmate Costello and beating him over the head with a pipe.

By myself I couldn't handle that gang so I ran to the cellblock door, unlocked it and gave the three-slam signal. Within seconds several officers, led by Jerry, arrived.

As Jerry led us up the cellblock stairs, the five attackers heard us coming and scattered. Jerry and I both had a good look at their outlines and profiles. Later I learned how easy it is to identify inmates by their outlines when you've been around them for awhile. Even on that occasion I thought I could pick the attackers out of a lineup. I was sure Jerry could; he got a better look at them than I did.

When we got to Costello he was still alive but in pretty bad shape from head injuries. While the other officers carried him to the hospital, I talked to Jerry. Both of us would have to file reports and I wanted to get the details straight. Together I figured we could identify the attackers and prefer charges.

"Jerry, I need the names of those guys for my report."

He seemed annoyed that I'd ask. "Hey, I didn't see anybody."

"But Jerry, I was right behind you. I saw who they were but I just don't know their names. You must have seen them too."

"Man, I told you—I couldn't see them."

He cut the discussion and walked away. For whatever reason, Jerry chose not to identify the inmates who had beaten Costello. He had to know who they were. A few months later I had put the names with the faces but by then it was too late. The incident served as stark evidence that, even when the guards knew who was responsible for violence, they might turn their backs. Clearly, the disease infecting Walpole involved others besides the inmates. Ultimately one could only blame management for their failure to maintain discipline. They had instituted permissive policies and then looked the other way when things went haywire.

A glaring example of their lax attitude was Johnny Regalado. From my first day it was plain he had the run of the Administration Building. He even slept there, having a special room in the basement instead of a cell in Population. Coming to work one day I saw a big black limousine parked by the Administration Building's front steps. One of the limo's opaque windows was rolled down a couple of inches; as I walked by I could see inside. There sat Raymond Patriarca himself, the reputed head honcho of New England's underworld. Next to him sat Johnny. No supervising officer was in sight.

When they saw I'd spotted them, they rolled up the window as if an officer had no right to eavesdrop. Knowing Johnny's status, I realized they simply wanted to talk and had no intention of going anywhere. So I just shook my head and reported for roll call.

Patriarca was out on parole and forbidden to associate with known felons. Johnny was serving life for murder. Yet Johnny was sitting outside the prison in a private car with Patriarca. They did this within a few feet of the superintendent's office, and nobody seemed interested. I could see why they even trusted Johnny to sweep out the armory. If he wanted to escape he didn't need a gun; he'd call Patriarca and have a limo sent for him.

While I wasn't happy with the Department of Corrections' philosophy as implemented at Walpole, I remained optimistic about my future. After I gained a little more experience, Hall would promote me into a management position. From there I could act on my personal insights and wield authority to help straighten Walpole out.

I never used my friendship with Hall to gain any advantage over my fellow officers. I saw them as brothers, all of us working in the same difficult situation. I had joined the guard's union and complied with its directives even though I anticipated moving soon into management. At that time I didn't know much about the union's workings; I never went to their meetings. From the talk among my fellow officers, I surmised that the union was a toothless puppy. So I respected the local as the voice of labor but, otherwise, paid little attention to it.

Three months after I started at Walpole, our local joined a statewide strike by state employees to get a new contract. With no particular sympathies for the action, I fell into line with the majority and walked the picket line. I realized that by doing so I risked my future with management, but I felt it my responsibility to my brother officers. Everybody didn't share my attitude: there were thirty-five scabs.

That strike lasted four days, and none of us were suspended or fired for participating. I felt pretty good about the whole thing. I'd demonstrated loyalty to my fellow officers without apparent damage to my career prospects.

Most new guards at Walpole didn't last ninety days. The ever-present danger scared some into quitting. Psychological pressure, weighed against the modest salary, weeded out others. A small but significant number of the rest sustained physical injury serious enough to force them off the job. With the attrition rate so high, once I got through my third month I found myself to be a veteran.

While still classified a junior officer, I'd accumulated enough seniority to begin bidding on permanent jobs on my own shift. When an opening occurred in Block A-2, old Death Valley, I immediately put in my bid. No one else bid with me, so I gained myself a home. And what a home!

I viewed the block as my sacred trust, my personal territory, its operation a reflection upon my competence. The fear of failing steeled me to the realization that many of the occupants had murdered their way into Walpole and could kill me without batting an eye. On occasion anxiety did arise, but I managed to hold it in check. I would not let inmates feed upon my fear. I had seen too many guards besieged in their own blocks, afraid to move from behind their desks. In desperation they would frequently bug their supervisors for bathroom breaks so they could spend a few minutes away from the tension. The inmates sensed what was happening and acted even more aggressively.

In actuality much of this threatening behavior by inmates was bravado. Most of them, especially in Minimum, did not run around berserk. They had no wish to lose their privileges by attacking someone out in the open. They acted threatening to maintain their image with the other inmates and discourage attack from the predators among them. This meant not allowing any insult or slight to go by without responding. The secret for an officer was to recognize when an inmate had been pushed too far.

If an inmate thought an officer had slighted him he might simply respond with verbal abuse. He might physically demonstrate his anger by refusing to respond to an officer's orders. Or he might attack, this often deferred to some later time when the officer could be caught off guard.

Scores of guard injuries—beatings, stabbings, scaldings, and so on—had occurred in Walpole during each year of its operation. Knowledge of this hovered over every officer and softened the approach of many to where the inmates could break most rules without fear of punishment. Management's reluctance to back up guards exacerbated the problem.

To sustain the effort required to maintain a strict attitude toward the inmates demanded enormous energy. Even I found my reserves drained over several months. I moved about with a caution bordering on paranoia. I'd always walk near walls, my back angled toward them to afford it partial protection, my head up, constantly alert for any unusual sight or sound. While crossing the yard or moving through the main corridor I avoided looking down even long enough to crush a lighted cigarette butt. I made sure no inmate walked close behind.

I maintained a constant alertness, honing my instincts until I moved about like a cat on the prowl.

I also made a special effort to keep in top physical shape. In high school and college I'd been an athlete; now I religiously played handball. I was rock hard and could move quickly. Still, I hardly posed a physical threat to most of the inmates. The majority spent hours in the prison's weight rooms building imposing physiques. This, of course, helped insure their survival among their fellows, but it also fortified their macho attitude, encouraged brazenness, and made the unruly that much more difficult to subdue. Picture being unarmed and standing up to an enraged Arnold Schwartznegger!

My first serious confrontation occurred within a few days during one of my trips to the tiers. It was evening, the cellblock dimly lit by lamps and TV's from individual cells. As I walked the third level I suddenly found myself standing face-to-face with George Burdock.

During my orientation days, Burdock had been pointed out, to me as one of the toughest of the inmates. A former organized crime hit man, he had been convicted of murder during the 60's and sentenced to the electric chair. By the grace of the Governor and the Massachusetts State Legislature, who together had struck down the death penalty before the sentence could be carried out, George now wandered Walpole's Minimum Section.

Everyone considered him a psycho, a loner who couldn't be controlled by any of the inmate gangs but who would do a "job" for price. As we stood there I remembered as a kid reading in the paper about the Charlestown/Somerville gang wars in which George wiped out a number of his adversaries. In those rumbles he'd lost three of his own brothers.

Knowing that George lived in a cellblock across the corridor and, according to regulations, should not have entered A-2, I gulped down my anxiety, squared my shoulders, and stated in a businesslike voice, "All right, George, you don't belong here. I want you to leave the tier and return across the hall."

He looked at me through narrowed eyes as if amazed I had spoken up. "Do you know who I am?"

"Yeah, I do," I replied. "In case you don't know who I am, the name's Mike McLaughlin."

"I know who you are." His reply reeked with disdain. Obviously word concerning me had already circulated the inmate ranks.

I didn't say anything further, not wanting to box him in verbally where he would be forced to defy me and turn this into a major incident. Instead I did something nearly as dangerous. I turned my back and walked away as if I assumed he understood and acknowledged my authority. To turn your back on an inmate in such a fashion is usually construed as the ultimate insult. In effect you're saying, "I don't think you're so tough that I should be worried about you."

With a psycho like George my action could've triggered an attack, so as I moved away I remained on alert. As I suspected, George had enough sense to use the out I'd given him. I hadn't backed him into a corner by standing there and demanding he move immediately. If he struck out at me, what could he gain?

By facing him on the tier in semi-darkness without backup, I'd shown him he couldn't intimidate me. I might in fact be as nutty as he was. If he attacked, he would likely lose his Minimum privileges and face banishment to Block Ten. For what?

Burdock left A-2 without further incident and never returned during my shifts there.

This incident drove home the realization that if I intended to continue walking the third tier I must develop a method to quickly escape from there should someone place me in serious danger. The layout offered only one route other than the stairs. I would have to jump.

I practiced jumping. The fifteen-foot fall ended abruptly upon solid concrete. One false landing, or a poorly executed roll, and bones could be broken. But the risk of broken bones had never frightened me in other pursuits, so I practiced until I felt confident I could execute the drop on a moment's notice. Naturally I only practiced when the block had emptied of inmates and no other officers were nearby. Had I been seen I might have found medics coming after me with a strait jacket.

I soon discovered that Burdock wasn't the biggest fish swimming in A-2. The biggest of all in terms of power was a diminutive, polite young man named Lyle Kramer. Officially Kramer was serving a term for having shot two policemen during a bank robbery. At the same time he faced an indictment for the murders of two women who allegedly knew of his involvement in another robbery. To top all this off he had earned extra time for art theft. The guy had an appreciation of the arts. He was an accomplished musician who once played with a famous rock group. Now he ran a group of a different sort—an inmate gang numbering over a hundred, affectionately referred to as "The Execution Squad."

How had such an outwardly behaved, inoffensive little fellow gained so much power? Why hadn't one of the brawnier inmates broken him in half and taken over?

First, money and connections with the outside. Second, reputation. Kramer exercised often in the gym, impressively demonstrating the validity of his claim to possessing a twelfth degree black belt in karate. In other words the Chuck Norris motto, "He didn't need a weapon, he was a weapon," applied to Kramer. At least, he had everyone believing it.

"The Execution Squad" reflected the personality of its leader. While the Minimum Section still experienced murders and frequent beatings, these usually took place under cover, without officers detecting trouble until the assault had run its course. This stood in stark contrast to bygone days at Walpole when gangs roamed the corridors in open defiance of officers. One, called "The Wrecking Crew," would file into a block, leave two inmates to guard the door and then go to work on someone. The lookouts would prevent potential witnesses, including single officers, from entering. By the time enough help arrived "The Wrecking Crew" would have retired, leaving someone inside dead or badly beaten. An assault like this would occur nearly every week.

The leaders of "The Wrecking Crew" had ultimately been caught and isolated in Block Ten, leaving the way open for Kramer and his smooth style. He had the Minimum Section in such awe of him that, if he ordered one of his subordinates to lead an action, all two hundred Minimum inmates were prepared to join in. Even inmates who preferred to remain apart dared not do so.

The guards knew the extent of Kramer's activities, but could never convince the administration that the guy was guilty of anything. After all, he seemed polite, cordial and well behaved. He was one of the few inmates who would openly carry on a cordial dialogue with administration. Ordinarily such behavior would get the inmate branded a "rat" and marked for a "hit". But Kramer showed no concern. Why should he? He controlled the Minimum Section, all the while leading administration to believe they had themselves a model prisoner.

Over time I came to see the motive behind Kramer's cooperation with administration. He was concerned about his pending murder indictment and needed someone of authority to put in a good word for him.

Eventually he did get support by helping District Attorney Delahunt recover a painting that had been stolen from the Museum of

Fine Art in Boston. Inmates joked that Kramer had duped Delahunt by having associates steal the painting so he, Kramer, could engineer its return.

Delahunt did speak in Kramer's behalf at the murder hearing. Delahunt's statement, plus the fact that all witnesses were either dead or missing, caused the charges to be dropped. Kramer is a free man today.

My first clue that Kramer was somebody special came from his cell location. The most powerful inmates in each cellblock occupied the most remote cells on the upper tiers. This gave them the most privacy, especially from officers. True to form, Kramer had gained possession of Cell 72.

One afternoon shortly after I started my new assignment I was sitting at my desk near the door when I spotted Kramer sitting in a chair on the tier outside his cell. He had leaned back, rested his feet on the railing, folded his arms across his chest, and was now staring down in my direction. At this time of day regulations allowed Minimum inmates to move freely so I saw nothing wrong in his sitting there. My eyes left him and routinely wandered the block.

Several seconds later when I again glanced up at him I found his eyes still trained in my direction. Only now a smirk had crept across his face. I looked around to see if he might be staring at something else. Behind me stood solid, featureless concrete. He had to be staring at me.

Anger started to churn my stomach. By this time the other officers had told me all about him. I could see his action as a move to intimidate and bring under his spell the new officer patrolling his domain.

I had already decided to treat Kramer like any other inmate so I reacted at once, almost without thinking. I rose and dragged my chair from behind the desk out into plain view. I made sure the overhanging tier still protected my head, but left my back facing the open cellblock door. There I sat down, legs crossed, arms folded, staring back up at him.

Now every inmate entering or leaving the cellblock had to pass directly behind me. In spite of that potential danger, I forced myself to ignore the foot traffic behind me, my eyes remaining glued to Kramer. In effect I was telling him that I cared more about establishing my right to be there than about protecting my back. I was also showing the inmates that I did not fear Kramer.

After a few minutes Kramer sent one of his runners out into the corridor. Within seconds the guy returned with Senior Officer Jerry in tow.

Jerry stopped just inside the door, took one look at the situation and snapped, "Hey McLaughlin, c'mere!"

Hesitant to break eye contact with Kramer, I nevertheless picked myself up and walked over to face Jerry.

With an annoyed look on his face he growled, "What the fuck you doin' sittin' out there? Get your chair back where it belongs and quit harassin' the inmates!"

"But Jerry," I complained, "look at him up there. He's staring at me. If he can sit out there and stare at me, why can't I stare at him?"

Jerry rolled his eyes up at the ceiling. "Just put your goddamn chair back and stop harassin' the inmates!"

The incident ended, only the first of many run-ins with Kramer. After that I watched him closely, waiting for him to step out of line. It took a few months. I knew he constantly smoked hashish in his cell but had never been able to catch him. One day I knew he'd just gotten a new delivery and hadn't had a chance to use it up. Something had interrupted, drawing him out of his cell.

In a flash I called a fellow officer, Mel Varney, and we swooped down on Kramer's nest. We not only found the hash in a pipe, but also a small scout knife. The presence of these items represented two major infractions that called for us to write a D-report.

To keep from losing privileges, Kramer brought in heavy artillery: a lawyer from the outside to contest me before the D-Board. The Board consisted of two corrections officers, one of them senior, and a civilian employee of the prison, in this case a female counselor. These hardly represented a group of juridical heavyweights, but Kramer wanted to keep his record clean.

As soon as Kramer turned his charming, innocent smile upon the lady counselor I could see my report faced rough waters. Kramer's attorney—hair styled, wearing a custom-made three-piece suit—lent an intimidating presence to the small, unadorned prison hearing room. In comparison, the rest of us looked like shabby maintenance people.

The Board's chairman, appearing somewhat overwhelmed by the attorney's presence, cleared his throat and began, "Officer McLaughlin, I have here a disciplinary report dated November 16th in which you and Officer Varney claim to have discovered a quantity of hashish and a small jackknife in inmate Kramer's cell. We have the items here. Do you have anything you'd like to add to your report?"

"No, Mr. Chairman. I believe the report states our findings clearly."

The chairman turned to Kramer. "Lyle, what do you have to say to this report?"

Kramer's attorney immediately stepped in. "Mr. Chairman, my client does not deny that the articles in question may have been found in his cell by the two officers. He does, however, deny any responsibility for them being there. He asserts that when he left his cell it contained no contraband. Someone, perhaps the very officers who have signed this report, planted the items there."

I bristled at the accusation. "Officer Varney and I reached the scene together. We can vouch for each other."

The attorney countered, "One would expect the two officers to stand together against a single, unfortunate inmate. We, of course, do not accept their claim of innocence. Even so, the possibility exists that someone else planted the contraband in my client's cell."

"I don't agree," I replied. "Virtually the entire time, I had his cell under observation. No one else went near it."

"Virtually? What does that mean?"

"I lost sight of the cell for a few brief seconds while in the stairwell rushing up to the third tier. But in that time I don't think it was possible for someone to slip into his cell and plant anything."

"You don't believe. And when my client left his cell where did he go?"

"He left the cellblock."

"You watched him walk along the tier, enter the stairwell, and walk out into the corridor."

"Yes."

"How can you be sure that no one slipped into his cell while you watched him leave?"

"I only had to watch him a few seconds."

The attorney groaned, shaking his head. "Mr. Chairman, this is ridiculous. This officer admits that during two different segments of time he lost sight of my client's cell. We contend that during either of those segments someone could have planted the contraband in my client's cell."

The attorney's argument shouldn't have stood up, but it did. The D-Board ruled in Kramer's favor.

Later, outside the hearing room, he paused to make conversation with me. By this time we had become well acquainted and he liked calling me "Mac," as he had heard done by my friends in the officer ranks.

"Well Mac," he said, "I hope there's no hard feelings, me beating you before the D-Board like this."

"Lyle," I replied, "don't misunderstand. You made fools of the D-Board, you didn't beat me. My job is to write a report when I catch you violating the rules, not to charge you with an offence or give you isolation time. That's between you and the D-Board. Just remember, if I find hash or a knife in your cell again, I'll write you up again."

Sure enough, a week later during a routine cell search I found the same knife in Kramer's cell. True to my word, I wrote a new D-report that forced Kramer, and his mouthpiece, to appear for another hearing. This time Kramer received support from a source no one would question. The D-Board called in Tom McCoy, the Deputy Superintendent responsible for dispensing with contraband items found in the prison.

In an annoyed tone McCoy told the D-Board, "That little knife is nothing. I gave it to Lyle. He needs the tools on the knife for a hobby of his. It's silly to think he'd use it as a weapon. You know Lyle. He doesn't need a little knife like that to defend himself."

The case went no further. Kramer was dismissed. The knife, however, for whatever reason, never reappeared.

McCoy failed to address the possibility that Kramer of anyone else could use the knife to fashion other crude weapons, the most dangerous of which were spears whittled from broomsticks. The blade or any of the sharp tools could have been sharpened into spearpoints or shanks (homemade ice picks). Or Kramer could have given the knife as it was to associates less skilled than he with hands and feet. In any case the rules specifically forbade the inmates to possess metal knives.

I soon came to learn that McCoy's tolerant attitude reflected the prevalent view in Walpole's administration. If at all possible, managers wanted to avoid punishing the "tough guys." They feared reprisals and/or organized general disobedience that could blossom into riots. Naturally these inmates picked up on this fear and felt encouraged to put their violent tendencies on display, thereby justifying management's anxiety.

On the surface the D-Board looked as if it could have been used as a kangaroo court against inmates. After all, two of its three members were officers. Instead, the D-Board usually protected the inmates. This happened because the chairman of the D-Board, the senior officer, was appointed by the Superintendent and was expected to apply management's view to the hearings. By following directions he enhanced his opportunities for advancement within the Department. In effect, management, not the members of the D-Board, decided how most cases would be judged. This resulted in an uneven distribution of punishment upon different inmates for the same offenses.

D-reports fell into two categories, those that covered infractions against prison regulations, and those classified as crimes under state law. The D-Board handled the former totally, including the meting out of punishment. The latter were reviewed by the D-Board and then forwarded on to the District Attorney for possible prosecution. In spite of the numerous attacks by inmates on their fellows and officers, seldom did we see convictions by the DA.

Punishment by the D-Board could take several forms. Least serious was the temporary loss of free periods, yard and canteen privileges. Isolation time theoretically hit the inmates harder, but in reality it proved to be a joke. Inmates did isolation time in their regular cells, minus TV and radio. But their neighbors were always willing to move their own TVs out of their cells into a position where the "isolated" inmate could see. They'd also turn their radios louder. While the "isolated" inmate lost freedom of movement, he remained well entertained.

More painful to inmates was the loss of visiting privileges. This had been known to trigger riots.

The ultimate penalty was transfer to Block Ten. Not all inmates looked upon this as negative. The problem was that Block Ten usually remained filled to capacity. In order to place someone there you first had to release someone else. No one resided in Block Ten unless he had proven himself to be extra dangerous. Therefore, to cage up one lion we had to release another back into Population. Overall the prison gained nothing in the exchange.

Because of the futility involved in defending a D-report against a powerful inmate, many of the guards had given up trying to enforce strict discipline. Why risk being slugged or stabbed over some minor infraction that would likely not be enforced by the D-Board anyway. Gradually of course, minor infractions increased and even major infractions slipped by unnoticed.

As I watched all this I came to realize that the guards weren't responsible for causing the troubles at Walpole by mistreating the inmates. If anything, the opposite was true. The guards had lost control over inmate discipline. Because administration would not stand solidly behind their officers, the powerful inmates could, in effect, determine against whom the rules would be enforced. Inmates with no influence faced the full impact of prison regulations, while the powerful got away with almost anything.

Recognizing this made me even more determined to keep guys like Kramer in line. In fact, I concentrated on the tougher guys and tended to treat the less powerful more leniently.

I would have liked to interdict certain inmate practices, but because the rules did not forbid them I could only stand by helplessly, no matter how disgusted I felt. Particularly appalling was to see many of the newer men requesting dental appointments to have their front teeth removed. They had been ordered to do so by powerful homosexual inmates for obvious reasons. What choice did these newcomers have? Either they requested the dentist to remove their teeth using anesthetics, or they'd have them knocked out in less sterile fashion with fist or foot.

Homosexuality in prison is difficult to comprehend unless you've seen its results. Inmates won't admit to partaking in it, yet a high percentage do. One quick clue to an inmate's involvement was to see him keeping all bodily hair shaved. Usually he did this in response to orders from a more powerful inmate. I found it strange to see big, macho inmates walking about with not a hair on arms, legs, or chest.

The new young inmate was virtually helpless to protect himself. One of the powerful inmates would latch onto him immediately and make him his property. When not using the new inmate himself, the powerful inmate might send him out to pay off gambling and other debts.

Love triangles developed with resulting violence, leaving inmates seriously injured. Some inmates known to provide homosexual services were even brutalized for being the object of unrequited love.

Even though I patrolled my tiers and tried to keep a close watch into the cells, the routine in the Minimum Section allowed so much freedom that the inmates could do pretty much as they wanted. Unlike Maximum, where inmates were confined most of the day to their cellblocks, the Minimum routine allowed inmates several hours during which they could move freely within their blocks, through the corridor, and to yard or gym.

To attain Minimum status an inmate had to hold down a job. A few of them served as maintenance men, runners in the corridor, or attendants in the hospital. Most, however, worked in the shops across the yard. Work schedule called for a three-hour shift in both morning and afternoon, unless an inmate went on sick call, had a visit, or attended one of the rehab programs.

In reality not enough jobs existed for all the Minimum inmates, and many spent their time in the shops getting paid ($.50 an hour at that time) to play cards or indulge in various forms of mischief. With only two guards assigned to supervise a shop that employed about a hundred inmates, some very frightening activities could take place.

A few years before I arrived, an inmate named Stanley constructed a powerful pipe bomb while working in the foundry. They never did find out what Stanley intended doing with his bomb. They'd had no inkling he'd made one until poor Stanley, in the process of assembling it, gave the cap one twist too many. The bomb went off with tremendous force, blowing Stanley all over the place. They continued finding pieces of him for months. A chunk of the pipe struck an inmate standing nearby and embedded itself in his forehead. Somehow he survived.

This wasn't the only incident of a bomb exploding in Walpole. Only a year before I arrived, an inmate died in an explosion in the print shop. The verdict on that one was murder, but they never found the perpetrator.

Since administration closely monitored the work programs, it had to know that not all Minimum inmates held jobs. Nevertheless, to placate inmates seeking a status change from Maximum to Minimum, administration went ahead and reclassified them, assigning them jobs that did not exist. Here again, management bowed to inmate pressure rather than following a well-thought-out procedure. As a result, men who'd committed the most henious crimes roamed freely, with idle time to indulge whatever might enter their minds.

The case of Peter DiLauro provided a perfect example of absurd inmate classification. When I took over A-2 I found him under my supervision. Peter had spent more than one segment of his thirteen years behind bars in Walpole's infamous Block Ten. Another refugee from death row (sentenced for killing a policeman), he had a history of fighting other inmates, threatening officers, and attacking employees. Prior to my coming to Walpole he had held medics hostage in the hospital. His explosive, combative nature should have kept him out of Minimum, but there he was.

My first run-in with Peter occurred one night while making the ten o'clock count. Coming up to his cell I found him sitting on his bunk with a bathrobe cord tied tightly around his left biceps. Peter had once been a longshoreman and a heavyweight boxer. He had arms like a gorilla. The cord had forced the huge veins in his forearm to bulge grotesquely.

As I watched incredulously, he calmly took a shank and began digging a hole in the largest of the blood vessels.

"Peter!" I barked at him. "What are you doing?"

At first he ignored me. He had pegged his cell, securing it from inside with a metal brace so officers couldn't open it. The inmates made these braces in the machine shop. The guards had devised a counter measure—a special crowbar that could apply enough pressure to force the door open in spite of the brace. These crowbars, however, were kept in the control room and it took time to obtain one.

Effectively locked out, I watched Peter carefully pick up a clear plastic tube, the outer casing of a ballpoint pen. The refill had been removed, making room for a white powdery substance. He proceeded to place one end of the tube into the bloody wound then bent over and blew on the other end until the powder had disappeared.

Finally he looked up at me and grumbled, "Man, I wish I had your veins."

"You'd have veins like mine if you didn't do things like that!" I replied. Then I shouted down to my companion officer, "Get the crowbar!"

By the time we opened the cell, "the works"—his drug paraphernalia—had been disposed of either down the toilet or out the cell window. We found nothing to confiscate. Peter was feeling too good to be offended by our intrusion.

Actually, we seldom laid our hands on the evidence of drug use. Often I had inmates blow pot smoke in my face as I walked by their cells. Other officers would ignore it. I always called for a key. The inmate would wait until I opened the door and then flush the butt down the toilet. Without evidence you couldn't file a report.

The incident with Peter, and others almost as bizarre, forced me to question certain of my concepts. I'd entered Correctons with every intention of being helpful to inmates. I wanted their penal experience to be a positive one. But you need some help from them. What good was my trying to help Peter by interdicting his drug use when he had no inclination to stop, and had such little respect for his own body? It was as if he lived in a completely different world.

I began getting an inkling of what had turned Peter into such a violent man when I observed his mother on her visits. They maintained a close relationship and she came to see him often. She hated prison authorities and, in spite of Peter's record, seemed to hold the view that Peter had done nothing wrong. Her outspoken, harsh demeanor was greatly appreciated by the other inmates. They showered attention upon her and called her "Ma." (A nickname to which the guards added, "Barker.") She appeared to eat this up, and would exchange banter with all of the inmates.

I remember her coming to visit Peter during one of his stays in Block Ten. Because of their temperament, Block Ten inmates spent their yard time in specially constructed wire cages. To reach the B-10 visiting room Peter's mother would have to pass by these cages. At the sight of her, those in the process of exercising would call out their greetings.

Once she called back, "Hey you guys, if they're gonna treat you like monkeys you should act like monkeys." She then leaned forward, balanced her knuckles on the ground and began walking on all fours like a monkey. The inmates found this hilarious.

While this incident seemed comical, it made me wonder if Peter had ever experienced the soft kindness that all of us need from our mothers. Lack of it may have gone a long way toward making him explosive and insensitive to the rights of others.

4 Merry Christmas

In my first seven months at Walpole five inmates were murdered, three in Block A-2. Two of the A-2 killings occurred after I had become its regular 3–11 block officer. One was a simple strangling—you begin to view these things in that light when they so frequently take on more gruesome characteristics.

In the case of James, we never did learn the identity of his murderer or the motive. In fact his passing seemed to evoke little concern among the administrators. As I'd heard Superintendent Butterworth once comment, "What do you expect in the big house?"

The second of these A-2 slayings drew more attention. I refer to the murder of Robert Perrotta, the killing later discussed in the 1986 Boston Herald article. Perrotta had been targeted for a hit by members of the gang he had run with on the outside. They believed he had been informing on them to the DA concerning a bank robbery.

Perrotta knew he was in big trouble, but he refused to sign the Protective Custody papers that would have isolated him in Block Nine from those seeking his life. Becoming a Protective Custody inmate carried a stigma, so most inmates sought P.C. status only as a last resort. Isolation in Block Nine might afford them excellent security, but they could never be sure that circumstances wouldn't eventually take them out of B-9. They might need to spend time in the hospital or be transferred to another prison. Wherever they went, their P.C. status at Walpole marked them as a stool pigeon and a target.

Apparently Perrotta feared this more than his precarious position in Population. I personally talked to him, telling him to stay within sight of the officers at all times. This, of course, was easier said than done.

The inevitable occurred Thanksgiving night. I happened to be in Avocation when the alarm sounded. I rushed back to my block to find officers gathered around Perrotta's nearly nude body. He had been drugged and then strangled. But even more gruesome than that, his murderers had torn his penis from his body and stuffed it into his mouth. Later the autopsy proved that Perrotta had been alive during the mutilation.

The 1986 article stated that one inmate was eventually convicted for Perrotta's murder. During my time at Walpole I saw no convictions for inmate murders. In fact, I never saw cases pursued vigorously. To be fair, in many cases evidence was lacking. Still, I sensed no tenacity on the part of administration or the DA's office.

Another inmate murdered? What do you expect? This is a prison.

Once, after five inmates had beaten a murder charge for lack of evidence, I saw their two counselors celebrating in the corridor. "They beat the rap! They beat the rap!" The counselors were actually doing a jig together, celebrating what they perceived to be a victory for inmate rights. I wanted to ask them if they'd forgotten that the murdered man had rights too.

Counselors refused to recognize that by helping their client avoid punishment, they condoned his aggressive behavior and allowed him the freedom to strike again. Perhaps isolating him would indeed undo any progress made in counseling, but what about those he might attack? Didn't we owe the well-behaved inmates protection from the incorrigibles?

Terror rather than sadistic hatred often instigated the brutal nature of the killings. One day a group of inmates told me a body was lying in the stairwell of my block. Before I investigated I told the officer in the corridor to call a medic. When I rushed to the scene I indeed found an inmate sprawled on the stairs with holes all over him. Later the autopsy counted 280 puncture wounds. As I crouched over him my stomach nearly retched at the sight. He certainly looked beyond help.

The medic and several officers arrived within seconds. As I watched the medic fumble around trying to find a neck pulse I saw blood begin to ooze from puncture wounds in the deceased's eyeballs.

"Jesus," one of the guards commented, "it looks like he ran into a whole gang. There are holes all over him. I can even see some in the bottom of his feet."

The medic shook his head to declare the poor fellow officially gone, then commented, "I don't think this guy ran into a gang. All those wounds look identical to me. I'd say they were made by the same weapon."

"You mean one guy inflicted all those wounds?" I asked. "What kind of sick mind would do such a thing?"

I received my answer a few months later. By that time we had a good idea who the killer was but had no evidence with which to press charges. One day I happened to be conversing privately with him about something else. I didn't consider him a particularly dangerous inmate so I probed to see if I could find out why he had committed such a ghastly killing. He seemed almost eager to talk about it, although he carefully avoided directly incriminating himself.

"Man, if you're gonna do somebody you gotta make sure you get it done. I mean, if the guy survives he'll be after your ass as soon as he gets well. Stabbing a guy with a shank can be chancy. You can't tell when you've hit a vital spot. So you keep stabbing and stabbing. Sometimes the fear of the guy recovering gets so strong your arm begins pumping all by itself, like a piston in a racing engine. You couldn't stop it if you wanted."

With this kind of mayhem constantly surrounding me, it wasn't easy to maintain my fearless, "slightly crazy" image, but I felt I had to do so if I was to last a few more months and walk out of Walpole in one piece. Two incidents come to mind where my radical behavior prevented potential harm to both me and my wife Karen.

One night in a quiet moment just before the ten o'clock lockup, a group of between eight and ten inmates surrounded me in A-2.

"Come with us," the leader ordered.

"What do you mean, come with you?" I responded.

"Don't resist or you're gonna get hurt. We're gonna take you hostage. We're fed up with how things are goin' around this place. We figure the big shots will listen if we're holding one of their screws."

Naturally I was scared, but I'd made up my mind shortly after starting at the prison that I'd never allow myself to be taken hostage.

"Hey, I'm not going anywhere."

Unperturbed by my refusal, the leader stated, "You're comin'. If we have to rough you up, we will."

"You'd better be prepared to do more than rough me up. You'd better be prepared to kill me, because I'm going to fight you to my last ounce of breath."

My words gave them pause. All of them stared at me curiously.

"I don't get it," the leader said. "Why would you rather die than come along peacefully? If we get what we want, you get out of this without a scratch."

"Simple. I don't think management knows how to properly handle a situation like this. On top of that, you guys are too crazy to trust. I figure something will go wrong. Then you'll work me over first before you kill me."

The inmates murmured but otherwise seemed to take no offense.

"You've still got a choice," the leader repeated. "Either come along or get hurt."

Standing there, looking him straight in the eye, I repeated, "You'd better be ready to kill me."

Tense seconds passed. Then, without another word, they turned and walked away. They simply had not been prepared to kill an officer. Killing me would have gained them nothing. If, however, I had shown fear, I might have given them the encouragement to carry out their threat. Had I gone with them, the emotional tensions that surround a hostage situation might have pushed them to the point where murdering me looked attractive. They certainly possessed the capacity. Some of them were serving sentences for murder. This incident taught me a great deal about handling serious threats.

A few weeks later another small group confronted me as I sat at my desk in the block. This group didn't look as agitated as the previous one but the looks in their eyes told me they meant business.

"McLaughlin," the leader said, "you've been coming down on us pretty hard, poking your nose where it doesn't belong. You're interfering with our action and we want you to stop. Maybe you don't care much about your own ass, but what about your wife?" He paused to see my reaction. "We can get to her, you know. I've got people on the outside who can stop by and see her. Do you want me to describe what they'll do?"

We locked intense stares. After a moment I reached over and picked up the telephone receiver. I dialed home, fully knowing that Karen wouldn't be there. As the phone continued to ring I turned my stare back on the inmate leader and spoke as if someone had answered.

"Let me speak to Harry, please . . . Harry? Mike McLaughlin. You know that life insurance policy you wrote for me on Karen a few months ago? I want to bump it up substantially . . . Yeah, a couple hundred thousand . . . No, I'm not expecting any problems."

I sat back in my chair, still glaring at the inmate leader. "I'm just taking precautions. Can you stop by the house with the paperwork in the next day or so? . . . Super. See you then." I hung up and folded my arms across my chest.

"You want to send somebody after my wife? Go ahead. With the amount of money I'll get from the insurance I can find myself all the women I want. So don't expect any special treatment from me. Now you'd better make yourselves scarce before I write you up for threatening an officer."

If they hadn't thought me crazy before, they surely felt convinced after that. Not that they believed I'd really called my insurance agent. They probably hadn't. Still, they did see a guard wacky enough to try such a stunt when his wife's life might hang in the balance. How could they ever hope to control me? In response to their threats I might do anything.

A number of the inmates found the pressure of their peers unbearable and sought various legitimate ways out of the institution. Many worked on their cases in the law library, seeking retrials. Some, after building a record of good behavior, requested transfer to other, less volatile prisons in the system. A few, who could not use either of these avenues and had a drug history, found even the environs of the state mental facility at Bridgewater preferable to Walpole. There, when patients acted nutty, the doctors prescribed as much medication as it took to keep them calm. Patients could space out all day rather than face a routine that exposed them to random violence.

I ran into one classic case of an inmate seeking this route to oblivion. A black man who wore his hair in a big afro decided one night to try to convince me he'd gone crazy. While making my ten o'clock count I found him standing naked in his toilet repeatedly hitting the flush button and saying, "I am a turd, I am a turd, I am a turd—"

I didn't take him seriously. Certainly not enough so to recommend him being committed to an asylum. Since I had no fear that he'd flush himself down the toilet I moved on to finish my count.

Two nights later on my count I found him waiting for me at the bars. He was brewing a cup of coffee in his cell and asked me if I wanted to join him. Naturally I declined, having learned that officers should never accept food or drink from inmates. He just shrugged and picked up a little jar which bore a familiar whitish liquid.

"You know what this is?" he asked.

Having seen semen often enough I replied, "Yeah, I sure do."

He then proceeded to pour the semen into his coffee and began drinking as if he'd just added cream.

The act reinforced my doubts concerning his mental stability, but I still did not see his actions as warranting transfer to Bridgewater. So I again moved on.

Not one to give up easily, this poor fellow gave it another try a few nights after that. This time when I reached his cell I found him holding a can of paint thinner which he proceeded to sprinkle all over his hairdo.

Finally putting down the can he said, "Don't go away, I want you to see something."

With that he struck a match, touched it to his hair, and POOF! Within a few seconds what had been an afro had become smoldering stubble. The flash fire had blistered his scalp hideously. He, of course, had mercifully passed out.

By the time we opened his cell the fire had extinguished itself. All we could do was administer first aid and get him to the hospital. I never did learn whether the ordeal was worth the pain; the next day administration granted his wish. We packed him into an ambulance and shipped him to Bridgewater.

A few inmates became so despondent over conditions that they took the ultimate step and committed suicide. Suicides occur in all prisons, but one that took place in Block Ten shook all of us. It showed the depth of depression a human being could reach.

One morning the officers came upon an inmate who had hung himself with his bathrobe cord. The cell layout made hanging oneself difficult; the walls and ceiling didn't provide any place to fasten a cord. This inmate, however, managed to hang himself by pure determination. He had wound his bathrobe cord through the bars, tied it around his throat, and sat down, allowing the pressure to cut off the flow of air through his windpipe. At any point he could have saved his life simply by rising to his feet. Instead he chose to endure slow, agonizing strangulation rather than face another day in Walpole.

The holiday season came and I looked forward to some relief from the pressure by spending time with family. We had always been close-knit, and this year I especially wanted my mother to have a pleasant Christmas. She had endured a great deal of anxiety knowing the danger I faced each day. I'm sure my father had concerns also, but he always came across as a strong guy who felt that a man had to live by the principles in which he believed.

Many inmates celebrated Christmas too. But on this particular Christmas Eve the Department of Corrections had a gathering on its hands it had not planned on. At Framingham, another prison in the system, a group of female inmates had taken guards as hostages and were threatening murder.

We heard about the incident just after the ten o'clock lockup. Supervisor O'Rourke came to us and asked for twenty volunteers to suit up in riot gear and accompany him to Framingham. Negotiations had broken down, necessitating aggressive action against the building where the hostages were being held. Since no other institution in the system had guards as well trained as those at Walpole, Commissioner Hall had put out the request.

The overture catered to our egos. Having faced so much violence together, a camaraderie existed among most of the guards, especially when someone stacked us up against officers of other institutions. The 3–11 shift under Lahoud felt particularly proud of its ability to handle tough situations. So in spite of the holiday, O'Rourke had more than twenty men to choose from.

For whatever reason, he passed me by, leaving me very disappointed. I had never taken part in a hostage incident and wanted the experience. Suddenly family and Christmas celebration slipped from my awareness. I approached one of my friends among the chosen and begged him to give me his spot. Amused by the desperation in my plea, he finally agreed. O'Rourke didn't balk, so I joined the others and we marched down to the armory.

Our armory carried the reputation for being the best equipped in the state. Both the State Police and the National Guard actually borrowed weapons from Walpole.

For this mission we gathered helmets, night sticks, shields, our special crowbars, handguns, shotguns, tear gas, and tear gas launchers with missiles that could penetrate an inch of oak before exploding.

Then we piled into private cars and began driving the twenty miles to Framingham through a heavy snowstorm. As is common when you put three feisty guys together on their way to adventure, colorful stories began to pass back and forth. The two officers riding with me had seen a lot during their years at Walpole.

As we approached Framingham Prison we saw dozens of State Police cars lining the road. Turning into the prison driveway we spotted the State Police, approximately seventy-five of them, standing at attention, looking very sharp in their natty uniforms and formidable riot gear. They had even brought along several attack dogs.

I found the sight both impressive and ominous, and wondered why the State Police hadn't already handled the attack. They carried a reputation for being highly trained and tended to perform their normal duties in a cocky manner. I'd always assumed they would be experts in dealing with prison disturbances.

My companions informed me otherwise. During such situations the State Police usually handled only perimeter duties. If at all possible, cleanup of the mess was left to the guards.

This still didn't make any sense to me. Why summon guards from twenty miles away when heavily armed State Police had already arrived on the scene? During the delay the hostages could have been killed.

I felt rather awkward when the twenty of us gathered in clear view of the State Police. Technically we carried the status of Special State Police Officers, but, in contrast to the troopers' spit and polish appearance, we could have just as easily belonged to the local sanitation department. The Department of Corrections had yet to issue a standard uniform to their officers.

We were escorted into the administration building, where the Framingham Superintendent and Commissioner Hall awaited us. If Hall recognized me in my riot gear he gave no indication. This was no time for casual conversation.

The talks had broken down over an hour before, triggering several subsequent threats by the inmates to kill the hostages. Hall now apparently saw no alternative to attacking the block.

The Superintendent directed our attention to a blackboard containing a layout of the cottage dormitory where the hostages were being held. He estimated that approximately fifty inmates were involved. Four of them were holding two female guards at knife point, tied back to back in an interior room. We closely studied this room along with the location of the entrance doors and the setup of the cells.

The briefing took almost an hour, during which I reflected how it would be for anyone to die on Christmas. Being a religious man, it struck me that Christmas and Easter might indeed be the best days for a Christian to die. I forced these fatalistic thoughts from my mind and concentrated on the issue at hand.

The strategy seemed obvious to everyone. The cottage featured an entrance door at each end. We had to reach both doors simultaneously, quickly break through, and rush to the holding room before the inmates could kill the hostages. To reach the doors we had to follow a path that ran from the administration building directly toward the cottage. After several yards the path forked, providing access to both entrances.

Cottage windows looked directly out upon the path making it virtually impossible to approach the cottage undetected, especially with floodlights illuminating the scene. We could've killed the lights but that would have alarmed the inmates, possibly into taking action against the hostages.

The Superintendent gave us one final instruction before clearing us to rush the cottage. He wanted us to remain undetected for as long as possible and, therefore, ordered us to refrain from making noise. This ran contrary to all the training we had received.

Once by ourselves O'Rourke quickly countermanded the last order and told us we would show the inexperienced Superintendent and Commissioner how to rescue hostages. We would march toward the cottage in perfect step, calling out our cadence, increasing our pace until at a full run.

All of us trusted O'Rourke's judgment. We all felt psyched. You could see muscles swelling, bellies tightening, and facial expressions turning deadly serious. Butterflies danced in my stomach as I realized that one mistake could cost two lives.

We lined up outside in two columns. I stood third in my line. The first man carried the shotgun, the second a crowbar and gas gun. I carried gas missiles and gas grenades. The other seven wielded nightsticks and carried shields.

As we moved out our heavy boots gave us good traction in spite of the snow. We could see several inmates staring out at us through the windows of the cottage. Our pace started slow, feet stomping, voices remaining deep and together. Each heavy footstep and thunderous cadence call made it sound like a giant monster approaching.

The pace steadily quickened and the cadence call increased in volume until we were running at full speed and yelling at the tops of our lungs. Each column took a separate fork and we did reach both doors at the same time. The crowbars forced each door without difficulty and we entered the cottage from both directions simultaneously. Once inside, the shotguns were leveled and the nightsticks began beating against the corridor walls for effect.

This onslaught so shocked the inmates that many had curled up on the floors of their cells or crawled under their beds to cry like babies. Those who could not get out of the corridor in time were quickly restrained, dragged to secure rooms, and locked inside. We found the hostages abandoned, still tied up, exhausted and scared, but not physically harmed.

The entire rescue lasted perhaps a minute and a half. Its shocking suddenness had caught the inmates off guard. The systematic execution of hostages ordinarily takes mental preparation. Our terrifying appearance momentarily stunned their thought processes, giving us the time we needed. Had we tried to sneak up on the block and been detected, anger instead of fear would have dominated them. The result could have been tragic.

Once we had locked up all the inmates and shaken down the cottage for weapons, we gathered together, proud of ourselves and congratulating each other for a job well done. O'Rourke faced a dressing down by the Commissioner for disobeying orders, but we anticipated it going no further than that.

When the Superintendent asked for a half-dozen volunteers to remain and assist with transporting the inmate leaders to a more secure area, I of course stepped forward. I was still experiencing such a high from the successful operation that Santa Claus and my family had slipped into the background.

A short time later I witnessed interplay between officers and an inmate that turned my stomach. As with all the ringleaders, this particular female inmate was led handcuffed between two Framingham officers, one male and one female. I walked about three paces behind, still wearing my helmet and with nightstick ready.

I watched flabbergasted as the aggressive female inmate resisted the officers in the same manner male inmates did at Walpole. She directed her hostility at the female officer. With her arms shackled, she whipped her legs around wildly trying to kick her female captor. Frustrated that her feet could not reach her target, she began spitting all over the female guard.

"You fuckin' cunt slut!" she shrieked, like some mythological witch. "I get my hands on you I'll tear your fuckin' hair—scratch your fuckin' eyes out!" She continued on and on, shouting one foul word after another.

I had come to expect such degrading, filthy language and hostile antics from the hardened criminals at Walpole, but coming from a woman they shocked me. At that point I still held the traditional men's view of womanhood.

Throughout all this neither officer took positive steps to put a halt to this behavior. I began wondering how much abuse they were willing to take. At one point I was tempted to step forward, put the inmate down on the snow and drag her the final two hundred yards to the lockup area. I saw her as having no right to walk as a person considering the abuse she meted out. But this was their territory, not mine, so I decided to observe how the Framingham guards handled themselves in terms of protecting each other.

This incident had a lot to do with the forming of my opinion that many inmates, by virtue of their behavior, forfeit all claim to being human.

After the two guards had locked the inmate up, the female officer began violently pushing her companion around.

"You bastard!" she shouted. "How could you let her do that to me without trying to stop her?"

Her sudden outburst surprised the male officer.

"Hey, I was waiting for you to do something. You didn't ask for help. I didn't want to embarrass you."

"You're full of shit! You just won't stick your neck out for anybody!"

I couldn't remain silent any longer.

"You both acted like damn fools! If this had been Walpole we would have put the inmate down on the snow and dragged her all the way to her cell. In the process she might have lost a few teeth. Anytime a good officer sees another being attacked, physically or verbally, he takes action, whether aid is requested or not. As far as I'm concerned, you're both disgraces to your profession."

Watching this incident gave me a greater appreciation of the camaraderie shared by Walpole officers, especially those on the 3–11 shift. Our lives often depended on each other, and we never let each other down. Once we sensed a fellow officer in trouble all personal differences were set aside. It shocked me to see officers from another institution lacking a similar loyalty to each other.

We finally completed our duties at Framingham just after 5 a.m. Christmas morning. Exhaustion had finally settled in, but, as I drove my two companion guards home, we celebrated our feat. Having saved the lives of the hostages, we considered ourselves heroes. The operation had proven conclusively that our extensive training had paid off.

I turned on the radio, curious to see if the incident might be covered on the news. Sure enough, we cut right into the middle of a detailed account. As the announcer spoke in glowing terms of the efficiency shown by the rescuers, our egos swelled even further. We commented to each other that it was about time corrections officers received credit for their professionalism.

Then the newscaster pulled out the rug. He attributed the entire effort to the State Police! He made no mention of the Walpole twenty.

The oaths and profanity reverberating through that car nearly blew out the windows. I recovered my composure first and offered a philosophical view. This was Christmas and we should enjoy inner peace over what we'd done. We hadn't volunteered in order to gain recognition. We had responded to the needs of fellow officers in jeopardy. Because of our efforts they would enjoy the holidays in the safety of their homes.

My words sunk in and the guys quieted. As we drove on, however, I continued pondering the circumstances that had given credit to the State Police. I could only surmise that they employed a more effective public relations officer than did the Department of Corrections. Prison guards always seemed to be portrayed as undignified blunderers with sadistic tendencies. Without decent PR this public view would never change. That realization was to be of great value to me later.

For me personally, Christmas Day ended up being a downer. After dropping off my two companions, I arrived home shortly after 6 a.m. I had a forty-minute drive home alone from Walpole. I used the time to unwind, to transform Mike McLaughlin from a stern guard into a loving husband. That day, in spite of intense effort, my guard personality would not disappear.

Karen had planned a full day of activities with our families and now much of this would have to be postponed. I needed rest and then faced my usual 3 p.m. shift at Walpole. That left little time for social activities.

As always, Karen took all this like a trooper, accepting my apologies and showing me understanding. But I still felt badly, both for having ruined her holiday and for having to sacrifice a normal Christmas with other family members.

I remember trying to unwind in the shower and to recapture my good feelings about Christmas. I asked God for courage, direction, and peace of mind. I took solace in knowing that the end of my career as a Walpole guard lay just around the corner. In the future, I would celebrate Christmas traditionally if only God would stand with me the next few months.

I left that shower feeling my prayer had been heard. I would have access to His strength. I had no inkling then how much I would need it.

* * *

After the incident at Framingham all lingering concerns that I might be a "rat" for Hall seemed to disappear. Having often watched me wade into danger at their sides, my fellow officers trusted both my loyalty and competence. They made me one of the guys, inviting me out for beers, sharing their views, and confiding in me. In turn, I assured them that my friendship with Hall might work to their advantage. I promised to keep our problems firmly in mind once I reached a position of authority. I would fight for the officers' rights, not knuckle under to the bureaucracy.

Faces appear before me now. Bob Furtado, Steve Adair, Carl Schofield, Mike Gilmore, and many like them, men who fought the good fight every day. In the months ahead I would get to know them much better. At that time however, we were just drinking buddies bound together by a common danger from which we saw no escape. In situations like that men often fall back on their senses of humor.

Sometimes the inmates provided humorous situations to break the tension. More often their idea of humor proved embarrassing or dangerous to officers.

One inmate managed to smuggle rabbits inside that he had caught in the prison yard. Before they were discovered they had given birth to little ones that were given to other inmates. Administration did not want inmates keeping pets, so we were ordered to round them up. Naturally some of them escaped and gave birth to more. For months we found our routines interrupted when one of the furry critters would be spotted. With the aid of the inmates they'd usually get away and show up again.

At one point the canteen, which sold canned food and sundry items to the inmates, began stocking Magic Shave facial hair removed. Within a short time inmates began using it to terrorize officers, who'd be walking by a cell when a gob of the stuff would strike them in the head. They would reach up, feel the gooey mass and begin to rub. The next thing they'd have a bald spot. Until we got the stuff outlawed, any officer conscious of his appearance had to take special precautions when making his counts. Some feared the Magic Shave more than the feces that the inmates routinely tossed at us.

Another prank the inmates thought funny was turning aerosol cans into flamethrowers. I'd seen James Bond do this in a movie. Apparently some inmate in Walpole had also seen the movie and thought it good for a laugh. With aerosol sprays plentiful in the canteen, the practice soon spread.

All they had to do was fasten a section of TV antenna to the nozzle of the can. Then press down the button, light a match to the end of the antenna, and WHIZ! A pencil thin flame would shoot out and travel as far as twenty feet. Several unsuspecting officers nearly got zapped on their rounds. The inmates weren't really trying to hurt them, just having fun with pyrotechnics.

The unwritten inmate code said when you wanted to do an officer some real damage, you did it directly. Still, inmate pranks did cause some serious injuries to officers.

At one point administration made the mistake of allowing "trustworthy" inmates to cook for the officers. All went well until several officers complained that a batch of beef stew tasted funny. Soon after, a half-dozen of them suffered stomach pain and had to be taken to the hospital. Upon investigating we discovered that the cook had thickened the sauce with a can of motor oil. On top of that he had been urinating in the mashed potatoes for days, having found that the resulting stain looked exactly like the one made by melting margarine.

Bob Furtado fell victim to another trick. Before officers would eat in the chow hall, they'd wash up in a small area just off the kitchen. One day Bob walked up to the sink and began lathering a bar of soap in his hands, all the while staring in the mirror. A moment later he unsuspectingly applied the lather to his face and began scrubbing. When he again opened his eyes and looked in the mirror he panicked. Bloody red suds covered his face. Once he'd rinsed it all away he found that his face was unharmed. His hands had suffered the damage. Someone had imbedded fragments of razor blades in the soap bar. Fortunately the cuts were superficial, but for days Bob could barely grip anything.

5 "Mike, Get Yourself a Sponsor"

After my sixth month at Walpole I decided I had gained enough practical experience to upgrade my resume and begin applying for management positions. I now had three and a half years in the field, divided between Youth Services, Middlesex County House of Correction, Shattuck State Hospital, and Walpole. I also had a Bachelor's Degree in Law Enforcement and Correctional Practices and was on my way to a Master's Degree in Public Administration. I though these represented impressive credentials for a young man of twenty-six.

I felt confident I could make an exceptional showing in the interview process. From my first day at Walpole I'd made mental notes of problems I saw there and had begun formulating solutions to present to Commissioner Hall. I figured that these suggested reforms would impress Hall with what I had learned and serve as powerful ammunition in interviews with his underlings.

By this time I had sorted Walpole's problems into two major areas. The first revolved around management's philosophy of dealing with inmates.

In school we had defined two major strategies for managing a prison, one based on treatment, the other on security. A treatment-oriented policy provided an atmosphere—privileges, programs, and so on—that encouraged rehabilitation. A security-oriented policy concentrated on maintaining discipline and preventing incorrigibles from inflicting further damage on society.

Theoretically, the ideal prison environment reflected both. But at Walpole I observed one view advancing at the expense of the other.

I'd always felt that the first obligation of a prison—especially a maximum security prison—is to isolate from society those individuals who had broken its laws. Only when these criminals proved they could return to society without posing a danger should they be released.

Naturally one couldn't expect an individual to change his habits and world view without being treated humanely and offered encouragement. But the primary responsibility for rehabilitation rested with the inmate. After all, inmates had, of their own volition, committed the acts that had gotten them sentenced.

My views fell completely in line with Commissioner Hall's philosophy as he had explained it to me when I'd first met him. Actually, he hadn't talked much about the security factor because, I assumed, strict security was a given. Instead he outlined an attractive, comprehensive plan in which inmates could pass from Maximum to Minimum Security in Walpole, then to lower security prisons, camps, halfway houses, and ultimately back into society. The key to unlocking these doors was good behavior. Inmates had to earn their freedom.

I had embraced Hall's plan completely. But at Walpole I saw that somehow the process had become inverted. The well-behaved inmates seemed to lag behind while the troublemakers received positive attention. I kept hearing administrators comment that if you punished a misbehaving inmate he'd only act up more. They refused to see that their attitude only encouraged more bad behavior.

I think perhaps the public uproar over the Attica riots a few years before, plus Walpole's violent history, had turned administrators paranoid. Hypersensitive to public opinion, they wanted to keep Walpole quiet at all costs. To them, pacifying the troublemakers seemed the only way.

I intended making that point in the interviews and ultimately to Hall. He had to be told that his program was being sabotaged by men who didn't share his vision. The program itself functioned, but the wrong inmates were passing through the system.

The second major problem I saw at Walpole centered around mistreatment of officers. Security suffered because officers' morale remained low. This couldn't be blamed on one lone factor. To start with, the prison was undermanned; even administration admitted this. Walpole had 240 officers but needed 300. Low salaries and high peril kept the number of qualified applicants down. As a result, regular officers worked long hours in an inadequately supervised environment. The consequences could be lethal.

At the same time these officers, most of whom intended a career in Corrections, saw bleak prospects for upward mobility. Corrections officers were ranked in three classifications: supervisors, senior C.O.'s, and junior C.O.'s. Civil service provided frequent exams to recruit entry level officers, but it had been several years since a civil service exam had been offered to junior officers seeking senior or supervisory status. Over half of the existing seniors and supervisors had been appointed by management. Although they belonged to our union, they would stand with management on every issue. Guards who intended to make their career in corrections—many in the process of starting families and buying houses—saw that to get ahead they must cooperate with management and do exactly as told, against their better judgment. Officers seemed to receive promotions based on their acquiescence to management, not seniority or test score. Naturally, qualified officers who were repeatedly overlooked became frustrated. But even then they dared not complain for fear of being harassed.

Uncooperative officers could find themselves pulled off their bid job (an assignment won by seniority) and assigned to another post that did not offer the best days off. Or they might find themselves put on the Doctor's List, which meant that each time they took an earned sick day they could not return without a doctor's note. Considering the cost of visiting a doctor, most men worked with heavy colds and stomach flu when they should have been in bed.

The toughest harassment tool of all was management's control of Industrial Accident pay. If an officer was stabbed by an inmate and faced lengthy convalescence, he was entitled to IA pay but usually would not receive it for months. During this time he was forced to go without income.

Why? Management claimed that once it filed the paperwork, everything was out of its hands. First the Industrial Accident Board had to approve the claim. Then it went to the Attorney General's office for review and final signature. The claim then returned to the IA Board who could begin issuing checks. Somewhere in this pipeline, guard injury claims always seemed to be held up.

Peculiarly, however, my fellow officers could cite a number of instances where injured officers friendly to management had received prompt payment. At that point I didn't feel qualified to hurl any charges, but I did see more than one officer bleeding through his bandages because he'd returned to work too soon.

As with the treatment policy, I felt confident that once Hall was told about the officers' problems he'd take steps to rectify them. I saw myself as his potential instrument for implementing these changes, especially once he and his subordinates saw my grasp of the situation.

I didn't feel comfortable going to Hall and asking him to bring me into his department. That was exactly the practice I intended to criticize. Instead I began watching the bulletin board outside personnel for job opportunities. The Department was required to post all its openings.

I kept looking for interesting mid-level management positions that listed qualifications I could meet and offered a decent salary increase. Periodically I'd find them. I'd send a cover letter and my resume to the department listed and copies to Hall so he'd know I was applying. Within a few weeks I'd be interviewed before a panel.

The nature of the questions told me that the interviewers were probably less qualified than I was to hold their positions. Since I was applying for positions subordinate to theirs, it appeared that breaking into management would be a snap. But nearly six months went by and during that time I received four interviews and four rejections.

Four job rejections may not sound like a large number, but I was a young man in a hurry. Six months in Walpole seemed like an eternity, and I had grandiose plans for myself. Besides, I had picked up this peculiar feeling in my interviews that the panel and the questioning were but a courtesy. The jobs had already been taken by someone who hadn't gone through the process. Could I be running into the same collusion the other guards had talked about? I had to find out and the only way to do so was to confront the Commissioner of Corrections.

Spring had arrived, a time for recommitment and rebirth. That's what I told myself as I maneuvered through the busy downtown Boston traffic that May morning. The sight of the Statehouse sent my heart palpitating. I hoped one day to make that structure my regular place of work. For now, however, I drove by, seeking a less official destination, the restaurant where Frank Hall had agreed to meet me.

Mixed feelings accompanied me on this drive. I felt grateful that Hall had responded cordially to my phone call and kept his previous promise to be available whenever I wished to discuss my career. I was even more grateful when he went out of his way to find an opening in his busy schedule. He ended up offering to meet with me for a late breakfast.

This seemed to say I still had his ear. Yet I couldn't shake the underlying ominous feeling that had grown during my frustrating quest to obtain a promotion.

I had known Frank Hall for over two years. Circumstances had brought us together at a Northeastern University seminar on Law Enforcement and Correctional Practices. I had attended both as a graduate student who had earned his undergraduate degree in that field, and as a professional who worked for the Middlesex County House of Correction. Hall was one of the guest panelists.

When Governor Sargent had recruited him a year and a half before, Hall had become one of the youngest Commissioners of Correction in the nation. He considered himself a "New Deal" liberal who believed "Government could still do things for people." Or so he told the press.

In the months that followed he became respected and popular throughout the state. He spoke frequently on television and radio and received praise for the organization and accomplishments of his administration from the most widely read newspaper in the area, The Boston Globe. When the Democratic Governor, Michael Dukakis, took over from the Republican, Sargent, in January 1975, he kept Hall on. This made Hall's appointment appear to be nonpartisan.

Hall's most notable achievement was the establishment of community-based treatment units known as halfway houses. The only bad mark against his record was the continuing violence at Walpole. He managed to evade heavy public criticism on the matter by pointing out that other prisons in the system ran smoothly. He contended that Walpole represented a unique problem that he would resolve over time. With his history of success, everyone believed him.

As he spoke at the seminar I found myself in general agreement with his views and eager to work under him. He'd outlined a program called reintegration. This did not deal with rehabilitation or in changing an offender's behavior. Rather it sought to provide an efficient means for cooperative inmates to move through the system and make a smooth transition back into society.

The idea involved establishing a network of stepping stones. Each would reduce the extent of supervision by a limited degree so that the offender could prepare for release gradually. He would escape facing the sudden shock of going from maximum security Walpole to the total freedom of the everyday world.

To implement this, spokespeople in the community would identify locations for, and help set up, reintegration centers. The Department would work with employers to arrange jobs. It would also bring families into closer contact with offenders so that spouses and children could gradually refamiliarize themselves with a long-absent loved one.

The program appeared to be well thought out, but I hadn't heard him address security considerations. I wanted him to flesh out the picture by describing how society would be protected from those who stumbled on their way through the program.

I figured one of the experienced professionals in the audience would ask the question. When none of them did, I finally put it forward and received a loud round of applause. This told me that many of these men had wanted an answer but felt reluctant to put Hall on the spot. If he wasn't their boss at the time, he might one day be.

Hall did not appear offended by my question. Instead he praised it and answered in a manner I found satisfactory.

At the seminar's conclusion I waited at the rear of the room hoping to meet him. He surprised me by coming forward, shaking my hand, and asking me about myself. My background interested him, and the discussion broadened to include our philosophies toward correctional practices. We found we shared very similar thoughts. I liked the man and I felt he liked me. Even so, I felt stunned when he invited me to join an elite new department he was forming within the Department of Corrections—The Security Management Team.

Naturally I was elated. In one fortuitous moment my career had received an enormous boost. The position with the SMT promised to be interesting, influential, and a perfect springboard into higher management.

I joined the SMT six months after fulfilling a school obligation. I was immediately sent to the Department's training academy for eight weeks of physical training and classroom instruction on how to deal with inmates. On graduation I was a Special State Police Officer. With that under my belt I was ready to cast off and face the adventures of my new career.

But suddenly all the glamour disappeared. Instead of becoming part of a team that traveled from prison to prison investigating difficult problems, I found myself assigned to Shattuck State Hospital. There I spent a boring year, seemingly floating in the backwaters of the Department. I gained little experience dealing with inmates and made little use of my education.

To his credit, Hall was willing to listen to my complaints. He invited me to a private meeting in his office where we discussed my career.

My request for transfer to Walpole startled him and he recommended that I reconsider. He could see no value in such a move. It would be a step backward that would expose me to an environment that had broken many men. Headstrong as always, I continued making my arguments until finally he gave in. I thought I had sold him on my own program and timetable for advancement in his department.

Now as I drove up to the restaurant, doubt haunted me. Had something gone wrong? Why had those under him stonewalled me?

We met inside and, after being ushered to our table, ordered coffee and a sweet roll. He had expected to buy me breakfast but I was too keyed up and eager to talk. Before he even ordered I began explaining my concerns. I reminded him that I had now spent a full year at Walpole and had recently applied for four management positions without success. Besides feeling discouraged, I felt dismayed over not getting anywhere when those interviewing me seemed less qualified than I.

I asked him, "What's going on? What can I do? Is there a future for me? Do you have plans for me? What do you suggest?"

He looked at me matter-of-factly and stated, "Mike, get yourself a sponsor."

"A sponsor?" I replied. "What do you mean?"

"Get a State Representative to give me a call on your behalf."

I sat there stunned, as if he'd slapped me in the face. What did a politician have to do with this? Hall himself had invited me to join the Department. Wasn't that "sponsor" enough?

"What about merit, seniority, and work experience? How does that fit in? Doesn't any of it count?"

He looked at me tolerantly and very curtly replied, "Mike, get a sponsor. My hands are tied."

Thinking about this after the shock had worn off, I wondered just who had tied his hands. He reported directly to the Governor's office. Did Dukakis stand behind this system of patronage?

Perhaps someone else would have backed off and tried to salvage something of the situation. I suffered from one of my frequent attacks of righteous indignation. Whenever that happened I lost all restraint.

I told him that I didn't know any politicians and that I didn't want to know any just for the purpose of gaining favors. I pointed out that many officers deserved a chance at various promotions. It was unfair that they should all need politicians to succeed. Political patronage was one of the major factors behind Walpole's unrest. I wouldn't become part of the problem. If I couldn't gain a promotion through merit I would rather not have one.

He heard me out and then stated that he hoped I would change my mind. I could see the conversation had reached an impasse. I stood up, tossed a dollar on the table and stormed out—my bridge effectively burned with the usual McLaughlin style. Maybe I should have belonged to a military demolition team.

As I drove to the prison my thoughts became a total jumble. What could I do now? What career plans could I make? Should I relocate to another state and seek a corrections position there? Should I leave corrections altogether? Should I study some other degree program and get out of the Department? Should I remain in the field and teach?

I even briefly entertained the thought of seeking a politician's help. But conscience quickly intervened. I'd never been able to respect any man who advanced in that manner. I could never feel any sense of accomplishment if I stooped to that device.

My mind finally drifted back to Hall. I wondered if I had alienated him by insisting on the transfer to Walpole. Might he not have remained the sponsor I needed had I followed the career path he had set for me?

That evening I felt awkward discussing the situation with Karen. She was fully supportive, yet underneath I knew her to be a pragmatist. As she put it, "Sometimes you have to play ball for awhile until you gain a position of authority. Then you can step forward and begin making the changes you want."

I could never see that view. Head down, straight ahead—that was my standard procedure for pursuing goals. I valued a clear conscience above all else and could not maintain one by playing ball.

Fortunately for our marriage, the pragmatist in Karen managed to tolerate my headstrong nature with a minimum of complaint, drawing on her own strength to keep us together. Had she not done so, I might not have made it through those years.

* * *

The first few days after my breakfast meeting with Hall I could perceive no solution to my predicament. Depressed, I fought off the urge to quit my job and continued searching within myself for some ethical way to mend fences. My family and all my roots were in the Boston area. I couldn't see myself picking up and leaving without exhausting every avenue. That would be like running away.

Then, out of a clear blue sky, an opportunity dropped in my lap from a totally unexpected quarter.

Around the prison I had begun hearing talk about the election for Walpole guard union president, scheduled for some six weeks hence. This year's contest stood in sharp contrast to previous ones. For once the guards felt they might have a candidate who would truly represent them to management. This had been far from the case in the past. They had come to expect their presidents to be manipulated by both management and the bosses of the statewide employees union, Council 93. The important interests of the guards always went unattended.

One evening after the ten o'clock count I sat with a half-dozen members of the 3–11 shift commiserating over the miserable safety conditions we faced. Safety always seemed to be of greater concern to those of us on 3–11 because ninety percent of the violence occurred on our shift. We also had fewer officers than the day shift. The 11–7 overnight shift had fewer officers yet, but they patrolled a locked-up prison and faced considerably less danger.

Not knowing the history of the union, I questioned why its leadership did not fight for safety reforms. I received a sobering story. For years their own union officers had been selling them out, including the president and the majority of his Executive Board, most of whom had sought their jobs merely for the opportunity to act like big shots. They enjoyed wheeling and dealing with both management and Council 93, who told them that if they laid down and didn't confront important issues, they'd be taken care of.

When they grew tired of Walpole they'd suddenly suffer injury, usually "slipping on the stairs and hurting their backs." After a perfunctory medical examination, papers would go through and they'd be granted early retirement at 72% pay. Many of them were barely forty years of age. A number owned bars, restaurants, or vacation homes in Florida.

Confront safety issues? For what? Demand that management apply a fair means of selection to fill job vacancies? Why? One of the past presidents had even resigned to accept a management position. How could the guards view that except as a sellout? How could they ever believe in a union whose leadership displayed such a poor sense of ethics?

This election promised to be a little more interesting. An outspoken senior officer on the day shift, Roy Scandia, had declared himself a candidate, promising to challenge management on the issues.

During his two years in office, the incumbent president, Al Costas, had followed in the paths of his predecessors. His close ties to Council 93 were public. He served as its sergeant-at-arms. Few of the guards liked him. Most had no illusion as to his loyalties. It appeared as if Scandia could beat him.

Scandia's candidacy had ignited interest among the 3–11 officers because we felt particularly vulnerable to poor management decisions. On a daily basis we also faced the toughest conditions. This had turned us into a tightly-knit group with a strong sense of pride. Naturally we were tired of being pushed around by management. Anyone willing to represent us in a crusade against the bureaucracy was worthy of support.

Scandia had convinced most of the shift that he would take a radical position and vigorously pursue the issues. This increased his appeal enormously.

But beyond that the 3–11's enthusiasm waned. Scandia's personality and language were often volatile. They feared that in the midst of important bargaining he might lose his temper and alienate those who had the power to grant us what we wanted.

While Roy's outspokenness appealed to the emotions of many of the guards, they recognized that it might backlash. Management might use Scandia's lack of tact as an excuse to quit talking completely.

We had been kicking these thoughts around for some time when one of the men suddenly said, "Hey, Mac, why don't you run for president? We need someone like you to talk for us. Someone who can pull a long goddamn word out of the hat during a discussion rather than just grunting and cursing."

"Yeah," another one chimed in. "You've got a way about you. You're getting your degree. That impresses even them. You can talk to management on their level. And you know what we're going through."

"But fellas," I protested, "it'll be next month before I've been here a year. Isn't there some service requirement attached to the office?"

"All you need's a year. You'll have that by the time of the election."

"But I've never even attended a union meeting."

"So what? Most of us have given up going. We'd go if we had something worth going for."

"But how can I lead the union when so many of you guys have much more experience and seniority? It doesn't seem right. Besides, who'd follow my leadership?"

"Hey man, we haven't had any leadership to follow. If you speak for us we'll be behind you all the way."

By now more of my fellow officers had joined the discussion. Most had comments, none were negative. I found it hard to believe that these guys were actually serious about putting forward a guy twenty-seven years old with barely a year in the prison and no union experience.

Other than what I'd learned in school I knew nothing about unions. I had no idea of how this one was structured, how its bylaws and constitution read. I didn't even know the responsibilities of its president. What power did he wield? How did he relate to Council 93? How did he initiate meetings with management? All of those questions hit me at once along with the biggest of all—could I do the job?

Still smarting from my meeting with Hall, my first inclination was to seek the presidency and then use the office to strike back at him. I quickly saw, however, that by doing this I'd betray the guys. They were asking me to carry forth our issues as a group, not carry on a personal vendetta.

I also found myself swayed by the proud feeling of being chosen their spokesman. The flattery exerted strong pressure, but I knew that if I accepted for that reason I would ultimately cheat myself. I must decide if this move would serve my own self interests. By definition, union and management stood diametrically opposed. If I made my bed with the union I must commit myself completely. I must give up all management aspirations and stop applying for jobs in the Department. After all the career plans I'd made the past few years, it wasn't an easy decision.

I took a couple of days to decide. The reality kept hitting home that Hall could have had me as a manager but had turned me down, with strong possibility that the door might never open again. What would I be sacrificing by casting my lot with my brother officers who had asked me to use on their behalf the very skills Hall had rejected.

One door had closed, another had opened. It seemed only logical to join with those who wanted me and could make use of my abilities.

Once I made the decision to run I still faced a tough fight with Costas and Scandia. Costas represented the old system. Business as usual. Favors for those who played ball. He appealed to a number of those with seniority, who had learned to play the game. Safety issues didn't mean as much to them since they'd managed to work their way into easier jobs over the years. Why rock the boat now with retirement just around the corner?

Scandia had the majority of the day shift behind him because of his personality. Volatile or not, once you got to know Roy you couldn't help liking him. I liked him myself, and I had to admire his dedication and courage for initiating the opposition to Costas during this campaign.

My strength lay on the 3–11 shift. But while they stood almost solidly behind me, the day shift complement outnumbered them by about 3 to 2. The overnight shift was the smallest of the three and it remained to be seen who its members would support. This also held for the fifty or so civilian workers—cooks, maintenance people, and so on—who were union members.

My biggest problem was image. I remained relatively unknown to those not on my shift. Because of my businesslike manner in the prison, I realized I had seemed abrasive and distant in casual contact. I also still had a few enemies from early days when I had questioned some officers' competence.

What I did have in my favor was a reputation for fairness, dedication, and courage. Even Scandia himself had recognized those qualities in me when I'd worked overtime for him on the day shift.

The entire campaign took place on the prison grounds. Costas and Scandia had risen above the status of block officers so they had more mobility during their shifts than I. They could move about addressing individuals and groups of officers in the process of performing their regular duties. On the other hand, I could not leave my post except for lunch or breaks, so I was forced to do most of my canvassing before and after my shift. Fortunately this did not hurt me with my shift because I already had the 3–11 pretty much sewed up.

Winning over the day shift proved to be a stiffer challenge. I remember my first meeting as a candidate with a group of them in the rec-room before roll call. I tried to gather as many as I could into a group. Since many had already decided for my opponents and others simply had no interest, they continued playing cards or shooting pool. Thirty or so did gather around me and began tossing legitimate questions.

"You're only a junior officer. You've only been here a year. Why should we vote for you over guys like Al and Roy who've got far more seniority and experience?"

"First of all," I replied, "Al hasn't been doing much of a job representing you. I'm not going to say anything bad about Roy. I'm sure he'd do a good job. I just think I can do a better one. I've studied labor relations. I believe I'm more articulate. Management has been ignoring you guys because you haven't had a president who is willing to carry a fight on their level. I promise I will."

"McLaughlin," one of them observed, "we know you're a friend of Commissioner Hall. How's a friend of the head of the Department going to do a good job representing us?"

"I admit, I was a friend of Hall's. But that's past history. Hall shafted me just like he continues to shaft you. We're not friends anymore. I'm ready to slug it out with him over a bargaining table."

"Are you saying," another asked, "that if Hall offered you a job tomorrow you'd turn it down?"

"I am. Furthermore, I'm willing to promise you that I will not seek out any management positions within the Department for at least a year."

I sensed my words had swayed some of them, but not necessarily enough to vote for me. Apathy hung over this group. The safety issue wasn't as crucial to them because they didn't experience nearly as much violence as we on the 3–11 shift. I also sensed that they were more hesitant to reject the status quo. Seniority had placed many of them on the day shift. They had seen loud-mouthed presidents come and go without changing anything. Why should they believe I'd be any different?

The overnight, 11–7, shift had a slightly different perspective. They didn't face the same safety problems as the 3–11 because overnight the prison remained locked up. I discovered that they were more interested in what I had to say about general benefits. They also had become used to being neglected by union presidents because of the odd hours of the shift.

"Look, you guys," I told a group of them after intercepting them in the corridor as they filed inside, "I intend to make fairness a cornerstone of my presidency. Every member will be treated equally by the union and every member should receive opportunities for job advancement from management commensurate to their work experience and seniority. I know that's not happening now, but I intend to fight for it."

"We hear you're just going to be president for the 3–11 shift," one of them shot back.

"I promise you that as president I will meet with every shift at least once a week to discuss problems. I intend to bring the three shifts together. We all work in the same place and face the same dangers."

Then came the same question. "What makes you think that with only one year's experience you can effectively represent us?"

I answered that question many times during those first weeks in June. Whether in the rec-room, in the corridor, or in the chow hall trying to win over the kitchen personnel, I answered it the same way. I could sense that I swayed a few votes, but apathy still hovered over the campaign like a dark cloud.

During the day I'd occasionally cross paths in the corridor with Costas and Scandia. I never saw either make much of an effort to win over the 3–11 guys. Costas presented himself as the candidate with connections—the handshaking, backslapping type. Scandia acted like one of the guys and sought votes on that basis. He knew what everyone was going through and was willing to throw these issues in management's face. Roy never took offense at me canvassing his shift. Costas, on the other hand, acted like I was trespassing. But he knew better than to say anything.

Actually Costas had been placed in a peculiar position. To him the Walpole presidency represented a titular post rather than one of substance. He already had a more significant union post with Council 93 that he would continue to hold even if he lost the presidency. His problem was one of losing face. If the Walpole guards rejected him, his reputation with Council 93 as a man who could control votes would diminish. Future ambitions with the Council might then suffer.

Management hardly paid any attention to the election. They hadn't had any problems with presidents before and they didn't anticipate any as a result of this election. To them the proceedings were little more than a nuisance that in minor ways disrupted prison routine.

About three weeks before election day my campaign focus suddenly shifted. It was then that I first saw a copy of the new statewide union contract that would soon come before the 48,000 membership for ratification. The document had taken four months to negotiate. It spelled out salary provisions, benefits, and working conditions that applied to all member locals, including ours. Over the next three years it would govern all negotiations with management.

I had heard that prior contracts had left the union completely vulnerable. Now, the further I read the more angry I became. In glaring fashion the contract favored the state, undermining the bargaining positions of its employees. I could not believe any union would give away so much. Union negotiators had even allowed different pay standards for current and future employees.

Language in the area of safety I found of particular concern to me:

> Section 1A: "The employer agrees to provide a safe, clean, wholesome surrounding in all places of employment. At least once per week the employer shall inspect the premises to maintain good housekeeping."

This section did not define a "safe, clean, wholesome surrounding," nor did its wording offer redress once the employer made his weekly inspection and declared the housekeeping to be in order.

> Section 1D: "If a tool, machine, or piece of equipment is defective, worn out, or dangerous to operate because of its condition, the supervisor shall not permit its use until authorized by his department head or his designee."

I read into this that if the department head authorized the use of an acknowledged faulty piece of equipment the employee would be expected to do so. It did not say anything about fixing the equipment.

> Section 1G: "When an employee reports any condition which he/she believes to be injurious to his/her health to the administration head of a work location, the administrative head shall correct the situation if within his/her authority, or shall report said complaint to his supervisor."

Great! And then what? What redress did the employee have if the supervisor failed to act or disagreed with the assessment?

The contract listed many more such nebulous paragraphs. The

bottom line was that management would allow us to complain about the absence of commonsensical safety measures, but they would acknowledge no specific standards. Everything was a matter of interpretation.

I saw at once that this wording would hamstring my efforts to negotiate safety improvements at Walpole. It would place me into the position of an advisor rather than an equal partner. I didn't know how I could combat this. Council 93 was getting out the word to all its 48,000 members, praising the contract and encouraging ratification. I only had the ears of the three hundred members of our local. It seemed futile to resist, but I still decided to make an issue of it in the election.

The day after I read the contract I went to the prison and expounded upon it to every officer I could corral. I caught small groups in the rec-room, single officers on break, and tables of them during lunch.

"This contract is a disgrace," I told them. "It erodes our ability to negotiate on wages, benefits, and safety."

As I sat with several of them in the dining room, one said, "Costas has been praising the contract and urging us to vote for it."

"Did he read it to you?" I responded. "He wouldn't dare. Listen to this."

Retrieving a copy of the contract from my briefcase, I read them the language that troubled me and explained why. By the time I'd finished many were shaking their heads. One of them voiced the sentiments that most of them held.

"So we vote against it, so what? We're just a small local. It's going to pass."

"Well I'm not just going to sit here. I intend to be your president and I can't be as effective in that capacity if I have to live with this contract. I'm going to visit the other prisons and see if I can get their memberships to vote against it too. Maybe I can start a movement."

And so I made trips to Concord and Norfolk prisons and managed to drum up opposition to the contract there. The two local presidents weren't happy to have me opposing them on their own turf, but my actions impressed the Walpole guards. When they saw me willing to make that serious an effort in opposition to the union's mainstream, previously disinterested guards began taking a look at my candidacy.

My attacks on the contract hit particularly hard at Costas. I was told that once I had made my objections clear to everyone, he couldn't make a campaign pitch without officers demanding to know why he supported the contract. When he tried to generalize by describing its merits with superlatives, the guards would have nothing of it. They threw up the specific points they had heard me hammering away at. Costas could not answer. Time after time he had to walk away embarrassed.

Within a few days it became apparent that his reelection effort had failed. Rather than face a humiliating defeat at the ballot box, he dropped out.

That left Scandia and me to battle it out. We were two men with similar views. But we had vastly different backgrounds and widely diverging philosophies on how to accomplish reform. Roy suddenly found himself facing the backwash of the wave that had swept away Costas. The membership wanted to hear his stance on the contract. He did oppose it, but he had difficulty articulating why. He also had trouble explaining why he had not been alert to the weaknesses in the contract before I had pointed them out. This did not speak well for his abilities to lead.

At the same time, the initiative and energy I'd displayed in opposing the contract had definitely impressed the quards with my leadership qualities. The election suddenly looked close.

The day of the balloting was a regular day off for me but I still spent much of it at the prison doing some final canvassing. Scandia and I met briefly and expressed sincere best wishes to each other.

The ballot box itself sat on a table in the rec-room. I placed myself nearby as the men arrived for work or checked out after their shifts. Many still suffered from apathy but I wanted to encourage them to vote. Some would say, "I'm in a hurry, I'll vote later on," or "I've already voted," as they punched their time cards and then hurried out. I knew they hadn't voted, but what could I do?

I sweated out that day. To most, the presidency did not look like much. But to me it represented a management position in the field of corrections, something I no longer had access to through the Department. Besides the valuable experience it would offer, I knew that often a management job becomes what you make of it.

That evening I had to break away from the prison to attend an important social engagement in Boston. I was too much on edge to enjoy myself. If I lost in the balloting I would be faced with the prospect of remaining a common guard indefinitely or seeking a complete career change. I didn't want to be faced with that.

I knew it wouldn't take long to count the two hundred to three hundred votes so I only waited a half hour beyond the voting deadline. Then I called the prison. I reached one of my staunchest supporters, Officer Mel Varney.

"Well, Mel?" I asked, holding my breath. "How'd I do?"

"You did all right, Mr. President."

"You're kidding. I won?"

"Yeah you won. The final count was 119–85. Not a great turnout, but we elected the right guy."

Elation shot through me and I started to laugh. "Damn, how about that! I won. I actually won. Mel, tell the 3–11 how happy I am, will you?"

"You tell them yourself tomorrow."

When I hung up and announced my victory to those in the room, I was showered with congratulations. But, as I stood there soaking up the attention, I felt a pang of fear. I had accepted the responsibility, now I had to deliver the goods. Where should I start?

6 Meet the Press

After my election as president I had to step back and reassess my entire posture in the prison. I could no longer view myself as a lone ranger, pursuing my own personal agenda. I now had a large family to look after, one that numbered nearly three hundred. This seemed like quite a responsibility to a guy who didn't even know how to run a union meeting.

My first day at the prison after being elected the guys of the 3–11 shift cheered me at roll call and asked for a speech. As I stood before them I seesawed between feelings of pride and humility.

"Guys," I said. "First, thanks. Without you solidly behind me I had no chance. Now I intend to fulfill all my promises. I have a lot to do and I'm going to need your continued support. I'm not due to be sworn in for a couple weeks, but as of this moment I'm going to start pushing hard to make Walpole safe and restore benefits to the officers."

Cheering interrupted me and suddenly I found myself too swept up by the emotion to continue. What more was there to say anyway? The time had come to begin acting on my promises.

As a final gesture they passed up a gavel to me. Staring at it I remember asking myself, "How do I use this thing? Do I bang it once? Do I bang it twice? Do I bang it at all?" Suddenly feeling stupid, I knew I had some research to do.

I immediately ran out and bought a copy of Robert's Rules of

Order, and read it from cover to cover. When I finished that I dissected the union constitution and bylaws. I'd been told that union meetings had not been conducted with any formality. I intended to change that. Familiarity with these items, added to my knowledge of the proposed union contract, gave me the necessary confidence to proceed with union business.

One of my first tasks was to begin building an image of strength and credibility with management. I knew their perception of my age and lack of experience would pose a problem right from the start. I could hardly hope to bargain with them if I acted like a pompous punk kid. At the same time I couldn't afford to act meek and malleable either. I had to establish myself as a figure unique to their experience—reasonable yet incorruptible.

To that point my contact with management had been limited mainly to cordial greetings in the corridor. Occasionally managers would give me direct orders to carry out, or I would escort inmates to see them. But the contact usually remained superficial, with them doing the talking and me politely listening.

Butterworth, Larker, Tinker, McCoy—I had become familiar with the faces and from personal observation had formed an opinion of their personalities and temperament. My strongest impression of them, however, had been instilled in me by my fellow officers, the majority of whom—and certainly most of the 3–11 shift—strongly resented the management group, considering them enemies of the guards and responsible for many guard injuries.

With this animosity existing, I knew I faced a long uphill struggle to fulfill my campaign promises concerning safety. From what I'd heard, the local was in disarray. It lacked unity. No previous president had ever tried to pull it together. They'd never talked of striking for safety. None had ever even spoken publicly against the Superintendent. Instead they had wheeled and dealed for their own individual benefit, occasionally tossing the membership a few scraps.

Without unity the union could never force management to implement changes. But unity could only be built upon trust of the union leadership, and building that would take time. Just how much time I couldn't be sure, but I knew I couldn't afford to wait for unity before beginning my crusade for reform. Certain things had to be dealt with immediately.

I'd won the election on June 15. I was to be installed on July 5. In between, on June 30, the vote on the statewide union contract was scheduled.

To me that contract remained an outrage. I could never make use of it to bargain for safety reforms. I had to put forth every effort to stop its ratification.

My trips to Norfolk and Concord prisons had stirred up opposition to the contract there, but even if I won all their members over to my view, we did not carry enough clout to stop ratification. The union membership in all three prisons numbered less than a thousand. As a portion of the statewide 48,000 membership, we amounted to just over two per cent. The leadership of Council 93 appeared to have a strong grip on the majority of the remainder.

About a week before the scheduled vote on the contract a group of my fellow officers gathered with me after the ten o'clock count. As we sat against the wall in the corridor waiting for our relief, I complained about the consequences of having that contract hung around our necks. I told them I didn't see any hope of fighting its passage.

Suddenly one of the guys popped up with what seemed like an outrageous suggestion.

"Hey Mike, why don't you call a news conference?"

I thought he was joking. "A news conference? For what?"

"Over the contract. Tell the whole damn state what you think of it. Put it on radio and television. Tell Unit Four not to vote for it."

In one way it sounded excitingly attractive. In another, very frightening.

"News conference?" I repeated, scratching my head. "How do I do that? I mean, who do I call?"

"Call all the local channels. The radio and the newspapers too."

He was serious, making it sound so simple I found it annoying.

"Hey," I told him. "I've never talked to those guys before. They won't come for something like this."

"Sure they will. You're the union president and this is news."

Next thing I know a couple more guys jumped in.

"Yeah, you just get on the phone and call. You tell them to come at a certain time on a certain date. You get out there and you talk. Nothing to it."

Seeing that these guys were serious started my stomach churning, so I got to my feet and began pacing. "A news conference?" I grumbled. "I can't talk to the press. Go on television? Me? I've never talked to those people before."

But the more I thought about it the more it made sense. People talk to the press all the time without suffering permanent injury. The contract certainly qualified as a news story. What better way to get the message out than to have the media carry it?

Even then I wouldn't promise the guys I'd do it. But by the time I got home it seemed like too logical an idea to allow my personal anxiety to inferfere.

The next morning I began calling the media and found them very receptive. Everyone said they'd come so I scheduled the conference for that afternoon just outside the prison.

The rest of the morning proved hectic. With my mind racing, trying to prepare myself to talk to the media for the first time, my hands seemed to have grown several thumbs as I struggled to dress myself. I had no idea of the hornet's nest I'd stirred up until my phone rang and I found an angry Fred Butterworth on the other end.

"McLaughlin, what are you trying to pull? You can't have a news conference on the grounds of Walpole without my permission!"

"Well," I asked innocently, "can I have your permission?"

"No! Now you better get down here right away!"

End of conversation.

It was time to leave anyhow. On arriving at Walpole, I went directly to Butterworth's office. He already had company. An irate Al Costas and the top officials from Council 93 had gathered there like a pack of wolves. As soon as the door closed behind me, Costas jumped down my throat.

"You can't do this! You have no authority to have a news conference!"

"Al, I'm president," I replied.

"You're not the president! I am! You haven't been sworn in yet!"

"Okay, so I'm president-elect. Same thing. I'll be sworn in after another week. I'm the one who has to live with this contract, not you. The guys don't like it. They think you sold them out."

"Well that's a union matter between the guys and me. We shouldn't be discussing it before the Superintendent."

"Hey Al, I didn't ask for this little confab. You're the one who started this. All I know is that I'm having a news conference."

"Wait a minute," Butterworth chimed in, "I haven't given my permission."

"Look Mr. Butterworth, if I don't have the conference here, I'll have it down the street. The news people are going to ask why we've changed locations. I'll have to explain."

His stare bore holes in me, but before he could say another word, Costas jumped back in.

"If you're going before the cameras, the Council and I are going on to oppose you."

"Be my guest, Al. It's a free country. All I know is that I'm going to tell everyone the contract sucks." I walked out of the office without another word.

Butterworth didn't try to interfere further with the news conference. Outside the administration building I met Chet Curtis, a major local newscaster, and we chatted until the cameras were ready. Then he began interviewing me.

After shaking off my initial nervousness, the exercise was a snap. Throughout, more and more newspeople arrived, setting up cameras and recorders. Newspaper photographers roamed everywhere snapping pictures. Little did I realize that I had orchestrated the exact type of event the Department of Corrections feared most.

Costas and the Council members made good their threat to share the limelight. They spouted the same line I'd heard from other contract defenders.

"McLaughlin's wrong. It's a good contract. We've worked long and hard through tough negotiations. It's going to be beneficial to all members—"

My final words were: "Don't be fooled folks. Brothers and sisters, I need your help. Vote against this contract. It's going to take a lot of our rights away. Let's vote it down and go back to the table. Give me an opportunity to help hammer out a better agreement."

Ultimately that news conference served more than one purpose. Through it I made friends with many of Boston's top newscasters and reporters. The prison administration had been stonewalling them for years. The newsmen sensed that important news was taking place inside the walls but they had no access to it. They saw me as a conduit for that information.

Three days later my effort met defeat when the statewide union voted to ratify the contract. Council 93, however, did receive a scare. The final count ended up far closer than anyone anticipated. For this I was given credit, thus initiating my reputation as the most vocal of the local presidents.

Al Costas had only a few more days of his presidency but he tried to make good use of them and drag me down. Claiming that my controversial media appearance had undermined the union's cause in general, he initiated a movement among the guards to have me impeached. Initially it received some support. Remember, I had only carried 58% of the vote. But ultimately the officers realized they finally had a president willing to stand up to both Council 93 and administration. That gathered the vast majority of the guards behind me. I replaced Costas as president without further opposition.

While my candidacy had awakened the guards to the possibility of building a strong local, I could see that their enthusiasm was tenuous. They obviously would be watching me closely to see if I would, or indeed could, bring the administration to battle. If I showed hesitance I could lose my support. But if I blundered forward without total unity behind me I could fail and lose my credibility. I had to carefully plan all my moves to build credibility with both sides.

The first obstacle I had to hurdle was the damned contract, in particular Article Twenty. Because of its ambiguity I'd never be able to prove administration in violation of it. How could I proceed?

It soon became plain that for the upcoming struggle the only weapon we would possess as a union would be our willingness to strike. In that situation the contract's ambiguous language could work both ways. Administration would find it as difficult to prove conditions "safe" as we would to prove them "unsafe." If the language made it difficult for us to force them to make changes, it also made it difficult for them to force us back to work.

But a new, inexperienced union president just doesn't persuade his members to walk off the job at the snap of a finger. Especially when they have never struck as a local before. True, they had fallen in line and walked off during statewide actions when heavy negotiators stood behind them. But never as a group of three hundred, with no guarantee of support from Council 93, had they dared strike against the State of Massachusetts.

The inmates provided an incident a week after I took office that pushed the officers to increased solidarity. My election had apparently stirred officer morale sufficiently to where some began enforcing rules more strictly. Inmates immediately saw the change and some decided to make their feelings known.

The strongest heat came from the Max-section where inmates had little to lose by mouthing off. Again, inmate leaders had reputations to protect. They couldn't allow officers to wrest control away from them.

One of the most cold-blooded individuals I met during my time at Walpole was Connie Mancuso. Another bank robber/killer who ran a formidable gang, Connie's record included an escape from Walpole, in which he had disarmed two officers escorting him to a court hearing. Mercifully he had handcuffed them to a tree and left, instead of blowing their brains out. After a short time he was recaptured and returned to Walpole. He immediately reassumed leadership of his gang.

Since his activities were restricted to the Max-section he never had to cross swords with the "Execution Squad," Lyle Kramer's gang that ran things in Minimum. Furthermore his behavior stood in sharp contrast to Kramer's. Mancuso was kingpin of his block and proud to let everyone know it. He himself did not dirty his hands, but he seldom tried to hide the fact that he controlled what went on.

Apparently during that early July he began feeling the officers' change of attitude and saw the need to demonstrate his power. He came right out one day and stated that if things didn't lighten up "a screw would die."

Three days later Officer Rutherford was cornered in Mancuso's block by three masked inmates and stabbed three times. Fortunately he was able to defend himself sufficiently to prevent further injury until help arrived. He eventually recovered physically, but ultimately his doctor recommended that he retire to avoid further psychological stress. The incident had turned him into a bundle of nerves.

It also put him on Industrial Accident Pay, something that would not be forthcoming for weeks. The inmates, of course, escaped identification.

I refused to let this incident pass off as another unfortunate injury. The guards were angry. We might not be able to apprehend the inmates involved, but we all felt the time had come to begin taking steps that would prevent such attacks from recurring.

I therefore went to Fred Butterworth and requested he call an emergency meeting over safety. Fred had nothing against meetings. He had made it a practice to periodically meet with union presidents and their E-Boards. He just wanted these meetings scheduled at his discretion and at his convenience. And he always demanded that an agenda be set in advance.

In this case he acted very cooperatively and met with us promptly. This was to be the first of many meetings with the Superintendent and I had a few things to learn, both about him and my E-Board. Most of the E-Board members were incumbents who had served long careers as guards, many terms on the Board, and had sat in on many meetings with Fred. They treated him like royalty operating from sacred ground, as if to challenge him might bring forth a thunderbolt from heaven. He in turn played the part, sitting back as he conducted the meeting, relaxed and noncommittal.

Even so, as I sat there I began to feel optimistic. I had expected to meet antagonism. Instead Fred seemed to acknowledge the validity of our concerns.

"Gentlemen," Fred began, "first I wish to express my regrets over the stabbing of Officer Rutherford. Having worked as a guard I can sympathize with how you feel about this unfortunate incident. I'm only too glad to talk to you about your safety concerns. Mike, if you'd like to proceed."

I sat forward in my chair.

"Mr. Butterworth, the factor that most encourages inmate attacks upon guards is understaffing. Currently we operate with approximately 240 officers. The extensive activity regimen of the prison is designed to be supervised by a full complement of 300. To operate twenty per cent shorthanded creates too many situations where single officers must face large numbers of freed inmates. Most of the time the inmates behave themselves, but when you continue to expose single officers in this fashion, tragedies like the Rutherford stabbing will inevitably occur.

"In my view, one way to compensate is for management to authorize more overtime. Unfortunately the Department has recently been taking steps in the opposite direction, trying to cut back on its overtime budget. This only puts officers in more danger.

"I don't pretend to understand the Department's fiscal problems, but if it cannot release the purse strings then it should curtail programs and cut down inmate freedom to a point where the officers available can provide adequate supervision. In the meantime we should seek to fill officer vacancies. As positions fill we can gradually reinstate the programs. The inmates will suffer some inconvenience, but I see that as less of a problem than officers being stabbed and beaten.

"To further prevent attacks, Mr. Butterworth, I request that you no longer require officers to make their counts alone, especially at night. Officer Rutherford was stabbed in exactly that situation. I'd also like you to consider pulling officers from elsewhere to escort the men making the counts. If necessary the counts could be staggered to give the escorting officers time to move from block to block.

"Finally, it is the officers' view that most violence is gang instigated. We feel that gangs could be disrupted and perhaps broken up altogether if we methodically separate the ringleaders from their 'soldiers.' We could do this by relocating various inmates to different cellblocks. In the Max-section, particularly, communication between cellblocks is difficult. Without direct contact no one could orchestrate mass violence."

Fred commented, "The gang leader might just build a new power base in his new cellblock."

"True, but this will take time. Once we get wind of it happening we can move him again."

Throughout my presentation Butterworth had appeared attentive. Now he pondered a moment before replying.

"Mike, gentlemen, there is no question that we are short-staffed here at Walpole and that this does place extra pressure on the officers. Recruiting of officers has always been a problem. As you know, the job is far from glamorous. We have tried many different techniques, but none has completely worked. We will try others. For now all I can suggest is that the guards union try to help us by putting out the word and instituting some recruiting efforts of its own.

"In regards to curtailing programs or altering prison routine, gentlemen," his brow furrowed, "I don't think that's the way to go. In fact, I think it would increase danger for officers rather than reduce it. An interruption of programs will cause frustration and anger. And angry inmates are always more likely to strike out than happy ones.

"Mike, I commend you for the thought put into your suggestions but I hope you can now see that they would likely have wide-ranging repercussions. I want to give them some thought before giving you answers on individual items. I suggest we meet again next week."

The delay didn't please me, but he had conducted himself amiably so I could hardly protest. I did not know that I had run head on into his favorite tactic—stalling an issue until the union simply dropped it.

It took three weeks for me to get us another appointment with him. I say "us," reluctantly for in that time I learned that most of my eight man E-Board was in management's pocket. All had just been elected by the same guards who had elected me, but I stood alone in terms of my commitment to the union. They had been elected based more on their seniority. That seniority gave them privileges with management they wished to protect.

During that three-week span more guards reported flagrant inmate threats. I met several times with my E-Board trying to unite us so that we could wield some strength once we were granted an audience with his majesty. But the E-Board stood firm in not wanting to push Butterworth on the hard safety issues. They were confident, or so they said, that Fred was doing all he could.

Facing this attitude I had no choice but to ignore the E-Board and fight Butterworth by myself. To do this I needed strong backing from the rank-and-file, so I met periodically with all three shifts to keep them informed of my activities and of my difficulties with my E-Board. The 3–11 shift, as always, showed solid support. The other two shifts had more dissenters, but slowly I gained ground.

Finally the day of the second meeting arrived. Before entering the Superintendent's office I took aside my E-Board once more. Fireworks ensued.

"Guys," I told them, "it's taken us long enough to get this appointment with Butterworth. I want you to strictly follow my agenda in the discussion. The topic will be safety and safety only. I do not want to be sidetracked."

My vice president, Art Kostner, replied, "Are you trying to treat us like little kids? We're supposed to be an advisory board, not a bunch of yes men."

"Nobody's asking you to be yes men. I just want to stick to the subject. The guys we represent want answers on safety."

"The guys you represent, maybe. Everyone knows you're just president for the 3–11 shift. Now you're trying to act like a dictator."

"Call me what you want. I'm just telling you I don't want you bringing up stuff like overtime, new uniforms, and IA money."

Perhaps Butterworth had picked up on our sullen mood for his prior amiable attitude had disappeared. That suited me fine; I had entered the meeting prepared to do battle. "Mr. Butterworth," I challenged outright, "you've had three full weeks to consider my suggestions. I'd like to know what you intend doing about them."

He stared at me coldly, fingers playing with a pencil. "I don't consider them workable. Disrupting prison routine would cause more danger than the officers now face."

He could have met with us two weeks prior as he'd promised to give us that answer. Restraining my anger I asked, "Just what do you intend to do to increase safety for our officers?"

"We're trying to recruit more officers."

"You told us three weeks ago that you've always been doing that."

I sensed his temperature rising a notch. "And we are. I *always* treat recruitment as a priority issue."

I took that to mean he saw nothing wrong with current efforts. He intended making no changes.

Suddenly Kostner tried to jump in.

"Mr. Butterworth, we know you're doing all you can."

I overrode him and in a firm voice stated, "Mr. Butterworth, considering your failure to implement any safety measures in response to my request, my officers will no longer walk the tiers by themselves to make counts or for any other reason."

Butterworth's complexion turned crimson. He pointed his pencil at me. "Your officers will obey the instructions of their supervisors or face suspensions. Those instructions will be to follow normal procedures for making counts."

I folded my arms across my chest, looked him straight in the eye, and replied, "Your threats don't frighten us. If you try to suspend anyone we'll initiate a job action."

He sat forward, an incredulous look on his face. "You're threatening a strike? Here at Walpole?"

"If necessary."

He fumbled for words and then threw his pencil across the room. "This meeting is over! Get out of my office!"

I rose to leave, but my E-Board remained seated.

"Are you coming?" I asked.

"In a minute," Kostner replied.

I shot an angry look at him. "It's pretty evident where your loyalties lie." Then I stormed out of the room.

Later I cornered them. "Why the hell did you stay in there? You're just a bunch of traitors, not only to me but to all the guys!

"Take it easy," Kostner responded. "We just wanted to ask about our overtime checks."

"I specifically forbade you to do that," I snapped.

"Hey look, we're not taking orders from any dictator." We continued wrangling for several minutes but settled nothing.

Because the E-Board wouldn't back me I couldn't organize an immediate job action. The 3–11 shift would have walked out the minute Butterworth threw me out of the meeting. The other shifts, however, still doubted me and with the E-Board still influencing them, they hesitated to take the step. It took two weeks of meeting with them every day to convince them to strike.

I then called Council 93 and told them what we were about to do. To this point they had been of little help to us. During one of my routine meetings with them I had suggested, "Gentlemen, I want to get together with you so we can form a general strategy concerning the safety issue. After all, my local is paying membership dues, entitling it to your counsel. You've got heavyweight lawyers on your payroll and access all the way to the Governor's office. We need your help now."

Their leader, Sam Frustaci, responded, "Sounds like a reasonable suggestion. We can make that the top item on the agenda at the next regular Council 93 meeting."

I protested, "Mr. Frustraci, that's one month from now. By then more inmates and officers will certainly be injured. Why don't we get together tomorrow morning?"

"Tomorrow?" he chuckled. "That's out of the question. We've got over 160 locals to represent. That pretty much fills our schedule for the month. Let's do it at the next regular meeting."

Obviously our plight did not particularly move them. I didn't waste my time trying to change their minds. Their schedule meant nothing to me. They were obligated to represent us. My guys needed attention now. If Council 93 would not step out front with us on the issue, I would drag them into it by initiating an action.

This was where they found themselves when they received my call. After I explained our position they had no option but to send negotiators to support us.

The morning of Thursday August 18th all but five of my guys walked out as scheduled and formed pickets on the perimeter of the Walpole parking lot. The work stoppage forced management to call in the Office of Employee Relations (OER) to mediate. The resulting meeting brought us to Boston where I sat beside the heavy Council 93 negotiators in the heated talks with Hall and Butterworth.

I had looked forward to this moment from the first day I'd sought the presidency. I sat across from Frank Hall, now not just an eager subordinate, but a rival in power. My presence at that table authenticated my claim to being legitimate spokesman for the guards. It proved that I couldn't be bought. It served as a statement that a new movement had taken over the Walpole guards' union.

The issues discussed at that meeting were the same ones I'd covered in Butterworth's office. No new points were raised. No new arguments made. This time, however, Council 93 presented them garnished with legal jargon that softened their impact.

In effect the two sides acted like two wrestlers feeling out each other's strengths. To management the big issue here was not safety, but rather balance of power. They'd had it all up until now. They didn't want to surrender any of it to the union. We weren't asking much more than a commitment to give us attention. Even that they resisted.

I could see bitterness in Hall's eyes as we exchanged several glances. This was the first time we had seen each other since our ill-fated breakfast. It seemed as if he felt I'd betrayed him. If so, the feeling was mutual.

The meeting lasted only a few hours. In the end we didn't win much tangibly. In return for cancelling the work stoppage, management agreed to set up an Ad Hoc Safety Committee that would meet monthly to discuss safety problems. I was to be a member. At the same time they agreed to discuss the overtime problem at the first safety meeting, scheduled for two weeks hence.

These seemed like small victories, but I knew they represented cracks in the dike. We had won them without incurring any suspensions; we had maintained unity; and we had established ourselves as having a voice in the prison.

A sidelight benefit, that at the time seemed more flattering than significant, was the media coverage. My face and name were becoming more widely known. This would become extremely important down the road.

Back at the prison the day after the walkout ended I found myself barraged with questions from the inmates in my block. They had never experienced a strike that had forced managers from the Department to walk around feeding them through the bars. Now they gathered around my desk, some to complain, others to satisfy their curiosity.

"McLaughlin, what the hell are you trying to pull with this strike crap? You had us locked up all of yesterday. No visits, no programs, shit food. What did you gain by that?"

"We received a commitment to improve safety around here," I replied.

"A strike over safety? What's so wrong about the place as it is? What kinds of changes are you going to make?"

I answered forthrightly, "We're going to break up the cliques by moving inmates about. You no longer will have the right to decide where you're going to live. We'll decide that for you."

Their comeback was, "That's not going to make a difference. Whether we live in A-1, A-2, or A-3, (these were Minimum inmates) we're still going to have our fun."

"If so," I responded, "then you shouldn't be concerned with us moving you."

Much of this was banter for at this point I still posed no threat to them. But I could sense them probing to see just how much power I might have.

As another offshoot of the strike I strained several friendships at the Department of Corrections. I had come to know a number of the department managers by taking their courses at the University. Our Walkout had forced their temporary transfer from comfortable Boston offices to the perilous tiers at Walpole. Most had either never been to Walpole or had left its environs several years before. My actions had turned them into waiters and busboys, serving men they ordinarily dealt with from an exalted position.

One night in late August the 3–11 shift gathered for a pit-party at a nearby park after work. We cooked hot dogs and hamburgers, drank a few beers and generally had a relaxed, pleasant time discussing our prospects for the coming year. Everything was informal. We even invited the State Troopers patrolling in the vinicity to drop in and share our food with us.

I finally excused myself around 3 a.m. and made the long walk to my car parked about a tenth of a mile from the picnic ground. I settled into my hot Camaro, which I kept in perfect running condition, and put on a Neil Diamond tape. I lit up a two-dollar cigar I had been given at the pit-party and steered my car out onto the highway. For one of the few times in the past year all seemed at peace.

Turning upon the main freeway that would carry me home, my mind drifted to the coming year and those safety issues I must fight for. Only an occasional headlight appeared ahead or in the rear view mirror. The motor hummed just beneath the sounds of Diamond's "Beautiful Noise," and the tires slapped the pavement in a soothing percussion.

Suddenly I heard a loud THUNK beneath the car. It felt as if I might have run over some object, but I hadn't seen anything. Now fully alert, I checked the gauges and found everything normal. The engine hadn't skipped a beat. The tires seemed okay. I had no problem steering. I was just about to settle back down when I looked in the rear view mirror. I nearly jumped out of my skin. Flames were shooting out through the trunk of my car!

I turned my head to get a better look. In that instant the back seat caught fire. I had but moments to get out—but I was travelling at sixty miles an hour!

I hit the brakes as hard as I could, at the same time steering the car onto the dirt shoulder. As I cringed forward trying to escape the flames licking at my back, a large post suddenly loomed in my path. I swerved into the guardrail and skidded to a halt, the car coming to rest at a crazy angle.

By that time flames were everywhere. I felt sure that I must be afire myself. The passenger seat was burning fiercely, blocking my other exit. My own door was partially blocked by the ground. Having no choice but to try to force it, I barely managed to open my door into the dirt some eighteen inches.

Squeezing myself through, I rolled out and continued rolling in the dirt in case any of my clothing had caught fire. Then I got up and ran. After perhaps twenty steps I heard a loud POP and I turned to see the entire car engulfed in flames.

Right there I dropped on the seat of my pants. I was still chewing upon the stub of what had seconds before been a full cigar. I could hear the now eerie sound of Neil Diamond's voice singing the final bars of "Beautiful Noise." The blaze politely waited for him to finish, then erupted with another POP. Flames began soaring eight feet in the air.

I just sat there gaping and mumbling, "My Camaro, my beautiful Camaro. How could this happen?"

Just then a car came along and stopped. The driver got out and approached the wreck to see if anyone remained inside. At first when I tried to call out my voice wouldn't work. Finally I rose and managed to shout, "Get away from there before you get hurt! There's no one inside!"

By this time a siren could be heard in the distance so the passerby jumped back in his car and drove off. Moments later a State Police car arrived in a rush, followed closely by the fire department. As the firemen attended to the wreck the trooper approached me.

"You all right?" he asked.

"I don't know," I mumbled, still in shock. "I don't think so. My car just blew up."

He looked at me closely and correctly concluded that I was confused rather than injured. When the fire was extinguished he led me back to the wreck and began examining it with his flashlight. The flames had gutted the car, leaving little more than twisted metal.

After a quick once over he whistled and commented, "From the look of the tires I'd say you had a blowout that forced you off the road. When you hit the guard rail your tank caught fire. That the way it was?"

"No," I replied, "not at all. I remember driving peacefully along and then hearing a 'thunk' under the car. That's when I saw the flames, not after I hit the guard rail. There was no blowout. I steered my car into the guard rail purposely to avoid hitting that post. If any tire blew it happened during the crash."

He looked doubtful. "Are you saying this 'thunk' caused the crash? What could it have been?"

"I don't know. It was just—just a 'thunk.' "

He heaved a big sigh. "All right, have it your way. I don't have time to look any further. My report's going to read, 'Blowout, tankfire, and I drove you home."

He kept his promise. When we arrived Karen heard his radio and was waiting for me at the door. Since my transfer to Walpole she had feared the arrival of such a car bearing news that something terrible had befallen me at the prison. To see me in one piece, even if I had lost the car, was a great relief.

The next morning I took her with me to see the wreck at a local garage. It was so completely destroyed that we walked past several times without recognizing it. Finally the proprietor had to point it out. At first glance, Karen fainted.

Once she revived I closely inspected what was left of the car and took some pictures. At that moment it occurred to me that the car had been firebombed. Having maintained it religiously, I could conceive of no reason for it to catch on fire. Gas tanks just don't explode. I had been completely alert. No collision or blowout had occurred prior to the "thunk." That strange sound, I now felt, was the tripping of an incendiary device attached under the back of my car.

When I reached home I called an old friend who still worked on the Security Management Team. The SMT had finally taken on the responsibility of performing investigations.

"Ted, I'm convinced my car was firebombed last night. I was traveling Route 128 on my way home from a union affair when the car went up right under me."

"Jesus! Are you all right?"

"Yeah, barely. I wonder if you'd do me a favor and look into this? I'm sure it has something to do with the prison."

"Mike, I'd be glad to. I'll pick up my partner and we'll head out immediately. Where's the car now? We'll give it a good going over, then I'll call you back."

After giving him the information I waited around the house for his call. One hour, two, three went by, before the phone finally rang.

"Mike, sorry it took so long, but I just got back from Connecticut."

"Connecticut? I don't understand."

"When we got to the garage we learned that what was left of your car had been tossed on a flatbed and sent to a wrecking yard across the state line. The garage owner said he'd gotten a phone call from you authorizing him to release the wreck to the flatbed driver."

"I never made such a call. I need the wreck for the insurance company. Besides that, doesn't he need paperwork before he releases a wreck?"

"He's obviously trying to cover his ass. Maybe he did get a call. Anyway, we jumped in our car and took out after the truck. According to the garage owner it had less than a half hour head start on us. I thought we might even catch it on the highway. I had my speedometer needle laying on eighty all the way, but that truck driver must've been pouring it on himself. I couldn't catch him in the sixty miles between the garage and the yard. Actually, I wasn't worried about that. I figured we'd find the car sitting in the yard.

"Mike, something's fishy all right. When we arrived the flatbed had been there and gone. I saw wrecks everywhere in that yard, many of them obviously waiting to be crushed. But when I approached the owner and asked about yours he told me it had been put through the compactor just minutes before. When I asked him what was the rush, he told me the truck driver had given him a little tip to do the job right away. He's never seen the truck driver before, nor did he get a license number.

"So there I was. No way of even knowing which hunk of metal was your car. Even if I'd been able to pick it out, there was no way to determine if someone had messed with it. I'm sorry. Nothing I can do but write in my report that I found no evidence of the car being tampered with."

Upon hanging up I again asked myself the question, how could this happen? How could a car be whisked away and crushed without permission? Someone had given the order. It had to be someone who wanted something covered over.

My insurance company had similar questions, but not out of concern for my well-being. The adjusters were angry at me for not giving them the opportunity to inspect the car. Consequently they ignored my accident report and used the one filed by the State Trooper. Since my policy covered fire but not collision, they agreed to pay for the glass only. Besides evidence of foul play, the little crushing episode cost me several thousand dollars.

Later, I pondered who might have initiated such a drastic step to put me out of the way. One was always tempted to blame the inmates. But the inmates had no access to my car that night. Any who wanted to get me could have done so more easily on the inside. It was unlikely they'd go through the trouble of taking out a contract.

I saw management as also likely innocent. So far our clashes had been minor. I had given them no reason to believe I'd become a major problem.

To me the most likely culprit was the statewide union. I had caused it major embarrassment by opposing the contract. Within its leadership politics and patronage were sacred practices. I had already blasphemed once and had given strong indication of continuing to expound heretical views. My suspicion, later verified, was that men existed in the union hierarchy who thought nothing of seeing a thorn forcibly removed.

7 Pushing on a String

The car bombing forced me to take a long look at whether I should remain at Walpole. Facing the danger posed by inmates on a daily basis was bad enough. But to be treacherously attacked, after I thought I had left the danger zone, was an alarming invasion of my domestic life.

Our car's destruction shook Karen to her foundation. During that first year I had returned home every night unscathed and virtually unmarked. She'd heard my horror stories and saw my chronic fatigue, but never grasped how closely death attended me until she saw the charred, twisted Camaro.

We discussed this harrowing experience at length one evening shortly afterwards. Karen didn't directly ask me to leave Walpole, but the plea in her tone was plain.

"Michael, you act like you're willing to die for that place. If it were a great and glorious cause, maybe I could understand."

"It's not a great and glorious cause," I said, "Though at the very least, it's a good cause."

Karen shook her head. "You're an incurable idealist. But getting obsessed with a prison? A place packed with crazies who'd just as soon kill you as look at you? I'm sorry; it makes no sense to me."

I saw no reason to rehash my ambitions concerning a career in corrections. Instead I told her: "Karen, I know this incident shocked you. It shocked me too. After all, I went through it."

"And I hope you learned a lesson," Karen said, her eyes shining with intensity.

"Of course I did. But I've had a little time to put it in perspective."

"And?" Karen asked warily.

"I honestly don't think I'm in any more danger now than before."

"Oh, Michael," Karen groaned.

"Let's look at things realistically," I said, trying desperately to persuade her—and myself—that I wasn't doing something abysmally stupid by staying on at Walpole. "I've managed to cover myself well on the inside. Now I have to be more cautious when I leave the facility is all. Believe me, the inmates have more and better shots at me than anyone on the outside."

She threw up her arms. "That's supposed to be comforting?"

She regained her composure before I could think of an answer good enough for the occasion. "Well, Michael," she said, "You may think it's routine to face up to those crazies with nothing more than a pencil in your hand, but it sure takes its toll on me."

"I know it does . . ." I began.

"I hate having to fret every day over whether you've been stabbed, whether you're coming home alive. I just hate it."

"I know . . ."

She cut me off. "You don't know, Michael. You don't have a clue what it's like, waiting day after day. Every time the phone rings when you're at work I think they're calling to tell me something terrible has happened to you."

I thought hard, trying to come up with a solution or at least some way to ease Karen's fears. I didn't come up with much. She didn't wait for me to put my feelings into words.

"All right, Michael, if you intend staying on at Walpole, I'm renting a beach cottage for the rest of the summer. The beach is one place I've always been able to relax."

"But except for my days off, we won't see each other," I protested.

"I don't like that part of it either, but if nothing changes I'll go bananas. I need a refuge where I can forget the danger you're facing. Since the car fire I haven't been able to get the idea out of my head that I've got to do *something* to preserve my sanity."

I felt miserable about the prospect of not seeing her except on my days off, and about having forced her to this extreme. Yet I couldn't come up with a better plan.

Reluctantly, I nodded my assent. She then startled me with another request.

"I also want you to increase your life insurance. I know that sounds cold under the circumstances, but I have a future to think about too . . ."

"I appreciate that . . ."

Karen went on, ". . . I've made it my business to be here for you no matter what. The way things are, something dreadful could happen any day and you wouldn't be here for me. Living under that burden, I think at least I deserve a measure of financial security."

Sighing, I again nodded. "You're right, of course."

She continued. "Now maybe you can understand better why I'm so afraid to have kids? I don't want to raise them all by myself. In the first place, it wouldn't be fair to the children. And just the thought of being a single parent scares the hell out of me."

Karen's refusal to have children came up after I started at Walpole. It troubled me deeply because I held the traditional Catholic value of raising a family. Karen supported my view even though she professed no religious preference. After we first married we delayed starting a family until I could settle into a stable career. Now it was clear that Walpole's dangers had altered her attitude completely.

The wives of Walpole guards deserved admiration for daily facing the same crisis. Police wives often say they kiss their husbands goodbye every morning knowing they might never see their man alive again. The Walpole wives must have felt an anxiety far more intense. Consider it in this perspective:

The people declared by our legal system to pose the greatest danger to society make up the population of the state's prisons. Among this collection of convicted criminals are about 12 percent who are considered to be the very worst. In Massachusetts, they end up at maximum security Walpole. So the guards there deal with the Commonwealth's most aggressive and dangerous men every hour of every shift.

Many of the guards experienced this as a normal work routine. Their wives, however, lived in the normal world and suffered constant anxiety. The profession suffered a high divorce rate.

Karen did not further resist my decision to stay at Walpole. Knowing my sense of loyalty, she had expected as much. I had given my word to the officers. Self respect would not allow me to break it or be chased out.

Resigned, she began implementing her own plans and pursuing interests she had neglected. This turned out to be wise, for the demands of my union presidency kept me at the prison before and after my shift, as well as on normal days off. I didn't allow myself time to be much of a husband. And still, Karen was always there when I needed her.

As union president, everywhere I turned I found myself facing obstacles. The union had never before elected a junior officer president, so administration tended to view my election as a futile gesture that would soon lose its novelty. First, I didn't possess the knowledge to be taken seriously and second, the officers would not continue accepting leadership from someone they outranked.

I'm sure management would have loved to turn its normal harassment techniques against me. But I already worked the most dangerous shift and one of the toughest blocks. Also, I never seemed to get sick so they couldn't use the Doctor's List against me. All they could do was make it as difficult as possible until I resigned, lost support of the officers, or my year ran out.

Riding herd on my guys proved to be an exacting task. Factions existed who either supported the administration or didn't have the guts to stand up for their rights. At the same time, I occasionally came into conflict with my own supporters because of a subtle difference in our philosophies toward management.

I didn't like the administration any more than most of them. But I was able to put aside personal feelings and focus on one overriding goal—imposing safe conditions in the prison.

Many of my fellow officers, most of whom had been at Walpole longer than I, had a slightly different perspective. They wanted to improve safety, but at the same time they wanted retribution. When they saw the possibility of gaining some control over the prison, the fires of defiance began burning in their guts. It became more important to defy administration as a payback from years of harassment than to obtain the safety measure that had triggered their protest.

In some cases their actions looked so silly that they undermined the union's credibility. For example, after the Rutherford stabbing the 3–11 officers got together at roll call and decided to wear brown shoelaces in their black boots one day and white shoelaces the next.

"C'mon guys," I groaned. "I'm trying to build some credibility for us. It helps if we look and act professional."

They still liked the idea and, gripped by herd psychology, decided to proceed.

Marty Trent, a fiery young veteran officer, spoke up. "Relax, Mac.

It'll twist Butterworth's tail a little. You know how he likes to see his officers neatly dressed."

Sure enough, at my next meeting with Fred he leapfrogged the Rutherford injury and went right to the shoelaces.

"You know," he said. "Your guys look like a bunch of assholes."

I did not reply. What could I say? I agreed with him. The action did nothing but draw disdain and unnecessarily place another little obstacle in my path.

You can't bargain if you appear unreasonable or rebellious. You can't negotiate if you become uncouth or vindictive. I took strong positions, yes, but on issues only. I never let prior grudges or personalities distort my view of the steps we needed to take.

Safety remained my driving consideration. I would do nothing to hamper our pursuit of it. I had no desire to "get" anyone unless he stood in the way of achieving our goal.

To handle the various factions within the officer ranks, I learned to employ certain rules. The first was to allow everyone an equal right to speak at union meetings.

My initial meetings usually drew only 30–40 members and often these were the most vocal. We'd gather at our meeting hall—a rented community room at a local bar.

I didn't like the environment and later shifted the location to the Walpole grounds. My E-Board sat with me behind a table, other members on folding chairs opposite. The numerous empty chairs staring back at me reminded me of how much work I needed to accomplish.

I always tried to follow Robert's Rules—calling for a Secretary's report, Treasurer's report and so on. Then I'd get to the issues and open up the discussion to the floor.

Of course, this invited frustrated loudmouths to voice points of view that, if implemented, would prove detrimental to the cause of safety. But I didn't wield my authority as president and shout them down. A sixth sense told me that I could never build unity if I prevented union members from voicing their opinions.

If the speaker turned out to be a blowhard I'd still let him rant and rave and make his point. Then I'd get up and calmly explain why his position made no sense. Usually this would embarrass the man, and make him hesitate to spout off again. By handling blowhards this way I showed the other members they would receive a fair hearing and encouraged their full participation in union activities.

One instance occurred where I needed even more than my

presidential authority to maintain control of a meeting. I knew I faced trouble when Barney Odwell stood up to be recognized. Barney's 350 pounds were piled on his 6′3″ frame and he had a bellowing voice to match. The issue before us was a routine matter now forgotten. But Odwell had other things on his mind.

"I'm tired of listening to all this piss-ant bullshit. There's only one thing that concerns me and that's how McLaughlin's running this goddamn union.

"He hasn't accomplished a fuckin' thing except to get management pissed at us. More guys are going on the Doctor's List; it's tougher to get your IA money . . ."

I'd heard enough so I tapped my gavel.

"Barney, the issue before us is not my presidency."

"It fuckin' well should be!" He pointed at me. "You're nothing but an asshole the way you're riding the union into the ground!"

I managed to control my temper.

"Barney, you're out of order. If you don't have anything to say regarding the issue before us, please sit down."

"Fuck you, asshole! You're not putting a gag on me! I'll stand up here and talk as long as I want!"

"Nobody's putting a gag on you but we follow rules here."

Flipping me off, he shouted, "Here's your rules! You want to shut me up? Come over here and do it."

Odwell outweighed me by two hundred pounds. He had a reputation for mercilessly beating up smaller men. I wasn't crazy enough to meet him on his terms, but if I backed down I would lose control of the meeting and, perhaps, the ability to control meetings in the future.

Slowly, my eyes never leaving his, I removed the gavel from the table and put it in my pocket. Then I reached into my belt and pulled out the gun I carried everywhere except inside the prison, a .32 Walther PPK. I placed my "piece" on the table where the gavel had been.

Odwell looked at me warily. "What's that supposed to mean?"

"Since you don't like Robert's Rules of Order, we'll try Walther's Rules of Order on for size," I said.

That took the wind out of the big man's sails. I never would've used the gun on him, but how could he know that? All the guys had seen my radical behavior in the cellblocks. None of them knew for sure what I'd do if pushed hard enough.

Another rule I strictly enforced was following the will of the majority. No matter how I felt about an issue, if the majority voted for it, I gave it my full support.

At first, I implemented this democratic practice by employing secret ballot. Then I found that this tended to shortcircuit my efforts.

We'd have a lengthy discussion on an important issue. One member after the other would stand up and voice an opinion in favor of the proposed action. Often the discussion would run its course without a single dissenting voice. Then the agreed-upon action would be defeated in the secret balloting.

I didn't believe that men should be allowed to veto proposals without either defending their views or at least declaring where they stood. So one evening I stood up and announced: "Gentlemen, from this moment on, all voting will be conducted by a show of hands."

A few murmurs rippled through the group, but none of those attending dared oppose my decree without revealing themselves as management sympathizers. Perhaps the new rule wasn't completely democratic, but it sure embarrassed people into standing up for something.

I had learned in school how to effectively defend both sides of an issue, and had been given just the right temperament to carry it off. Of course I expected the same type of loyalty from the membership. This meant supporting job actions. Scabs are the termites of any union and I made it quite clear that I hated them and would do everything in my power to run them out of the prison.

We had our share of scabs, but I was heartened that the number had dwindled since the statewide strike the previous year. Those who crossed our picket lines were usually men who had been raised to a position of authority by management and looked forward to easy duty on their way to retirement.

I understood the situation of these supervisors, but refused to condone it. After all, we all had careers at stake. I could not justify anyone, for the sake of his career, placing another man in physical danger. Once I established my strength as president, I made this quite plain, even to the point of defying supervisors on work matters. I was risking suspension, but I felt that making a point for the union was worth it.

One supervisor had a long history of disregarding union decisions. He felt my sting during lunch in the chow hall. The sixty of us from the 7–3 shift were eating together when in he came, walking nonchalantly as if he was one of the guys.

Conversation stopped as we watched him enter the chow line and receive his meal. His arrival surprised us because he usually spent meal time with the other supervisors. Now, not only did he join us, but he chose an open seat right in front of me.

He didn't say anything, but one close look at him destroyed my appetite. I couldn't believe he'd have the guts to sit at our table. I glanced around at the rest of the officers and noticed that many had resumed conversing, apparently having decided to ignore the intrusion. I couldn't.

I stood up and said as loud as I could, "Maybe you'll eat with a fuckin' scab, but I won't!" I then picked up my tray and turned it over atop his before walking out. For a brief moment the room went silent. Then fifty-nine other guards walked out behind me, leaving him alone and in need of a new tray of food.

I could've been suspended for that, just like I could've been other times when I ignored direct orders from supervisors concerning my job. I always obeyed reasonable orders. At times, however, certain supervisors and seniors threw their weight around trying to impress upon loyal union people just who was in charge.

Whenever I encountered such orders I'd tell the supervisor, "I don't take orders from fuckin' scabs." Then I'd walk away and do what I knew was needed.

I didn't care about being suspended or fired. The job had value to me only if I could accomplish safety reform. Besides, management didn't dare try to remove me over a minor issue for fear of solidifying the union behind me.

As president I didn't always take the side of individual guards against management. I expected officers to do their jobs. If they faced justifiable discipline I would represent them, make sure their punishment was reasonable, then chew them out in private.

Most of these little confrontations took place because of improper grooming or demeanor on the job. Some guys would come to work in scuffed boots or wrinkled uniforms that made one wonder if they'd slept in the woods all night. I'd tell them, "Hey, man, get it together. You're representing all of us. Don't come to work looking like a bum."

Occasionally guys would get caught reading, or even dozing at their posts. In these cases they'd get a sharper tongue-lashing from me than from management.

"You're here to do a job and do it right!" I'd tell them. "When you let down, you not only let down the inmates and management, you let down your brother officers. You could get one of us killed!"

Often I dressed down officers with much more experience than

I, but I didn't care. Nor did I care if they were friends or supporters. Somebody had to tell them to shape up and often I was the only one of their peers with the guts to do so.

Unlike previous presidents, I never wheeled and dealed to gain favors for individuals at the expense of the entire membership. What was good for one was good for us all. When management saw they couldn't divide us by offering favors to individuals, they hardened against us as a group, forcing us to fight for everything.

One example of management's stubborn insensitivity was its stance on industrial accident pay for injured officers. As mentioned before, injured officers facing months of convalescence also faced an extended loss of income.

When I investigated, I learned that the claims were being processed promptly by the Industrial Accident Board but became hung up in Attorney General Bellotti's office. I never received a reasonable explanation why, but I did notice that management seemed able to free the logjam for people it favored.

Without income the injured officers almost always returned to work before they were ready. Management could have showed some mercy by assigning them easier duty until they had fully recovered, but this didn't happen. These officers really needed to stay home, but they couldn't continue doing so with no money coming in.

The union tried to help by taking collections and even loaning small amounts, but this could meet only a small part of the need.

Knowing I didn't have the strength to take on the Attorney General, I took it upon myself to try to relieve the pressure on the guys by coming up with a private insurance program.

Coincidentally I received a phone call from an insurance agent representing a private insurance firm. He had previously negotiated an insurance package of the type I was looking for with some of the prior presidents. He told me the deal had fallen through but he thought he'd try again. When he explained what he had to offer, I was elated and invited him out to the prison to discuss it in detail.

He arrived the next day and I escorted him down into the basement rec-room where we could be alone. He then proceeded to outline a plan where, for a small premium, members injured would receive insurance checks in lieu of their IA monies.

When the IA checks finally came in the insurance company would be reimbursed. In the meantime the injured officers would be receiving income while convalescing and could take time to recover without wrecking themselves financially. The premiums being paid in would accumulate almost as if in a bank account and would be refunded when the employee terminated.

"Everything sounds great," I told him, "but how big a premium are we talking about?"

He smiled at me. "that depends on how much you want."

"What do you mean?" I asked.

"How much of a kickback do you expect for yourself?"

I gave him a hard look. "I don't want anything for myself. I just want my guys covered by income insurance from the third day of their injuries at the cheapest possible cost."

He looked surprised. "I put this identical plan together for one of your predecessors, but they wanted too much for themselves."

"In terms of dollars?" I asked incredulously.

He smiled at my naivete. "Yes, we're talking about money."

"I don't go for that stuff. You can forget about kickbacks."

"Okay, since we're just talking straight premium, I can let you have the plan for around four dollars per member per month."

"That's fantastic," I said. "Put it in formal form so I can present it to my membership and I think we may have ourselves a deal."

After he left I sat there shaking my head. Here was another case where the best interests of the guards had been sacrificed to the personal greed of prior union leaders. Maybe I was naive and idealistic, but what kind of man would stoop to making money off his brother officers' blood and desperate need?

When the proposal arrived a few days later I called a special membership meeting. The turnout was disappointing, just over a hundred, and most of those who came displayed no great enthusiasm. Nevertheless I wasted no time calling the meeting to order.

"Gentlemen, I called you here tonight to hear about and vote on an insurance program. It will provide income to all members injured on the job while they wait for their Industrial Accident payments from the State. For only four dollars a month . . ."

As I proceeded to rattle off the benefits I sensed growing interest in the group. On finishing, I opened the floor to questions. There weren't many, but two of them acted as roadblocks.

The first was Marty Trent. Fiery as ever, he got up and demanded, "Why should we have to pay four bucks a month to cover our asses when all the while the State is holding the money that's due us?"

"Marty, I agree. We shouldn't have to. But there's nothing we can do right now to speed up the IA payments. As of today, if a guy gets hurt he'll have no income for who knows how long. It's not right, but that's the way it is. Believe me, I'm going to keep fighting to straighten out the IA money problem. But in the meantime this insurance will help our guys over a lot of problems."

"Maybe so," he retorted, "but I still don't buy it. I figure management will look at this insurance as a sign we've caved in. They'll hang up our IA money even longer."

Murmurs of agreement rose in the gathering. I even found myself in sympathy, morally. But practical considerations weighed heavily in the plan's favor.

Marty continued, "I say that instead of us bleeding ourselves financially, we show some balls and start hitting management hard on this bullshit. If necessary, we hit the street."

Scattered shouts of approval greeted this suggestion. Still, I sensed that the audience contained a large number of cooler heads who saw value in the insurance.

Then Vern Warstler stood up. Vern had been in the Department a long time and had seen union presidents come and go. He'd supported Scandia in the election and had made it clear that I still had not gained his trust.

"We've heard about these deals before. Every time something comes along looking good, somebody's getting a kickback. I don't like the idea of putting up my money to line somebody else's pockets."

"Vern," I responded, "I assure you that I'm the only one who's talked to the insurance man. Nobody's getting a kickback."

"Even if that's true, the temptation's always there. Somewhere down the line somebody's going to get itchy fingers. It always ends up that way."

A few of the others voiced opinions in favor, but those two questions torpedoed the plan. I could hardly believe it. After feeling so proud of having procured the plan for the guys, it lost in a close vote.

During these months of dogwork I continued to look for opportunities to change the members on my Executive Board. Clearly, the E-Board's support was essential before the heavier issues could be tackled with a reasonable hope of success. I knew I'd never change the minds of its current members. I had to have them replaced. Like everything else this took time and maneuvering.

Union by-laws stated that members of the E-Board were to be up for election every year just like the president. As my "cabinet," they were entitled to accompany me to meetings with management, in theory to give a more comprehensive view to the discussion.

Due to the toothlessness of the union, however, the positions had always been looked upon as prestigious rather than influential. E-Board members were never held accountable for their dealings with management. The guards had not elected them based on their stance on the issues. Rather, the guards chose guys they liked or who had been around a long time. They didn't expect the union to accomplish much anyway. So why should it matter?

Typical of the stubborn dinosaurs inhabiting my E-Board was my vice president, Art Kostner. Art had served on the E-Board for several years now. He was an "old screw" with some thirty years of experience.

At one time Art had worked in the guard ranks with Fred Butterworth himself. He still considered Fred a friend. Now, as he approached sixty and with retirement close, Art Kostner moved about the prison at a slow pace. He performed his job methodically, as if resigned to the dangers around him. He certainly wasn't about to support action that would embarrass Butterworth, especially with Fred in a position to make his last years easier.

Members of the old school had been brainwashed long ago to accept a protocol that placed management on a pedestal. Strikes? Over safety? The old timers had put in their years and survived. Why should there be changes now? They even found it difficult to speak up to Butterworth. If one took that bold step he exercised meticulous politeness.

Publicly accuse Butterworth of doing a poor job? "Our Superintendent? Outrageous. He's put in thirty years. We're supposed to protect guys like him."

I saw this attitude in our early safety meetings. Butterworth usually appeared calm and collected, like a king entertaining petitions from his subjects. He didn't seem to resent us putting forth our issues. In the process of doing so I'd watch him stare off into space as if his mind had wandered elsewhere. When I'd finish he'd inevitably say, "Yeah, Mike, that's a good point. Next issue."

I'd respond, "Wait a second. If that's a good point, what are we going to do about it?"

Before Fred could answer, members of the E-Board would jump to his defense. "He said it was a good point. He'll get to it. Don't get excited."

The first time this happened I stopped my E-Board outside Butterworth's office and lit into them. "You're supposed to be on my side. Why were you defending Butterworth in there? We'll never get anything accomplished this way."

Kostner answered for all of Butterworth's stooges on the E-Board. "It just doesn't seem fair for you to be attacking the Superintendent."

"Why not," I demanded.

"Because he's a victim of the Boston bureaucracy. You should make waves with the Commissioner's office, not him."

"I intend to," I said, "but that doesn't exonerate Butterworth. Many of the problems we face are the direct results of decisions made here. He's in charge. He's responsible. He's here every day. Instead of bucking us every inch of the way, you'd think he'd go to bat for us with the Department, especially since he used to be one of us."

Kostner said, "He hasn't taken your issues to heart because he doesn't agree with you. Besides, he thinks you're too young and inexperienced to be president."

"My age is none of his business. I represent lots of officers who have heavy experience, so when I present an issue I voice their views as well as my own—he certainly can't claim they don't know what's wrong with this place. Besides, any moron can see the problems around here."

Kostner just stood there eyeballing me sourly.

To rid myself of barnacles like him I had to discredit them with the membership. I knew it wouldn't come easy but from then on, every chance I got I'd tell the guys which E-Board members weren't supporting me at the safety meetings. Those individuals would then find themselves confronted by officers demanding an explanation. The E-Board member, of course, had none to give other than to admit he didn't support majority opinion. Gradually the pressure mounted until they resigned.

When one would do so I would post a notice asking for applicants. After I gathered three or four names I would convene the remaining E-Board members and hold an election. I didn't always get the person I wanted, but I did get someone willing to support the majority opinion.

I did violate this protocol in one case when I avoided posting the opening and went out and recruited John Scandia. Even though I'd defeated him in the election, John remained popular with the membership. I respected him for having initiated the movement to unseat Costas. I also felt it would be a unifying gesture to bring him aboard.

One day I pulled him aside in the corridor and said. "John, I've got an opening on the E-Board. If anyone deserves to be on, you do. Why don't you join?"

"I don't know, Mac," he replied. "The guys didn't want me for president. Why should they want me on the E-Board?"

As I suspected, he was still smarting from the election loss. I was grateful for the chance to resolve any hard feelings.

"John, almost half the guys did want you for president. Those guys will feel that much better if they know you're representing them on the Board."

He went for it and from that time on became a valuable Board member. His appointment also encouraged the membership to further close ranks behind me.

Once a majority of my E-Board supported me, I convened them and set specific guidelines for the safety meetings with Butterworth.

"Guys," I told them, "We'll never gain anything if we go into these meetings divided. We must present a united front to the Superintendent. Now I know I've been accused of being a dictator, but I promise I won't force my opinions on you. If we have differences on the issues we'll resolve them together, privately, by vote beforehand. The majority opinion will be the one we'll represent. No bickering in front of Butterworth."

Kostner and his remaining three allies didn't look happy. They knew I now had the votes on the Board and would therefore be presenting my position on most issues. But there was nothing they could do officially to resist. As president, I theoretically had power over the E-Board. To defy me would betray their oath as members.

Yet even then, Art Kostner could not get himself to cooperate. In meetings he would still interrupt and take management's side or, in his wishy-washy manner, attempt to soften our presentation. After he'd violated our rule several times I finally confronted him at a regular E-Board meeting.

"Art, I don't like to do this, but I must forbid you to speak at our meetings with the Superintendent."

"Forbid . . . ? You can't do that!"

"Yes I can. My authority to do so is in the bylaws."

For the first time I saw Kostner worked up. I found it a refreshing experience.

He snarled, "What do you expect me to do, sit in there like a dummy?"

"I expect you to support the majority opinion. I told you that before; you refused to comply. Now I'm telling you again, keep your mouth shut or don't come to the meetings."

Embarrassed and outraged, he attended the next few E-Board meetings but sulked throughout. Then he quit coming. Ultimately, in the next election he was defeated in his effort to retain the vice presidency. Bob Furtado took his place, a major step in the right direction for us.

Even as I undermined Butterworth's strength with my E-Board, I also gradually postured myself on an equal footing with him psychologically. He still saw me as a punk kid and would address me simply as "Mike" or "Mac" during our meetings. I had learned in my labor relations courses in school that you don't allow management a higher level of respect than they show you. This gives them power they don't deserve. So finally, after a half dozen or so meetings, I decided to stake out my territory.

The agenda for the meeting did not look unusual. Basically we intended discussing the progress made on issues already presented. Butterworth had, as usual, sprawled back comfortably in his chair. He had no reason to expect anything unusual to happen.

"I can see we're all here," he noted. "Why don't you begin, Mike."

I took a long look at him before saying, "Fred, last month we asked you to look into the status of the new officers' uniform . . ." I went on but could see that my words weren't registering. He reacted to my use of his first name as if I'd slapped him across the face. At first he went white. Then I thought I saw cold hatred in his eyes.

Even the complexions of several E-Board members had lightened considerably. I'm not aware of any Department employees at the prison ever calling Butterworth by his first name.

It took him some minutes to get over the shock. When he did so he did not admonish me. A bright guy, he immediately saw the game I was playing. From then on, no matter how much he didn't like it, it remained "Fred" and "Mac."

I also had to put an end to another disrespectful practice of his. He allowed his secretary to constantly interrupt our meetings with phone calls. He seemed to be telling us that the meetings held low priority compared to his other responsibilities. It didn't take long for me to get fed up with this and decide to show him that we considered our time valuable too.

Before one meeting I pulled aside steward Mike Gilmore.

"Mike, we're going in to Butterworth's office at ten. Keep an eye on the clock. Give us about ten minutes, then call his secretary and ask to talk to me. After we hang up wait another ten or so then call again. Do so every ten minutes until the meeting breaks up."

Seeing mischief in the wind, a grin crept across his face. "What am I calling about?"

"Union business, of course," I replied, deadpanning.

"Ah-ha. Okay, Mac. You got it."

A short time later we took our usual positions in Butterworth's office and he opened the meeting. As I presented the first issue I kept one eye on the clock. The discussion proceeded routinely until exactly ten minutes after. Then, BUZZ!

"Excuse me, Mac," Fred interrupted, picking up his comline. He spoke into it. "Yes?" He suddenly frowned in puzzlement and glanced at the phone as if it was giving off a foul odor. Then he held it out to me. "It's a call for you."

"Thanks," I said, taking the receiver from him. "Hello?"

"How you doin', Mike?" Gilmore asked, his voice tinged with mirth.

"Great," I replied. Then I proceeded commenting as if involved in a serious conversation. "Yeah, un-huh, right."

"You still want me to call back in another ten minutes?" Gilmore asked.

"You bet," I said. "Thanks for calling."

Gilmore followed instructions, interrupting the meeting twice more. After I hung up the third time, Butterworth proposed, "Mac, why don't we have my secretary hold our calls. We can get a lot more done."

"That's fine with me, Fred," I replied.

That day I left his office wearing a big grin, knowing I'd won another victory. The phone prank and my placing myself on a first name basis with him may seem like piddling, childish games, but they put us on an equal footing with him and claimed our right to respect.

By establishing a safety committee, management had relieved pressure on itself without actually initiating safety reforms. We could not very well threaten to strike without giving the committee time to act. But as a member of the committee I could clearly see the Department skirting the issues, tossing out tidbits to appear well meaning without doing anything that mattered.

The Department's first and only significant concession came nine days after our first job action. It decided to permit the Superintendent to use as much overtime as he deemed necessary to properly man the shifts. After that, however, the safety meetings bore little fruit.

In the meantime we fought and won some battles on minor issues. Fighting them was necessary to maintain both our newly won credibility and our morale.

For example, in spite of a liberal policy toward facial hair in the other prisons of the system, Butterworth continued to demand that all Walpole officers come to work clean shaven. Again, we were being held hostage by his old-school mentality.

When asked his reasoning, Butterworth claimed that gas masks did not fit properly upon bearded faces. This seemed like a flimsy excuse, especially since other prison Superintendents didn't seem concerned. Also, the navy used gas masks and had allowed beards for years.

Knowing I'd get no further talking to Butterworth on this issue, I put it on the back burner until the next meeting of the Department Safety Committee in Boston with Commissioner Hall. Butterworth was not in attendance, but union presidents from all the other prisons were. The meeting proceeded routinely without heavy topics arising so I felt it a good time to broach the subject of facial hair.

"Commissioner, is there some reason the Walpole guards are faced with a different grooming code than that at other prisons? My guys are forbidden to wear beards and mustaches and they'd like to know why."

My query drew a blank stare. Even if he'd wanted to, Hall would have found it awkward to defend Butterworth's policy in front of the other presidents.

"I don't know why. It's never been brought to my attention. I have no problem with facial hair. The grooming code should be standard throughout the system. I'll have to talk to Superintendent Butterworth."

I followed up: "Does that mean my guys have your permission to wear beards and mustaches?"

"Yes, as long as they keep them neat and trimmed. I'll send you a memo to that effect."

I did receive the memo a few days later. Whether or not Butterworth was copied in or even informed verbally, I don't know. In any case, he dug in his heels.

Subsequently two of my guys heard about the new policy while on vacation and returned to work with full beards. Like an alert watchdog, Butterworth spotted them before they reached roll call and confronted them with the alternative, "shave or go home."

Marty Trent was one. He immediately sought me out and asked, "What do we do?"

I told him, "Go home. I'll get you paid for the time you miss."

At this time the guys still weren't sure how much strength I'd gathered. For that matter, neither was I. But I knew I'd get them paid even if I had to pay them out of union funds.

Since verbal promises and written memos had proven to be ineffective in this matter, I decided to go through the official grievance process. Because Hall had backed us on the issue I skipped the normal first two steps and filed the petition directly with his office. Sure enough, four days later I received a call from his office informing me indifferently that we had won.

Within hours Marty Trent returned to work with his beard intact and a grin on his face. He patted me on the back and said, "I couldn't believe it. Butterworth called me personally and told me I could return to work with full back pay. Man, did he sound embarrassed."

The other officer returned with a similar story.

To me this little victory served as nothing more than further consolidation of our union's strength. Facial hair? I couldn't have cared less about it. I'd much rather have had broken light bulbs replaced. But you win what you can. As in sports, it keeps momentum on your side.

The incident also taught me to avoid head-butting with Butterworth and deal directly with Hall's office. From the beginning I built a highly successful record for winning grievances. During my time in office we won 92% of them. This happened because I refused to carry forward a grievance unless I knew it was legitimate.

Even though many grievances arose over simple day-to-day matters that seemed easily resolvable, management made sure it would take several weeks to settle them. The procedure for pursuing a grievance was designed in four steps. At any of the four, management could acknowledge the validity of the grievance and agree to make the necessary changes. Seldom did this happen. Usually they made us fight our way through all four steps.

In Step One the grievance went to the Superintendent, who had ten days to render a decision. He usually took the full time before ruling against it. We'd then move on to Step Two, the Deputy Commissioner of Administration, who was allowed twenty-one days to consider our claim. Again he usually took the full time before ruling "no." On to Step Three, Commissioner Hall, who was allowed fourteen more days. A negative decision by him would send us on to the Office of Employee Relations (OER), where they had twenty-one additional days. If they also ruled against us I could appeal and force them to grant a hearing. But this would be at their convenience, often several weeks down the road.

I learned patience dealing with grievances. Steps One and Two proved to be absolutely useless to us. We simply went through the motions of filing the paperwork, then waited the month until we could move on to Step Three. Once we got to Hall's office we could at least expect a review of the case. Over time we did win a number of cases at Step Three. But most of our victories were at Step Four. I came to expect it and didn't allow the unreasonable delays to discourage us from filing.

As the year went on, inmates became even more aggresive toward guards. Previously, most inmate attacks had occurred spontaneously from random causes. These were the acts of frightened, frustrated men trying to deal with untamed emotions. Now, however, the real heavies sensed something afoot with our union and felt threatened. In particular, they'd heard we were trying to identify them officially. This they couldn't tolerate.

Ever since the first strike these inmate heavies had been watching us closely. My comments concerning prison reform had gotten back to them and eventually they individually took me aside.

Typical was a brief conversation I had with Connie Mancuso in his cellblock. Just his talking to me showed his power. Inmates who valued their necks just did not talk privately to officers.

"McLaughlin," he said, "If you're smart you'll back off."

"I'm not backing off," I replied. "We're going to see that changes are made whether your kind like them or not."

He shook his head. "Don't say you weren't warned. We have the power here. Don't interfere. You're involving yourself in something a lot bigger than you. It's a simple matter to get you out of the way."

Their threats seemed to be borne out by increasing attacks on officers. One officer was struck by rocks and buckets thrown down upon him from a tier. Another officer was badly scalded on his face, shoulder and chest by boiling water thrown from a cell. Before the officer could get away, the same inmate split his head open with a stick.

In the future Butterworth would blame this inmate violence upon my inflammatory comments. In a way he was right. I had thrown down the gauntlet to the inmates and stated, "We've had enough."

I knew they would pick it up. They had to in order to protect their kingdom. But I couldn't let that worry me. If you're tired of trying to avoid a treacherous dog that is terrorizing your neighborhood, you must confront him and prepare yourself for one hell of a fight. You may sustain injury subduing him, but once the struggle is over you will be totally free of the stress he caused. Peace and order can then become the norm. That is how I viewed our coming struggle with the inmates.

Actually, many of the weaker inmates liked me and felt sympathetic to my posture on prison reform. They had witnessed my unbending toughness with the heavies but had experienced a slight leniency when I dealt with them.

When I caught one of the weaker inmates being rowdy I'd try to give them a break by firmly saying so everyone could hear, "Don't do it again or I'll lock you up." Or, "I'm going to write you up," and then I'd never turn in the report. My eyes told them what my voice dared not, that I was willing to give them a little break.

Often they'd acknowledge my gesture with a half-smile or a little nod. Even if they didn't go that far I could see relief in their eyes. As time passed I saw many inmates who were tense and paranoid in the presence of other officers become totally at ease in my presence. They didn't have to say anything. In a prison you learn much more from watching body language and facial expression.

The powerless inmates had endured years of intimidation at the bottom of the pecking order and had given up hope of escaping their miserable existence. I could sense that most did not believe that I could effect the changes I proposed.

They certainly couldn't help me. At any moment one of them could have been given the order to kill me and they would have been forced to obey. Still, they acted as friendly and courteous as circumstances allowed and provided me one service—a lifesaving one.

As the months went by I found myself the recipient of numerous tips. These, I'm sure, reflected plots to have me killed. Since I always acted upon them, I escaped having to painfully discover whether they were genuine or not.

The tipping process was simple. I was walking down the main corridor when an inmate passed and mumbled, "A-3." That's all. He didn't pause or make eye contact but kept moving as if nothing had passed between us. But that simple utterance put me on full alert. I knew serious trouble awaited me in A-3.

After becoming union president I had the freedom to move about the prison on union business. This was an enormous advantage that allowed me to avoid trouble spots without showing fear or revealing I'd been tipped. Naturally I didn't want to blow my pipeline by revealing that someone had tipped me.

In this case I was on my way to A-3 to talk to the block officer concerning union dues. I could have called him out into the corridor, but since the matter wasn't urgent, I decided to avoid attention. I crossed to the far side of the corridor, gave the open entrance to A-3 a wide berth, and continued on down toward A-1 before reversing my course. I did not return to A-3 until I received another tip two days later that the hit order had been lifted.

Over time I came to recognize a certain mechanism in operation that generated these tips. Gang leaders just didn't broadcast the fact that they'd ordered someone to kill an officer. The order would be passed secretly. Probably the reluctant designated hit man himself passed on the information. But he couldn't do so outright. The next time he saw me he was supposed to strike. If he failed, he would likely be hit himself.

His only out was to make sure he and I did not see each other. His restricted movement gave him an excuse for not carrying out an attack as long as I didn't blunder into his presence while the order remained in effect. Therefore he needed to get word to me. For this he'd use a friend. I'm certain I was spared many such attacks because inmates worked together to tip me.

Sometimes I received information that an inmate was about to be hit. When I got a tip like that, I did my best to prevent the killing. One afternoon while manning a tower, the Senior in the corridor phoned me. He'd heard that someone was about to be hit in the yard.

This particular tower carried a full complement of arms, including a submachine gun. Ordinarily on tower duty I only kept a .30–.30 rifle loaded. With murder about to be committed below, I shoved a clip of ammunition in the submachine gun and lowered the glass window to give me a field of fire. There I stood, the machine gun trained down on the yard ready to fire.

The inmates spotted me and immediately recognized the unusual nature of the situation; tower guards just never brandished machine guns. But instead of moving away, they gathered as near to the tower as possible. In a short time over a hundred of them stood there staring up at me and yelling, wanting to know what I was doing.

I remained deathly silent, my eyes carefully searching the yard for any hint of a murder about to take place. After about fifteen minutes of this the phone rang again. I picked it up and was greeted by the excited voice of Andrew Larker.

"McLaughlin, what the hell do you think you're doing?"

"Andrew," I replied, "I've been informed there's going to be a hit in the yard. I'm trying to prevent it."

Larker shouted back, "You put that machine gun down at once and stop intimidating those inmates!"

My voice turned cold. "Andrew, I consider my tip reliable. As far as I'm concerned nothing's going down in this yard while I'm up here." I hung up the phone.

A few more minutes went by with no further action in the yard. Then I heard loud knocking on the door.

"Yeah!" I called out, not daring to take my eyes off the yard.

A muffled voice called back, "Mac, Larker sent me to relieve you."

Still holding the machine gun, I opened the door for Officer Bill Esposito. At first he had a sheepish expression on his face. Then when he saw the gun he went pale.

"So Larker sent you to relieve me," I said.

"Yeah, he wants you to report to him pronto."

"Did he tell you what's going on?"

"He said you think somebody's going to be hit. He thinks you've gone nuts."

"Randall called me a little while ago and said he got a reliable tip. If I were you, I'd keep my eyes open." I held out the machine gun. "You want this?"

"Hell no!"

Before leaving the tower I unloaded the machine gun and put it away. Then I reported to Larker's office. He was waiting for me outside in the corridor.

"McLaughlin, have you lost your mind? Pointing a machine gun at unarmed inmates! We'll have lawsuits up to our eyeballs! How many times have you been ordered not to intimidate the inmates!"

"I intimidated them so they wouldn't commit murder."

"And if you'd seen one in progress I suppose you'd have blown away five or six of the innocent just to stop the attacker!"

"The point is I didn't have to shoot because I intimidated them."

"Admit it, you get a big thrill out of intimidating inmates because you hate them."

"That's not true, Andrew."

He waved his hand at me in disgust. "I don't want to look at you anymore. Report down to Randall in the Minimum Section. He needs a corridor relief officer."

Great, I thought. He could post me anywhere, but he sends me down to face the very inmates I'd threatened. In a few minutes they would be coming back in from the yard.

As I feared, there I was, standing conspicuously in the corridor as they filed inside. As soon as they saw me they started gathering around. Most looked angry. Nobody likes having guns pointed at them, especially men who have frequently used them. They weren't looking for explanations. Their questions were accusations.

"What were you doing up there with the machine gun?"

"Who did you think you were going to shoot?"

Fortunately Randall called for reinforcements and enough guards arrived to discourage the inmates from getting physical.

Another case of management indifference to inmate danger did not turn out so well. I first heard of the situation when officer Mel Varney came to me.

"Mac, this morning inmate John Davis came to me looking for protection. He said he owes fifteen bucks to inmates Jackson and Frazier for three Talwin tablets he got from them last week. (The small Talwin tablets always caused us trouble because they were easy to smuggle in and circulate.)

"Davis hasn't got the money," Mel went on, "and he's sure they're going to kill him. I figured it would be best if we moved him out of B-1 away from the other two until he straightens out the debt."

Varney shook his head in disbelief. "But when I proposed this to Larker and Butterworth, they refused. They claim nobody's going to kill Davis over fifteen dollars, especially not Jackson and Frazier."

I said, "If they think Jackson and Frazier are so angelic, why do they keep them in Block One?"

"Beats me. Anyway, Davis is hustling his ass trying to come up with the money. What can we do?"

"I don't know what to tell you, Mel. It's not a union matter. Alert the Seniors and hope Davis works it out."

A few hours later a doorslam in B-1 brought us all to the aid of John Davis. Too late. He had been strangled.

Outside in the corridor, another inmate stood by, shaken.

"Fuck, man," he told me. "I was on my way with the fifteen bucks. The deadline was only last night. Couldn't they wait a little longer?"

His question accented the stark prison reality that powerful inmates have their reputations to protect. Debts, no matter how small, must be paid on time.

Sadly, no indictments or convictions ever took place for this murder, even though the deceased has fingered the likely killers.

The above two instances point out that, contrary to the view of many, the guards usually showed more concern for the well-being of the inmates than the administration did.

As that first year drew to a close, I felt gratified at what had been achieved even though we had not been totally successful. We didn't accomplish a great deal visibly in the prison and still the vast majority of the membership treated me with great respect. I had remained their incorruptible, legitimate voice, and they showed their appreciation in many ways. Most gratifying was their eagerness to shield me from physical danger. In Walpole that meant a lot.

Sometimes their protective instinct reached comical proportions. In one instance I was standing in the corridor just outside Block Two talking to Connie Mancuso over some matter now forgotten. After a few seconds I felt something striking the back of my leg. When I turned around I found little Mikey Duggan, one of Mancuso's mischief-making stooges, standing on the opposite side of the closed gate, urinating on my trousers.

Immediately I ordered Mancuso back into his block, then stomped down the hall toward Andrew Larker's office. On the way I ran into Carl Schofield, a respected Senior Officer who commanded our Tac-team. When Carl heard what had happened he escorted me to Larker, all the way calling out, "He pissed on our president!"

Between the two of us we raised such a stink with Larker that he agreed to shift Duggan to Block Ten. Perhaps the infraction did not warrant the punishment, but all of us had experienced enough of this sort of thing. We did not enjoy being targets for human waste.

Duggan kicked, begged and cried all the way down the corridor. As it turned out, Larker transferred him back to Max after a few days anyway.

8 McLaughlin, You're Under Arrest

Many important safety-related problems demanded union attention during my first year. For that reason I hadn't yet tangled with management over the Doctor's List issue, even though it bred heavy resentment among the guards and posed a threat to prison safety. Suddenly, in my eleventh month, circumstances forced my hand.

Officers at Walpole got fifteen paid sick days each year. Any days not used were carried over to the following year. Work benefit guidelines placed no restriction on the use of sick days.

For those who exceeded their sick-day allotment, management had created the Doctor's List. Once placed on this list, an officer couldn't return to work after taking time off sick without a note from his doctor. I could see the reasoning, even though I didn't agree with it. The list discouraged men from claiming sickness as an excuse to take random time off. The approach seemed juvenile, but not completely unreasonable.

Management, however, took the List a step further. They arbitrarily added to the List officers who still had unused sick days on the books. Consequently these officers were forced to see a doctor and pay a fee every time they took a sick day. They literally couldn't take two hours off near the end of a day to get some relief from a cold without being forced to return with a note the next day. Obviously they had not abused their sick time. Why were they being treated as if they had?

The regulation proved to be more than annoying. At times it created dangerous situations. Men wobbly from flu or bad colds would remain at their posts even though they were incapable of functioning at full capacity. In that condition they tended to overreact or react improperly to inmates, thereby endangering themselves and fellow officers. The managers should have ordered them home so they could recover more quickly, not held them hostage to the Doctor's List.

But because management both distrusted the guards and resented the union, they used the Doctor's List as a punishment tool against men who had shown themselves to be troublesome union members. By the spring of 1978 nearly forty percent of the officers had been placed on the Doctor's List. Resentment might run high, but what recourse did officers have? The union had never stuck up for them on this matter.

Then a case arose that forced me to change my priorities and focus on this issue. I was sitting at my desk in a cellblock late one afternoon when the phone rang. Picking it up, I found Officer Leon Usher on the other end. He'd been off a few days with a bad throat.

"Leon, how're you doing? You still sick?"

"I'm feeling okay, Mike. I tried to come to work this afternoon but Butterworth sent me home suspended. He's got me on the goddamn Doctor's List now. And I've got days left on the books."

"Maybe their records are fouled up. Did you ask them to check?"

"Yeah. Their records aren't screwed up. Even they show me with three sick days left. How can they put me on the Doctor's List?"

"They're not supposed to. What did Butterworth say?"

"That I've been abusing my sick time. How can I be abusing my sick time when I've got days left?"

"You're not and he knows it. You're just a good union man, that's all."

"Yeah, but it's going to cost me. He won't let me come back without a doctor's note. That's going to cost me twenty or twenty-five bucks."

Something on my gut level told me the time had come to take a stand.

"Leon, don't bother getting a note. Stay home. They've got no right to apply the Doctor's List to your case. I'm going to file a grievance. We'll go over Butterworth's head, all the way to the Office of Employee Relations if necessary."

I put together the paperwork that evening and delivered it to Butterworth's office the following morning. As was inevitable, he withheld a decision for the full ten days allowed, then ruled against. No words were exchanged between us. I received the paperwork in my mailbox.

The Area Commissioner followed the same procedure during Step Two, forcing me to move on to Step Three, Commissioner Hall. Again the paperwork went out, and again I marked the fourteen days off on my calendar, fully expecting Hall to deny us at the end of that time. Meanwhile Usher sat at home without a paycheck coming in.

I felt guilty about that so at the end of two weeks, in spite of it being my day off, I put in a call from home to Hall's office. I reached his Deputy of Administration.

"What can I do for you, Mike?" she asked cordially. We had a difficult relationship because she knew little about prison operations yet was forced to defend the Department.

"Hall is due to give us a decision today on a grievance concerning Leon Usher. I wonder if you could check on the paperwork for me."

"It just came to my desk. I have it in front of me."

The sound of papers being riffled came through the phone. Then she said, "According to this, the Commissioner has ruled in Mr. Usher's favor."

"I almost dropped the phone. "Did I hear you right? We won?"

"That's what it says. His suspension is lifted and he'll be reimbursed for all pay lost. I'll have the paperwork in the mail to you later today."

"Boy, is that good news, thank you. Gotta go. I've got calls to make."

Elated, I first called Usher. "Leon, I just got word that we won in Step Three."

"No shit?"

"Your suspension is lifted and you'll be paid for all days off. You can report to work tomorrow."

I could hear the relief in his voice. "Man, that's great. I was really getting worried. Mike, thanks."

I next called the prison and reached Mike Gilmore.

"Mike, guess what. We won the Usher case."

"In Step Three? What's with Hall? He suddenly going soft?"

"I don't know," I laughed, "but I'm not going to ask him. This will be a big lift for the guys. We've set a precedent. Do me a favor and get all the stewards together so they can circulate the news. Tell them also to start putting together a list of other guys who've been put on the Doctor's List unfairly. Now we can gradually start pursuing their cases."

Word swept quickly through the guard ranks and in the process into Butterworth's pipeline. He had not been informed of Hall's decision. Now he initiated several phone calls that turned this case upside down. I received one of them.

"What are you doing telling Leon Usher to come back to work? You've no right to do that when he's still on the Doctor's list."

"Fred," I replied, "Commissioner Hall has just ruled in our favor. The Doctor's List does not apply to Usher's case."

"I've heard that talk but I don't accept it. I just called Usher to tell him to stay home. As far as I'm concerned he's still suspended! You haven't won anything!"

As soon as he hung up I again dialed the Commissioner's office. Again reaching his Deputy, I entreated, "I need someone to contact Fred Butterworth and tell him about the Usher decision."

"Mike," she replied sheepishly, "I've got bad news for you. After your earlier call, Fred Butterworth called here. Boy, was he upset. He talked with the Commissioner for a long time, and got him to change his mind."

"What?" I caught myself after having almost shouted. "Changed his mind? After rendering an official decision? I've already told all my guys. What's he trying to do, make a fool out of me?"

"I'm sorry, Mike, really."

I quickly gathered my things and drove into Boston, arriving at the Commissioner's office just before 1 p.m.

Hall greeted me politely and said, "I'm sorry this misunderstanding occurred. My Deputy should never have released details of the decision over the phone."

"Frank, you changed your mind. How come?"

"As long as the paperwork was still in this office it was my privilege to do so."

"Look, we both know you originally ruled in Usher's favor. I don't appreciate you letting Fred Butterworth change your mind."

Hall's back stiffened. "I'm sorry, but he made sense. I made my decision. I don't want to discuss it further."

Frustrated, I faced a tough decision of my own. I could back off and run the grievance through Step Four with the OER, but this would likely mean another three-week delay. After that we'd probably face another appeal. In the meantime, if I allowed Hall to jerk us around like he'd just done the union would lose any respect it had gained.

My option was to threaten a work stoppage and drag the OER into the controversy right now. But were we as a local ready to hit the street?

I had been building support for eleven months, but I hadn't concentrated on the Doctor's List as one of our main issues. Without briefing and preparation the men might not be willing to walk off. Further complicating the matter, Walpole was forty miles away. Even if the officers sympathized with the cause, did I have enough influence with them to initiate the job action by phone? I dared not break off contact with Hall and return to the prison for fear of losing the momentum of my presentation.

Swallowing hard, I decided to take a chance.

"Frank," I said, "My guys are firm on this. We're tired of being held hostage to the Doctor's List. They told me that unless you reinstate the original Usher decision at once, they will initiate a job action at 3 p.m."

At first shocked, he abruptly turned angry. "You can't come in here and extort a decision from me. I will not reinstate Usher. If you think you can pull off a strike, go ahead. It won't get you anywhere."

"All right," I told him, "then I suggest you contact the OER. That is, if you don't want Walpole paralyzed for a long time."

He fixed me with a withering stare. Then I turned and left his office, sweat beginning to break out. I had just officially announced a strike that the proposed participants knew nothing about.

Hurrying to a nearby phone, I called into the prison and reached Mike Gilmore.

"Mike, bad news. Hall's bailed out on us. He's reversed the Usher decision. We're back where we started."

"What the hell happened?"

"Apparently Butterworth got upset and did a number on Hall. Hall bought it."

"Shit!"

"Listen, I'm standing out here in the open so I can't talk long. I want to take the Department all the way to the wall if necessary. I hope you guys are behind me."

"Sure we're behind you. The guys will all be pissed when they hear this."

"Then listen closely. Catch the 3–11 at roll and tell them not to go to work. I've already told Hall they're going to strike. The 3–11 should stay outside until they see me in person. Got that? In person!"

Gilmore said, "Okay," but I wanted to leave nothing to chance, so I went on, "I may call again and instruct you otherwise, but don't take my words seriously. I'm about to go into meetings and I'm not sure what kind of pressure I'll be put under. They may try to force me to delay, but I want this issue dealt with today. Even if I seem to give in, by standing firm you'll force an immediate decision on them. Remember, don't return to work until you see my sweaty face."

Gilmore assured me he understood. He had proven himself to be a good trooper in the past so I felt reasonably confident now, especially since the 3–11 shift would fire the opening volley.

Around 2:30, the forces of battle gathered in Hall's office. Council 93 sent lawyer Joseph Spataro and chief negotiator Sam Frustaci to represent me. Hall's Assistant Commissioners Larry Meacham and Mike Fair joined him. Fred Butterworth arrived from Walpole. The OER was represented by a new labor relations specialist, Ira Cobb, who had been imported from out of state by Governor Dukakis.

Cobb's reputation for union-busting had already intimidated Council 93. Frustaci warned me that the guy was "tough and a bully."

This carried little weight with me. I felt that Frustaci himself was a bully, and therefore easy to bully. Besides, how could I fear any law abiding citizen when I walked among hardened criminals every day? I could've shown Frustaci some real bullies by walking him down the corridor at Walpole.

An urgency hovered over the Usher meeting because I had set a 3 p.m. deadline. If something wasn't decided quickly and the 3–11 shift didn't go to work, Walpole's afternoon programs would be disrupted. This possibility always seemed to strike fear into members of the Department. The inmates might get upset. Heaven forbid.

We sat at a long conference table, the Department people lined up on one side, myself, my E-Board, and the Council 93 people on the other. Significantly, Ira Cobb sat next to Frank Hall. Theoretically, the OER was supposed to be an impartial body. We believed otherwise. Cobb's placement at this meeting fortified our suspicions.

I could see in the smug facial expressions of the Department people that they didn't believe I could control a job action at Walpole from Boston. They knew I'd been with Hall since early afternoon. It would take tight control from me and strict loyalty from my men to engineer the threatened walkout. Since we had yet to put those attributes on display, they suspected I was bluffing.

Cobb rapped the table with his knuckles and opened the meeting: "Gentlemen, you've put me in an awkward position. I've been called here to mediate a job action that is not yet taking place." He glanced at his watch.

"At this moment, we are technically still in the grievance mode," Cobb went on. "Commissioner Hall has just exercised his prerogative and denied a grievance in Step Three. If Local 451 chooses, it can still file the paperwork with my office and we can avoid a potentially embarrassing scene."

Cobb looked at me. "But as it stands, I can't rule on a grievance this afternoon. I'm here to mediate a strike—and there's no strike. Where do we go from here?"

Hall broke in. "Mr. Cobb, the president of Local 451 has declared that a job action will begin at 3 p.m. Personally I doubt whether he's foolish enough to try to pull it off, but as a precaution I thought it best to call you here so that the prison would face a minimum of disruption."

Hall turned to Fred Butterworth. "Fred, what was the status at Walpole when you left?"

"Everything was quiet and running smoothly. A few of the 3–11 shift had already started to arrive. We saw no indication of a job action."

Spataro and Frustaci cast me sick glances that made it clear they felt embarrassed. Hall's eyes appeared even more challenging. The Department people's smirks widened, and they began mumbling to each other and ridiculing me in undertones I was supposed to hear. One comment expressed all of their opinions.

"How can this twit threaten to strike over a bird turd issue when his guys aren't behind him?"

I didn't respond, and they continued having a good time at my expense. But they didn't dare leave.

Cobb, Hall, and Butterworth sat there bantering like victors, waiting until 3:10 when the 3–11 shift should have assumed its posts.

At that point Hall quieted the others and told Butterworth: "Call the prison and find out if anything's happened."

Fred crossed the room and picked up the phone. As he dialed I sat in my chair trying to look cool. But under the table my fingers were tightly crossed. I could only hope that Mike Gilmore had been able to carry out my instructions.

A score of accusing faces glared at me as Fred finally made contact with Assistant Deputy Stanley Tinker. In a confident voice Fred asked, "Stanley, what's the status there? Everything okay?"

A frown crept across his face. "Yeah . . . Uh-huh . . . I understand. All right, Stanley." The cockiness had vanished from his voice.

After hanging up he announced in an embarrassed tone, "The 3–11 didn't go in. They're playing cards in the rec-room."

Jaws dropped. "God damn it," somebody shouted. Oaths rang out in the room. Hands slapped against the table in frustration. Their eyes asked what their voices dared not. How had I managed it?

I could hardly believe it myself. I muttered under my breath, "Thank you, Mike Gilmore."

Without further delay we proceeded with the discussion and I immediately took the floor.

"Mr. Cobb, we could have avoided this proceeding if the Commissioner had not allowed Superintendent Butterworth to push him around . . ."

"Wait a minute," Hall snapped. "Nobody pushed me around. It was my decision to make.

"Nevertheless, you reversed your previous ruling on the Usher grievance. That set my guys off."

Hall looked at Cobb. "I discussed the matter with Superintendent Butterworth and he made several good points."

"Like what?" I demanded. "How can anybody reasonably argue that Leon Usher deserves to be on the Doctor's List when he hasn't used up his allotted sick time?"

With curled lip Hall turned to me. "I remind you that the Doctor's List was created to discourage the abuse of sick time. Paid sick days are to be used to convalesce from illness, not for business or as days off.

"Superintendent Butterworth felt that Usher had abused sick time in the past and therefore added him to the Doctor's List. All Usher must do is provide evidence he was sick in the form of a doctor's note. What's so unreasonable about that?"

"Doctor's visits these days are exorbitant. You, as Commissioner, know how much we're making."

He ignored the dig. "The way I see it, if a guy's so sick that he must take time off he probably should have a doctor look at him anyway."

"I don't think that's any of the Department's business. What I want to know is, what gives the Superintendent the right to arbitrarily add someone to the Doctor's List without a hearing or any consultation with the union?"

"It's a management tool. We're running an institution. He's the Superintendent. We can't have a judicial proceeding over every little thing."

"Little to you, maybe. You don't have to shell out the twenty or thirty dollars for each doctor's note."

He shrugged. "If a few of the innocent are being hurt, I'm sorry. But we have reason to believe that numerous guards have abused their sick time and that the Doctor's List acts to prevent it."

"What it does is discourage seriously sick men from going home. They pass their illness on to other guards, or perform their duties in a substandard manner. People get hurt; the prison suffers."

"I think we on management level can determine what's best for the prison."

"I think we're finally getting to the real issue here. You object to the union having anything to say about the Doctor's List."

"I won't dignify that with a response."

The issue seemed clear cut. We had already made the basic arguments. But, because of maneuvering, the discussion dragged on. Hall called several drawn-out private caucuses with his people giving us the impression that he might be willing to bend. But each time he would return to the table as obstinate as ever. I, of course, held my ground just as stubbornly.

In the meantime the clock approached 6:30, an important time because the evening program schedule at Walpole started at 7:00. And, to repeat, management feared disrupting the programs.

Considering his reputation, Cobb sat through the proceeding with surprising patience. He listened intently and even though he spoke little, at times I thought I sensed him leaning in our direction.

Someone had obviously briefed him about Walpole's schedule for suddenly at exactly 6:30 he took the floor.

"Gentlemen, I think you've just about exhausted your arguments. We're not going to do anyone—certainly not the prison—any good by dragging this out. I'm ready to put forth a proposal that I think everyone can live with."

Both sides hung on his words. We all recognized this as a watershed case.

He continued, "I propose to reinstate Leon Usher; compensate him with all pay lost due to his suspension; remove him from the Doctor's List; and wipe his record clean. The Doctor's List will remain in effect under the supervision of the Superintendent's office. Each case will be judged on an individual basis."

In effect he was ruling on the grievance. It put us back into the position we'd occupied after Hall first ruled in favor of Usher. On the surface it didn't look like much, but I saw it as a great victory and accepted at once. Usher would get what he deserved and I had demonstrated I had firm control over a union that meant business.

Hall, of course, recognized it as a defeat. Badly disappointed, he could do nothing because Cobb reported directly to Dukakis.

Then Cobb said, "Mr. McLaughlin, I'd like you, Mr. Frustaci, and Commissioner Hall to join me for a private conference."

We followed him into an adjoining room where he turned to Hall.

"Frank, McLaughlin has stepped way out of line by leading a strike. In effect he just forced me into a Step Four grievance decision that I should have been given time to ponder. Punishment is in order. What do you suggest?"

Flushed with anger, Hall firmly stated, "I want him fired!"

"Now wait a minute," Frustaci jumped in. "That's awful drastic. After all, you did rule in his favor. What about transferring him to one of the prison camps?"

I couldn't believe my ears. How could they dare proceed with this outrageous discussion right in front of me? And Frustaci! Some kind of defender he'd turned out to be.

Unable to take any more, I interrupted and said, "If you think my guys will let you fire me or ship me off to the camps, you're crazy. I haven't done anything to justify it. The Commissioner is the one who triggered all this by changing his mind."

Hall remained determined. "Mr. Cobb, I want him fired."

Cobb scratched his chin in thought. Then finally he glanced at Hall and shrugged.

"Frank, I'd like to see him punished too but," he paused, "I think it's in the best interest of everyone to drop it."

This so frustrated Hall that I could see tears filling his eyes and his hands shaking. My challenging him had severed any bonds of friendship that might've still existed between us. He wanted my head, and Cobb had prevented him from taking it.

My fate decided, we went back out to rejoin the main meeting. With 7 p.m. approaching, the prison program schedule was on everyone's mind.

Looking pleased with himself in spite of the outcome, Cobb

handed me the phone and said, "Okay Mike, call the prison, get the 3–11 back to work and we'll call it a day."

Instead of taking the phone I cast him another of my innocent glances and shook my head. "Mr. Cobb, you don't seem to realize how important this issue is to my guys. They're upset about Usher and the Doctor's List. It'll take more than just a phone call to get them back on the job. I have to go there and explain the decision to them."

He stared at me incredulously. "Did I just hear you say you can't make a call and put your guys back to work?"

I shrugged. "I'm afraid so. My guys will want to hear about your decision from me in person."

I suddenly got my first view of Cobb's fiery temper. He reached down, lifted the conference table up high, then banged its legs back to the floor, sending pencils and ashtrays flying. "Who the fuck is in charge down there? I thought you were in charge! I thought I was dealing with the head of that union! Who's running that place?"

"Well I am, I suppose," I replied. "But understand, this is bigger than us. These guys are mad. I'm just their spokesman. I can't push them around. Once I tell them what's going to happen to Usher, I'm sure I can convince them to go back to work."

He threw his arms in the air. "How long will it take you to get there?"

"Forty minutes, at least. You don't want me to get a speeding ticket, do you?"

He stared at the ceiling. "All right, get there as soon as you can, then call me as soon as those guys are back to work."

I didn't reach the prison until 7:45. It took me just 5 minutes to get the 3–11 back to work. To the chagrin of management and the inmates, programs for that evening had to be canceled.

The Usher case opened the way to undermining the Doctor's List. Unfortunately we could never completely eliminate it. We had to fight each case individually. But we did remove many of those who had been unfairly listed.

The behavior of my guys during the job action made me proud. The prison had not gone without supervision. The dayshift had patiently remained at their posts until relieved without knowing the details behind what had triggered the confrontation. This took trust in me and loyalty to the common goal. I came out of the episode with a new feeling of strength, determined now to force the safety issues.

The safety committee had been meeting now for some ten months without making any changes of importance. We couldn't even get management to buy enough lightbulb replacements.

Lighting in the blocks always posed a problem because inmates frequently broke or would paint over the bulbs. They said the lighting interfered with their sleep. For some this may have been true, but at the same time good lighting interfered with covert violence.

Other basic improvements also went no further than the discussion stage. Among them we requested the installation of panic buttons, especially in the visiting areas, to eliminate the archaic practice of signaling trouble by banging doors.

Another suggestion was the establishment of a regular shakedown schedule, particularly in the Max-section. Again, no soap. Naturally if you couldn't make progress on basic items like these you weren't going very far on safety in general.

Less than a month after the Usher decision a situation arose that pushed me into a safety confrontation with Walpole's management. In the safety meetings management had come up with the term "Critical Minimum." This referred to the fewest number of officers that needed to be present in order to maintain the normal prison routine. Deputy Superintendent Andrew Larker, in particular, loved this term.

I had no problem with the concept itself, but rather with the figure decided upon by administration. I saw it as much too low. In spite of my objections, administration stood fast behind their figure. Time after time I complained that one area or another was understaffed. Larker would give me his cheezy little grin and say, "It's not under the Critical Minimum."

Ironically, the understaffing problem came to a head in Butterworth's absence, on the first day that Andrew Larker was left in charge of the prison. Andrew had shown himself to be highly conscious of his authority and eager to exercise it. Unfortunately his temporary assignment as Acting Superintendent didn't improve his judgment to match his increased authority.

I first learned that a problem existed as I stood with the rest of the guys at morning roll call. We'd had a bad run of illness and injuries in the ranks, but today the room looked even emptier than usual.

Supervisor O'Rourke read off the names and I could see furrows of concern creasing his brow as time and again he received no response. When he finished he scratched his head and feverishly went to work with pencil and eraser trying to adjust assignments. I could see he wasn't satisfied with the final list, but 7 a.m. was almost on us.

"All right, fellas, quiet down," he said. "Here's the bad news. We're down some forty officers."

O'Rourke paused to allow a rash of murmurs to subside. "You know what that means. Watch your ass today and do your best to avoid trouble. We don't want anything heavy breaking out that we don't have the manpower to put down.

After waiting for quiet through another outbreak of grumbles, O'Rourke went on, "I'll try to keep the corridor and blocks covered, but you know how things go. Once we break up I'll go to Larker and request he hold over officers from the 11–7 shift and call in some from the 3–11. In the meantime, be careful."

O'Rourke's hands were tied. He was taking the proper steps. The prison had to continue functioning. Everything depended upon how Larker responded to the emergency.

A group of grumbling officers entered the prison that morning. I could do nothing but commiserate with them. I too would be working under increased pressure. As union president I needed the freedom to move about so I no longer worked a regular assignment. Today I coincidentally had been assigned to my old block, A-2. I would have to work it alone rather than with a companion officer.

My familiarity with A-2 helped me keep the block under control but it demanded my full attention. I did not see any extra officers arriving but had difficulty breaking away to check on the full prison status. I knew the prison programs were in full swing and that inmates roamed everywhere without enough officers to properly supervise them. Had a major disturbance occurred we would have been hard pressed to put it down.

Finally after a couple of hours I managed get myself relieved and walked down to Larker's office.

"Andrew, what's happening on this manpower shortage?"

"Well, Mac, it's a problem. I tried to talk the 11–7 shift into staying over, but I couldn't get any volunteers. They've been working a lot of overtime lately. Now they claim they're exhausted."

"What about the 3–11?"

"They've been overworked lately too. I doubt if they'd want to come in either."

"Call them. We need help."

"All right, I will."

His attitude seemed reasonable so I went back to my block.

By late morning I still saw no sign of additional officers. I kept track by calling around to various points in the prison. I received nothing but complaints about the pressure everyone was feeling. The Max-section in particular faced an explosive situation. The inmates there had gotten wind of the shortage and were acting even rowdier than usual. With the Max-corridor undermanned, the block officers faced real danger.

Worried, I again broke away and marched down to see Larker.

"Andrew, how're you doing on getting the 3–11 officers in?"

My query seemed to annoy him. "Look, Mike, I'm in charge here. Let me worry about this."

"No," I replied. "With my guys in danger, I have to be worried about it. Now how're you doing?"

After giving me a cold stare, he said, "I haven't been able to find any volunteers."

"In that case, the next thing to do is order them in. We can't continue running the prison this way. My guys are in danger. Order the 3–11 shift in now, and in the meantime cut back some of the programs. Let's contain the inmates where we can properly supervise them."

As usual, any suggestion of tampering with the program schedule raised hackles. "I'll worry about running operations. I'm not going to cut the programs. I'll find some way to get more officers in."

I looked at him doubtfully, but could only accept his promise and return to my post.

The day dragged by with pressure mounting and still no extra officers arriving. Fortunately no serious altercation took place, but the prison felt like a powderkeg waiting for a spark.

Finally around two o'clock I spotted an officer from the 3–11 shift arriving. I immediately approached him.

"Did Larker call you in?"

"No. I just happened to come in early and they sent me inside to help."

I felt my blood starting to boil and repeated, "Larker never called you?"

"No, and I was home all day. I didn't have anything to do, so I would've been glad to come in and help."

His words sent me storming back down to Larker's office. Pointing at Larker, I accused, "You've been putting me off all day. I don't believe you've tried to call anybody. You don't care what happens to my guys. Now either you get some extra people in here at once or I'll straighten this situation out myself."

Larker exploded. "You're as much responsible for shortstaffing as anyone! If you were doing your job you'd be working harder to recruit more officers for this place! So don't complain to me! You do your job and let me worry about how to use the officers we do have!"

I couldn't believe what I'd heard. Finally I shouted back, "Since when does the union have the right to hire people? I've been complaining about your stupid 'Critical Minimums' for months, and now we're under 'Critical Minimum!' Recruiting staff is management's problem, not mine! And don't try to tell me how to run my union!"

Furious, I turned and walked out. Larker's office sat adjacent to the control room so I had a long walk back to A-2. By the time I got there I knew what I was going to do.

With most of the Minimum inmates still at work call, the blocks and corridor were relatively empty. I checked around to satisfy myself that the corridor officer could handle things by himself. Then I locked up my block and handed him my keys.

"I've got union business to attend to," I told him.

Before he could respond I started back the way I had come. I marched past inner control, past Larker's office, all the way into the Max-section. There, I immediately approached Officer Wayne Northrup, the Senior in charge of the corridor.

Northrup always handled his job responsibly and did not allow others to push him around. In this case he saw me steaming and listened attentively when I took him around a corner to explain.

"Wayne," I said. "I'm here on union business. I'm going to take control of the corridor. Don't interfere."

"What's going on?" he asked.

"Just trust me and stay out of it."

He shrugged and stepped back. "Okay, Mac."

I then proceeded down the corridor, stopping at each Max cellblock and issuing the same order to the officer inside.

"Step out into the corridor, please, and secure your block."

All seven officers did so, locking the block grilles behind them. They still had good vision into the blocks, but could no longer be reached by the inmates. More curious than anything, the inmates gathered at the grilles to see what was going down. This I didn't care about.

I stood in the center of the corridor in clear view of all seven officers, who remained standing outside their respective blocks. Raising my voice, I said, "Fellas, I don't have to tell you that all day long we've been working understrength in unsafe conditions. That's a clear violation of our contract. I do not want you pressing your luck any longer. As union president I'm ordering you to remain out of your cellblocks until the 3–11 shift relieves you. I guarantee you there will be no suspensions."

They all looked relieved.

I no sooner had finished my address when Assistant Deputy Tinker came rushing up. Poor Tinker could never seem to keep rein on his emotions. Since he was a frail-looking elderly man, I always feared that one day he might bring a seizure upon himself. Considering the flushed look on his face, the possibility looked even greater today.

His eyes darting from one officer to the other, he shouted, "What're you guys doing out of your blocks?" Receiving no reply he started pointing. "You! You! You! Get back in your blocks!" When still no one moved he scurried up to one officer and ranted, "I'm giving you a direct order, Mister! Get back in your block!"

I had followed behind Tinker and as he was issuing his order I emphatically shook my head from side to side and pointed at the floor as if to say, "Stay right where you are."

The officer responded, "I'm sorry, Mr. Tinker, but upon orders of my president I'm not allowed to reenter my block."

"Orders of your president? I'm giving the orders here! I'm in charge! I'm Assistant Deputy! You'll be suspended if you disobey."

"I'm sorry, Mr. Tinker, but I have to listen to my president."

Sweating noticeably, Tinker rushed up to the next officer and repeated the same threat. He received the same response. Finally realizing he would get nowhere this way, Tinker glared at me and angrily gestured, "Come with me!"

I followed him all the way to Larker's office. When Larker saw him puffing like a marathon runner, he came around his desk. "Stanley, take it easy. What's the problem?"

Tinker resumed his ranting. "McLaughlin's causing trouble again. He's supposed to be running a block in the Minimum Section but he came down to the Max-end without permission and ordered all the officers out of their blocks. Now I can't get them to go back."

Larker looked like a hunter who had just cornered his prey. A smile spread across his face. He leaned back against his desk and folded his arms across his chest.

"All right, Mike, what do you have to say for yourself?"

Seeing his smugness, I blew up. "I've been on your case all day about us being undermanned. I don't believe you did anything to relieve the situation. As far as I'm concerned you placed this prison in serious jeopardy. I ordered the guys out of the blocks and they'll stay out until the 3–11 shift comes in."

It was now 2:30. In another thirty minutes the arrival of the 3–11 would have relieved the crisis. Larker could have backed off and avoided further confrontation. But he refused to budge one inch. Obviously he envisioned this incident as a means of striking at me and the union.

Straightening up he said, "All right, Mike, I want you to leave this institution immediately." When I started to reply he continued, "Under threat of arrest, you leave this institution at once!"

The look in his eye told me that further discussion would be fruitless.

"I'll stop just long enough to get my briefcase," I told him.

I stomped back down to A-2, and as I retrieved my keys from the corridor officer told him, "I've got to leave. Call the Max-section and tell them to prepare for a strike."

I then entered A-2 and locked the grille behind me to keep the several inmates who had filtered back from work call from having access to the corridor. As I fumbled to stuff papers in my briefcase, they saw my agitation and approached.

"Hey, man, what's going on?"

"Just back off and mind your own business," I curtly told them.

Some went back to their cells, the others backed off a few paces. All knew me well enough not to interfere.

My briefcase packed, I picked up the phone and dialed my favorite newscaster. When the receptionist at the station answered, I said, "Let me speak to Les Collins, please."

A moment later his voice came on. "This is Les Collins."

"Les? Mike McLaughlin. I thought you'd like to know. There's a strike at Walpole."

"Strike? When?"

"Right now. I've just been thrown out under threat of arrest, so I can't talk. Do me a favor and call the other stations to let them know."

I'd developed such a close relationship with one of Boston's leading newscasters that I knew he would provide that service.

The inmates had only heard my side of the conversation but it had been enough to raise their ire. I heard them growling to each other, "Strike? Another night without programs or visits?"

Some of them began rushing about trying to hustle cigarettes and other goodies in case they were locked in. Others again came forward.

"Did we hear right? You're having another fuckin' strike? What is this shit?"

"I told you to mind your own business," I repeated. Then, before they could do anything further I turned, unlocked the grille, and exited. If they had acted together they could have prevented me from leaving, but my animated, businesslike demeanor kept them at a distance. Even so, as I walked down the corridor toward the main trap they serenaded me with insults and epithets. "Fuckin' punk" seemed to be the day's favorite.

A few minutes later as I entered the administration building, I ran into Mike Gilmore.

"What're you doing out here so early?" he asked.

"Mike, I can't talk to you," I replied. "I've been thrown out of here under threat of arrest."

"What do you mean, threat of arrest? Who's going to arrest you?"

"I can't talk, Mike, I've got to leave now."

He followed me out into the lobby and grabbed my arm. "You can't just leave without an explanation. What's going on?"

I stopped. "We've been working shorthanded all day. The guys have been under tremendous pressure. Larker promised to bring people in but he didn't even try. Finally I got tired of his bullshit and ordered the Max-officers out of the blocks. Now Larker's ordered me out of the prison under threat of arrest."

"What are you going to do?"

"I don't know yet. I'll figure that out after I leave. I'll probably call the Council 93 lawyers and go from there."

"Well don't go until you tell the 3–11 shift what's happened. They're at roll right now."

"Mike, I can't do that. I'll get arrested."

He pulled me along. "Nobody's going to arrest you. We'll see to that."

He led me down the stairs to the rec-room where some fifty or so of the 3–11 officers had gathered. I felt like I was interrupting a sacred ceremony, Roger Lahoud addressing his shift. When he saw me that old twinkle entered his eye and he stopped in the middle of his briefing.

"Oops, wait a minute fellas. Your illustrious union president is here. I believe he may have something to say to you. Mr. McLaughlin?"

He stepped back and I assumed his position. "Thanks Roger.

Fellas, all day long the day shift has been working in fear. We were short nearly forty officers, and yet we were forced to continue a full program schedule. You can imagine the pressure. I asked Larker to call you guys. He claims he did but could get no volunteers. Did any of you guys get called?"

They all shook their heads.

"I didn't think you had, so about a half hour ago I ordered the Max-officers out of their cellblocks. Larker then threw me out under threat of arrest. I have to leave directly. As soon as I talk to our lawyers I'll let the stewards know what's happening. Have a good shift."

A few minutes later, down the street from the prison, I called Council 93 from a pay phone. I reached Sam Frustaci. At this time he and I were still getting along.

"They have no right to threaten you with arrest. We'll come down right away and straighten this thing out."

I immediately felt better and called into the prison to check with Mike Gilmore. He told me, "Right after you left, the 3–11 shift voted not to go to work. We're not going to stand idly by while Larker pushes our president around. The guys are hanging around in the rec-room waiting for your orders."

Gratitude and pride welled up in my chest. These guys were truly behind me.

"Tell them to hang tight."

So it was on to Boston again. Less than thirty days after the Usher case the same cast of characters gathered in Hall's office again.

This time the discussion centered on the Critical Minimum sheets. These clearly indicated that I had grounds for protest that day. Even Hall couldn't contest that. He was willing to back off and set up another committee to investigate the short staffing problem.

The big argument developed over how to deal with me. Hall told Cobb, "McLaughlin has no right to take over the prison corridor or to issue orders concerning prison routine. Especially when his orders are in direct contradiction to orders given by managers. He can grieve anything he wants, but he can't take action on his own authority."

"What was I to do?" I asked them, "leave my officers exposed until one of them was badly hurt or killed?"

Hall shot back, "The situation was not that dangerous. You overreacted and in the process risked a backlash from the inmates. From that you deserve severe punishment."

The poor inmates again. I was tired of hearing that line. What about the officers?

Cobb led Hall off into a brief private caucus, then sent for Frustaci and me. I entered that same private room with a little trepidation. For some reason the blank walls reminded me of a cell.

Hall was puffing heavily on a cigarette, but otherwise looked much calmer. Cobb looked cool. He got right to the point.

"Mike, I have no choice but to agree with the Commissioner. That leaves us three options. One, we can terminate you. Two, we can reassign you to the prison camps. Or three, we can suspend you for two weeks. I'm not sure what Commissioner Hall wants to do."

Hall frowned. He knew exactly what he wanted. "I want him fired, right here and now! I don't want to be faced with dealing with him again."

This time Frustaci came to my rescue, making a case for me and even shouting at Hall. After a few minutes, Cobb decided he had heard enough. He looked at me and said, "So you really think you're right?"

"I know I'm right," I replied.

"Why don't we see just how right you are. Would you be willing to put your reputation on the line and allow your case to go before the Labor Relations Board? Their decision would be final. If you lose you face the two-week suspension."

That seemed fair enough to me. I felt sure I would win. It certainly seemed better than fighting termination or a transfer to the camps.

"All right," I replied, "I agree."

Hall suddenly went berserk and shouted at Cobb. "Wait a second! You can't do that! I want this guy out of here! Don't you know the problems he's causing at Walpole? He's instigated work stoppages! He's disrupting prison routine! He's agitating the inmates! The prison's locked up again tonight! For what? He doesn't belong at Walpole or anywhere else in the Department of Corrections!"

Cobb waited for him to finish and then stated, "Sorry, Frank, but that's my decision."

Hall sat there for a moment, hands shaking, tears running down his cheeks, rage oozing out of every pore. Then he started ranting again.

"Ira, the Governor wouldn't like this decision. He didn't bring you here to cave in to the union. You're supposed to support the Department."

Frustaci and I glanced at each other to verify we'd both heard this serious slip of the tongue. The OER was supposed to be an impartial agency. Hall had just verified our suspicions that the OER had become nothing other than another arm of management.

Cobb remained firm and after Hall composed himself, led us back to the main meeting. He announced:

"Gentlemen, the OER, the Department of Corrections, and the President of Local 451 have come to an agreement. Commissioner Hall has made a special commitment to address the shortstaffing problem at Walpole. He has also agreed to place the question of punishment for Officer McLaughlin before the Labor Relations Board. I think this is a lenient posture. In my view Officer McLaughlin could have been terminated for his actions in the prison this morning. Instead, he may get off. The worst he can get is a two-week suspension."

My E-Board erupted. Vice President Bob Furtado spoke for them.

"Why should he face any punishment? He was doing what was right. If you think we're going back to work with a suspension hanging over our president, think again."

"Now wait a minute," Cobb said. "McLaughlin's already agreed to this."

"We don't care what he's agreed to. We're not going to let him sacrifice himself."

"Mr. Cobb," I interrupted. "I think it's time I caucused with my E-Board."

"By all means," he said, flustered by this sudden resistance.

Once the door of the private room closed behind us I said, "Guys, I know you're trying to help me, but you just might cut my throat. We know I did the right thing, but they just might have the legal grounds to get rid of me."

"They try that," Scandia snarled, "and they'll have a real uprising on their hands."

"What are you going to do? Walk out without any legal grounds?"

Nobody answered, and in the silence I went on. "How long could you stay out? You know it's illegal for state employees to strike. They could force you back and you'll have lost everything."

I looked around at their downcast faces and said, "The best thing for all of us is for me to go before the Labor Relations Board. They're not going to rule against me. Even if they do, what's a two-week suspension? I could use the time off."

"I hate like hell to let the bastards get away with this shit," Scandia said. A couple of others grumbled a little more, and then they finally agreed. A short time later the meeting adjourned and we left feeling that we had another victory under our belt.

I didn't have to appear before the Labor Relations Board until several weeks later. By then I found the appearance more a nuisance than a problem. I was pursuing other, hotter issues.

To my surprise, the LRB ruled against me. As it turned out, my suspension was a paid vacation because the guys took up a collection to defray my salary loss. I spent most of the time at home catching up on union paperwork.

9 Your Goon Versus My Goon

Our successes against Hall and Butterworth came just before our local's presidential election. The guys wanted me back for a second term. I wanted to return, especially since I had just begun making headway on safety.

I won the election in a landslide and my E-Board and I rewarded ourselves by attending the nationwide convention of AFSCME (American Federation of State, County and Municipal Employees) in Las Vegas, Nevada. Conventions like these are usually one-third work and two-thirds play. Considering how hard we had worked the several previous months, I felt we more than deserved our share of the latter.

We returned home relaxed, invigorated, optimistic, and a bit poorer. This mood abruptly turned into concern moments after we stepped off the plane at Boston's Logan International. As I walked through the terminal a headline in the local paper caught my eye.

Still No Pay For State Employees!

Looking closer, I read that some of the Commonwealth's employees faced their third straight week without a paycheck. The article stated that budget negotiations between Governor Dukakis and the Legislature were stalemated. The Commonwealth was running out of spendable funds, and no one could project when the crisis would be settled.

I dropped my bags and stood in front of the newsstand reflecting on the implications of the article. Having been out of touch in Vegas for eight days, I knew nothing of the situation.

Grinding my teeth that the rat race had caught up with me almost the moment I stepped off the plane, I walked over to a bank of telephones and called Council 93. I reached one of Frustaci's assistants.

"I just got back from the Vegas convention. I hear there's a State budget problem. How does this affect Walpole?"

He replied, "This doesn't concern you. Unit Four (Walpole's local) is being paid. This only concerns the other locals. Don't worry about it."

I immediately picked up reticence in his tone. He wanted to keep me out of the matter, probably because I'd built a favorable reputation among the other local presidents. I suspected that Frustaci didn't want me and my big mouth undermining his influence over those officials.

Stubbornly, I probed further. "How is it we're being paid and they're not?"

"The Department of Correction still has money in its budget."

"How long can that last? Look, this is going to spread to us eventually. What's going on?"

Begrudgingly he explained, "The State has no budget because The Governor refused to sign the one proposed by the Legislature. Dukakis wants a rider attached that would allow State funds to be paid for abortions."

Besides the fact that I was a practicing Catholic who opposed abortion, I saw the deadlock as absurd on other grounds. Why should State employees be deprived of their paychecks on account of a touchy issue that had nothing to do with the work they did?

The State Police, for example, had not been paid in a month. It seemed only reasonable that Dukakis should fight out the abortion issue separately and let his employees be paid.

After hanging the phone up, I pondered. Should I get involved? Why ask for more trouble? I'd already stirred up plenty recently. Maybe I should let those directly affected stand up for themselves.

By the time I had driven home, I decided to stay on the sidelines and, as a loyal member of AFSCME, support whatever action it might decide to take. The impasse dragged on into the following week.

Then AFSCME organized a giant protest march on the State House on a Wednesday morning. A crowd of 8,000—state employees and close relatives—gathered on Beacon Street in downtown Boston. They marched up Beacon Hill toward the Capitol on a warm, bright summer day.

The marchers were dressed casually in summer garb. Many carried signs, some to announce affiliations, others to voice protest. Numerous baby carriages added to the confusion.

I saw a sprinkling of uniformed guards from various prisons, and estimated that 300 corrections people were there. Most locals were well represented. Ours was too, even though we hadn't yet missed any paychecks.

A large number of State Police wives waved signs that proclaimed who they were. Many had babies in their arms.

We approached the Capitol in an orderly manner, marched up the steps, and pushed our way into the main foyer. As the building began to fill, several State Representatives and Senators came out of their chambers to see what was happening. The marchers immediately surrounded them and stated our theme, that the abortion issue should not interfere with the passage of the budget.

The legislators listened sympathetically, but most of them looked wary and responded cautiously. They all rattled off a similar line, refusing to take responsibility for the stalemate.

"Yes, we know the position you've been put in. We feel for you. But it's out of our hands. The issue rests with Governor Dukakis, Senate President Harrington, and Speaker of the House McGee."

These three had hastily scheduled a meeting with our union leaders to discuss the budget in relation to the stoppage of paychecks.

Trying to maintain order, several of the Capitol Police moved to strategic positions in the huge chamber. Two posted themselves outside the legislative chambers, two outside the Governor's office, and a handful at the main entrance. For safety reasons they had standing orders to limit the number of people in the State House.

But the marchers, determined to participate, crowded the police aside and kept pouring in. Soon the foyer became a solid mass of humanity. Everyone remained reasonably orderly, but they soon took up the chant, "We want our pay! We want our pay!"

As a local president I was privileged to stand with Frustaci and Spataro as they waited outside the Governor's office. The meeting was due to take place momentarily. People pressed forward, eager for a glimpse of the principals. Soon we began to feel like sardines.

The two Capitol Policemen kept trying to protect the Governor's office but the press of bodies pushed those of us in front against the doors until I could feel them beginning to bend.

Suddenly, being crushed to death was a real possibility. I joined with others in shouting for order. After a few precarious minutes the pressure eased, leaving no one seriously hurt.

Still, the chanting continued. "We want our pay!"

Then the doors opened and a policeman escorted Frustaci and Spataro inside. When the doors closed, some of my guys began growling. None of us trusted the Council 93 leaders, certainly not behind closed doors.

Then Bob Furtado shouted out, "Hey Mac, how come they didn't allow you in there?"

Mike Gilmore jumped in, "Yeah, we want our representative in the meeting!" Soon all the corrections officers started chanting, "We want McLaughlin!"

Due to my highly visible activities over the last year, lots of AFSCME members knew who I was. They quickly picked up the chant until over a thousand voices were shouting, "We want McLaughlin!" The noise was deafening.

After a few minutes the Governor's door opened again. A policeman stepped out and asked, "Who's Mike McLaughlin?" When I identified myself, he stated, "Come with me please, the Governor wants to see you."

The noise had been so tumultuous that Dukakis couldn't conduct his meeting. Now another loud cheer arose as the policeman escorted me in.

I was flattered to have Dukakis greet me at the door and shake my hand. He quickly introduced me to the others in the room and then took his seat at the head of a conference table. All other seats were taken so I stood off to one side, admiring the antique furniture, the old colonial decor, and the large portrait of Samuel Adams that hung behind Dukakis' desk. Because of the noise outside nothing happened for a few minutes, I spent the time fantasizing that the governor's office might one day be mine.

The furor outside finally subsided, allowing the meeting to proceed. Frustaci said, "Most of our members live from week to week. They don't have large savings to fall back on. The budget must be passed so they can get their paychecks. What can be done to end this impasse?"

Dukakis remained silent, so Speaker McGee spoke up.

"We understand your dilemma, but the budget crisis affects the entire population of the State of Massachusetts. We've been fighting a deficit problem in this state for the past three years. I can't convince my members to go for cuts in other human services and then buy an abortion rider. Many of them represent Catholic constituencies. They'd be tarred and feathered."

Senate president Harrington added, "I face the same problem. The abortion issue is too hot to be tossed in the budget as an afterthought. It needs to be debated on its own. I won't consider trying to get it passed. I think its dirty pool to tack it on at a time like this."

Dukakis sat patiently, hands clapsed on the table, waiting for the exchange to conclude. As the others spoke I'd studied his expression. I could have sworn that he had tuned them out.

When his turn came to speak Dukakis stated in effect, "I will have an abortion rider attached to the budget or we will not have a budget."

More than his words, Dukakis's attitude shocked me. He gave not the slightest hint of being willing to bend. He didn't offer to negotiate. He didn't say anything to give me hope that he had any concern at all for the state employees.

"Well," McGee sighed, "I'm willing to go back and talk to my members again. I don't know what good it will do, but maybe someone can come up with some idea for a compromise."

"Not me," said Harrington. "If you, Governor Dukakis, veto the budget as is, I'll press to override that veto. And I think I've got the votes to do it."

"Override?" Frustaci groaned. "How long will that take?"

Harrington replied, "At least a week, maybe two."

"During which my members will go without paychecks."

Harrington shrugged apologetically. Dukakis remained stone-faced. No one had anything else to say.

The talks had been useless. None of the three major parties were willing to present alternatives. I had entered the room expecting to witness a back room deal that would solve the budget issue. Instead I witnessed an extension of the stalemate.

And yet as the meeting broke up everyone acted like old chums, smiling, shaking hands, and congratulating each other over having had a constructive meeting. Had my hearing gone bad? What had they resolved? No, I had heard right: the state's employees might not be paid for weeks.

Minutes later Frustaci, Spataro and I emerged from the office to face the crowd waiting in the foyer. I remember feeling somber and perplexed. Frustaci on the other hand, carried himself like a conquering Caesar celebrating a triumph. Someone handed him a bullhorn and Frustaci used it to address the crowd.

"Ladies and gentlemen, once again our union has shown what unity can accomplish. Because of our march today we were able to meet with the Governor and present our side on this budget stalemate. We emphasized to him how important we are in the running of this state.

"We told him in no uncertain terms to pay us. He tried to argue but we stood firm. Finally he listened. The budget's going to be passed. You can go back to your locals and tell your members that you'll be paid by Monday."

Cheers erupted.

Frustaci's last statement again started me wondering about the effectiveness of my hearing. Paychecks on Monday? This was already Wednesday. Nothing said in Dukakis's office had given me any hope of a settlement by Monday. I could only stand there and shake my head.

Immediately a couple of my guys saw my pained expression and called out, "Hey Mac, what went on in there anyway?"

"Yeah," another one said, "we want to hear from McLaughlin."

The demand triggered another eruption from the crowd. "We want McLaughlin!" again reverberated through the State House. Frustaci had no choice but to surrender center stage. He must've had terrible misgivings turning over his flock to the outspoken rooster.

I declined the use of the bullhorn and waited for the crowd to hush. Then I told them:

"I don't know how Sam came to the conclusion that the issue has been resolved. I heard no indication at all of a settlement inside. The Governor didn't bend; the Legislature didn't bend. The union couldn't do anything to bring them together. There's no budget now. There may not be one for two more weeks. I don't know when anybody's going to be paid."

My words struck the crowd like a slap in the face, turning it into a surly mob. They chose to believe me, not Frustaci. Angry shouts arose.

"Liars! Crooks! Sellouts! The Union sucks! Get out of our sight!"

The uproar reached such proportions that Frustaci and Spataro faced serious physical danger. They had to retreat back into the Governor's office and use Dukakis's private elevator in order to leave the State House.

The crowd stood there confused, asking, "Where do we go? What do we do?"

I raised my hands to quiet them and said, "Let's get all the presidents together and plan a mass strategy. Sam was right about one thing: we must stay unified." Slowly they dispersed.

Having watched Frustaci's performance, my guys remained behind. They looked angry and ready to do something.

"Well, what now?" Marty Trent asked.

"Go to work," I replied. "We haven't missed any paychecks. Naturally we'll support the others as best we can, but as long as we continue receiving our pay we must continue working." The following day, a Thursday, was our next scheduled payday.

Thursday came, but as we half expected, our paychecks didn't. The Corrections budget had run dry just like the coffers of the other departments. In reaction, the sentiment from the previous day took over. A movement swept the ranks to go on strike.

I found myself in an awkward position. I didn't want a strike over payless paydays. Most of the other state employees had already gone without pay for two weeks, yet had not gone out on strike.

The money was as safe as if it had been banked. I expected the budget issue to be resolved soon. I did not want to risk blowing our union credibility over such a petty issue when I had spent so much effort posturing us for a push on safety. An aborted strike over delayed paychecks could set us back months.

The guys would not listen. Their recent successful job actions had given them a false sense of power. A large majority began to say, "No pay, no work."

I met with all three shifts, trying to reason with them. "We haven't gotten our paychecks this week and I'm not sure when they'll come, but I feel confident it will be soon."

Skepticism gripped them. They did not trust politicians or management. "How soon?"

I didn't try to deceive them. "I don't know exactly when. I'd like to tell you Monday. I'd like to tell you a week from now. But in all honesty I can't. All I know is that they're trying to resolve the issue. In the meantime we're forming a strategy among locals throughout the state so we can flex our muscles together."

It seemed as if they hadn't heard me. "Hey, if we don't get paid we're not working."

"Fellas, Walpole can't stand alone. No other local feels this way. We've got to remain part of the statewide team to have any impact."

They refused to budge. To a man the 3–11 shift refused to work. I wouldn't allow one shift to put us on strike. A majority of all the officers would have to vote for the action before we'd implement it.

Although the other shifts had dissenters, the majority appeared to favor a walkout. I had no choice; I had to call for a vote. It was held the next day and I couldn't believe the result. My advice and entreaties had counted for little; seventy per cent voted to strike.

"What do I do now?" I asked myself. I had always promised we'd live by the majority opinion. Yet if we struck so soon we'd be out on the streets alone. Our credibility would go up in smoke, along with the scant progress we'd made on safety. How could we possibly win?

With great misgivings I swallowed my disappointment and helped organize the picketing schedule. At midnight, the officers turned in their keys and walked out of the prison. I handed out signs voicing our protest over payless paydays and we set up picket lines on the far edge of the parking lot where the highway feeds the prison driveway.

As could be expected, our action infuriated the Department of Corrections. When I checked in with Council 93 the next morning Spataro told me, "The DOC tried going to court to get an injunction against you, but the judge told them you're within your rights. They can't expect you to work if they don't pay you."

"Well, that's something positive," I sighed. "Do we have any union support in this?"

"A couple of small locals have gone out."

Meager support. But, the court's decision bolstered my morale, as did the presence of the press. We received wide coverage because it appeared that the three hundred Walpole employees were carrying the fight all by themselves for the entire 48,000 member AFSCME.

In the interviews I not only blistered Dukakis for his stubborn position on the budget, but I took the opportunity to blast him in general for his stance on corrections and law and order.

"First Dukakis appointed men to prison management who don't care about the safety of the public. They care even less for the safety of the state employees who operate the prisons in conformance with the justice system.

"Even when it became clear that his appointees wouldn't protect the public, Dukakis still supported them. These are the men who allow violence to run rampant in the prisons.

"I blame Dukakis, the man ultimately responsible for corrections, for the continuing tragic saga of inmate deaths and officer injuries. Our governor has a lot of blood on his hands.

"Now he expects us to continue putting our lives on the line in the dangerous environment he created without even paying us. I can't believe this man's arrogance and insensitivity."

The press gobbled this up and further bolstered our image with the public. Meanwhile talk at the State House continued without apparent result.

Initially my guys stood firm on their picket lines, but as the days passed they began getting testy. In particular, they resented the State Police crossing our lines to provide security for the prison. The Troopers had been hit harder by this budget crisis than anyone. How could they dare cross the picket lines of one of the few groups standing up for the rights of everyone?

Galling us even further, we knew the Troopers would remain on the perimeter of the prison and man the towers only. The press, of course, would praise them for courageously keeping order, but we knew the State Police, if at all possible, would avoid going near the inmates.

While the strike continued, Walpole's management tried to intimidate us. They sent out people to take photographs of the picketers and to list names. We could only assume that those identified would be added to the list targeted for management harassment.

A few days of this and our initial bravado wore off. My guys began to reevaluate whether it was worth inciting management against them and sacrificing pay in the process. What could they, a small local, do to change Dukakis's mind?

On the fourth morning of the strike members of the day shift approached me as I arrived at the picket line. One said, "This is ridiculous. We're going to get paid in a few days. They owe us the money."

Another broke in, "We're going back to work. Standing out here is getting us nowhere."

A third said, "Maybe the 3–11 shift wants to continue this crap, but we don't."

Their words angered me. I had made these very same arguments the day before they'd voted to strike. They'd ignored them. Now they were going to crumble as a group directly in front of management? Hall, Butterworth, and Cobb would never take another of our job actions seriously.

"No," I told them. "No one's going back to work unless the majority votes to do so. The 3–11 shift by itself didn't put us on strike.

Seventy per cent of you guys voted to do so. I'm willing to call a vote this afternoon, but no one goes back to work before then."

I set the time for 3 p.m. at the entrance to the prison parking lot. In the intervening hours I sat by myself fretting over how I could salvage some credibility. I had put a lot of effort into the strike, an action I didn't agree with. Now they were trying to force me into a flip-flop. How could my guys do this to me?

The meeting was well attended. Two hundred and fifty guards showed up, causing a minor traffic jam in the driveway and filling the area with cars. All recognized the convertible I had recently bought and gathered round.

As the guards continued to arrive, the front door of the Administration building opened and out stepped Andrew Larker, Tom McCoy, and Stanley Tinker. Apparently some rat in our ranks had informed them of this break in our unity, and they wanted to enjoy our dissension first hand. They strolled down the steps and across the parking lot, taking up a position just beyond the swelling crowd of officers. All three smiled broadly, sensing they had won a great victory.

As for me, my morale dipped even further when I noticed that nearly every officer had come dressed in uniform ready to work. Still, I had prepared myself to speak and the sight of Larker's gloating face rallied me to one last effort.

Since I had no lectern, I stood up on the front seat of my car. Media cameras started rolling. Management's ears perked up. I had no planned speech. I just decided to speak from the heart. "Fellas, I can see that most of us are here. We even have our friends in management over there listening. I understand there's been a lot of grumbling the last day or so. Apparently some of you no longer want to be out here. You'd rather be inside working, earning money, even if you can't collect it for a few days."

I shook my head from side to side. "Just a few days ago I came before all of you and told you we'd be getting paid soon enough. I advised you to let the Council handle this matter. The budget would soon be signed. The money we'd earned was as good as in the bank. We had only missed one paycheck. Other locals who had missed three were continuing to work. No one else would support us if we went on strike.

"Yet, by a seven to three margin you voted to put us out here. You put me, your president, on strike and in a spot where he had to defend a position he didn't agree with.

"What else could I do but go to bat for you? I tried to come up with all the reasons I could to claim it made sense. I defended us to the press, and in the process I attacked Dukakis and called our management names. I put our credibility as a local on the line in front of everyone because you voted to put us on the street.

"You didn't listen to me when I advised against striking, now you're telling me we should call this off without anything being resolved."

I pointed at Larker and his group. "Look at those people over there. They're taking our pictures; they're trying to intimidate us; they've been getting us hurt inside. Now they're eating this up. You guys are embarrassing me, and I don't appreciate it.

"As far as I'm concerned you put us out here until we get paid. You can go back to work if you want, but I'm not going to make myself look like an ass. I won't go to work until I get my check.

"Now I'm calling for a vote. Those of you who want to stay out here with me, raise your hands."

With the cameras running; with the management people eagerly watching in anticipation of my humiliation; all 250 guards raised their hands. I did not see a single dissenter.

"All right!" I shouted, "then let's cut the nonsense and set up the damn picket lines!"

As the guys picked up their signs and reassumed their positions in line, I saw Larker and his people shaking their heads in disbelief. How had I managed it? How could I, in a two-minute speech, rebuild a united front from such a demoralized group? I have no answer. You'd have to ask my guys.

After everyone had dispersed, the press interviewed me. This time even national television participated.

I was asked: "How do you feel about the Governor's promise that you'll receive your checks this coming Monday?"

I replied, "He said we'd receive our checks last week and we didn't. Why should I believe him this time?"

They prodded further. "Are you then saying the Governor's word is no good?"

"As far as I'm concerned, the Governor's word has proven itself to be no good in the past. I'll believe it this time when I receive my check." With that I walked away.

On the following Monday Dukakis's promise was kept. We got paid so we all went back to work. Although I had not wanted to strike, an odd turn of events had again worked to our advantage. I sensed we had become more unified than ever.

The next night I held a union meeting and in the process of recapping what had happened, brought up an issue that had been gnawing at me for several months. I'd had enough of the State Police interfering in our job actions by crossing picket lines. They too belonged to a union, one with similar interests to our own. Yet they acted in a gutless way by refusing to respect our strikes.

I therefore addressed my guys, "Fellas, I'm a little tired of the State Police. Think back to the Framingham hostage situation when we put our necks on the line and they got all the credit. Every time we initiate a job action they cross our lines and act like they're patrolling the prison when we know they never go inside. They act like bigshots and the press praises them.

"We've just finished striking over payless paydays, trying to get checks for them as well as for ourselves. Yet they had the balls to cross our lines again. They didn't even send any of their guys to march on the State House. They sent their wives instead. These guys are nothing better than a bunch of scabs, and I want permission to send them a letter telling them so."

Everyone yelled their support. "Yeah, write the letter. Let's send one."

Having foreseen their approval I had already sketched out a draft. I held it up.

"I've already written one," I said. "It reads as follows:"

"Once again the State Police have stabbed their brothers, the Walpole guards, in the back. While we of Local 451 risked our jobs walking a picket line in defense of the rights of all state employees, the troopers hid in the background, then treacherously crossed our lines to aid the persons depriving us all of our paychecks. Even when we marched on the State House they didn't have the guts to make an appearance even though they were suffering more from the budget crisis than anyone. They sent their wives and babies instead.

"The Troopers have shown disloyalty to union ideals too often. They allow others to do the real fighting while they skulk in the shadows looking for opportunities to take the credit.

"Their actions this past week reveal them to be gutless scabs willing to hide behind their wives' skirts when there's fighting to be done. We suggest they take a course in labor relations from their wives since the ladies seem to know more about proper union behavior than their husbands."

After reading the letter, I glanced up into eager faces. More cheers. "Yeah, yeah, we approve that! Send it!"

So I did.

A few days later we received an angry, threatening reply by phone, not by letter. The State Police wouldn't go on record with what they had to say.

"We'll stop you wise guys every time you get on the street. You won't be able to get to the corner drugstore without one of us pulling you over. Better plan on getting home late from now on because we're on your case. And plan on starting out for work early too. You think you got problems now, just wait. You haven't seen trouble yet."

Unfortunately, I didn't take the call. The guard who did lost no time spreading the word.

My guys suddenly didn't think my letter was such a good idea after all. Sensing the prevailing mood, the Executive Board met in an emergency session without me.

When I cornered Mel Varney later, he told me, "Mike, I didn't like the idea of sanctioning you."

"I heard the vote was unanimous."

"I had to go along. We couldn't see any other way to get the troopers off our asses. It looked like we'd be spending the rest of our lives parked beside the road trying to square things with pissed-off state cops."

"So you threw me to the wolves instead."

"Mike, there's no way we could get you off the hook—you signed the damn letter. This way, at least we've saved the rest of the guys a lot of hassle."

"I resent your sanctioning me a hell of a lot. But what really burns my buns is that you sent a written apology without my authorization or knowledge. Besides being a stab in the back, it tells the State Police that we have a serious split in our union."

"There's no split—except over that letter. The guys are behind you 100 percent."

"Yeah, sure they are."

"Mike, I'm sorry as hell." Mel did a little embarrassed shuffle. "What else can I say? It's done."

The State Police were delighted to get the letter. It let them off the hook too. To make good on their threat they would have had to harass the three hundred men in our entire local. They didn't have the manpower to do it without neglecting their other duties and attracting public censure. Now they could concentrate on just one guy—me. They could handle that easy.

From then on State Troopers stopped me constantly. I counted over fifty times during the next few weeks. They only found three violations they could cite me for, but the pressure was relentless.

Whether I was on my way to the prison or going shopping with Karen in the car, inevitably a trooper would loom up behind, lights flashing, and pull me over. Most were polite about it so I didn't get too angry. I knew they were operating under orders.

After performing a routine check on license and registration, they would engage me in light conversation, often on innocuous subjects like weather and sports. Sometimes it would drift to union business. I even had Troopers apologize and express regret that their union didn't have the guts ours did.

Usually they'd just delay me for half an hour or so. But for the times they caught me speeding or making an illegal lane change, I paid a stiff price. Speeding is costly in Massachusetts. It took me five years to finish paying the surcharges on those tickets.

I subsequently learned that my picture and license number were displayed on the dashboard of every patrol car in the state. A few years later, Karen met a Trooper on a camping trip. Upon identifying herself she received the response, "Mike McLaughlin's wife? You mean license number _________ ?" He rattled off my license number from memory. My letter had certainly made a lasting impression on the Troopers. Okay, so it wasn't the smartest thing I ever did.

A month after I'd sent it I attended a political rally for aspiring Governor Ed King. There I ran into a high official of the State Police Union. During the meeting I noticed him staring daggers at me, but I still decided to try to patch things up. At the first opportunity I approached him and formally introduced myself.

"Yeah, I know who you are," he replied. "I know you're a fuckin' asshole. To send a letter like you did, you must be crazy. Don't you have any brains at all? Calling my guys scabs. You know, we're fighting for our contract too."

I tried to get a word in but couldn't make myself heard. He continued calling me names and making aggressive gestures.

Finally I said, "Look, all I was doing was getting you mad so you'd fight for the kind of contract you deserve. If you guys get a raise, we get a raise. Why can't we work together? Why can't we have one union? Why must we stay separated? The State has us both where it wants us. But it needs us both. Let's recognize that and work together."

He wouldn't listen. "You think you guys are so tough. I should send a goon out to teach you a lesson."

I don't like being threatened. I was experiencing enough of that crap on a daily basis.

"Is that supposed to scare me?" I responded. "Screw your goon. Send him. Send five. I don't care. That doesn't change matters. You're still scabs and a bunch of sissies."

His jaw twitched and his face turned an even deeper shade of red. "You know, I oughta have you fuckin' killed."

"Go ahead. Try it. I've heard that shit before. I'm still here. You don't have anybody with the guts to do it. That's why every year you guys try to get a law passed to carry guns in the prison. We don't need to carry guns inside the prison. You show me how tough you are right there."

He snarled, "Keep your eyes open for our goon."

I retorted, "Send your goon any time. I'll have our goon meet your goon, how's that? You think your goon is tougher than our goon? We're supposed to be adults. Do you realize we're talking like kids?"

Finally I walked away, shaking my head. I'd been talking to a top official in state law enforcement and he'd threatened my life like a Max-inmate at Walpole would. Now he played a major role in trying to elect a new Governor. What a sad statement about politics.

I did take his threat seriously and, fortunately, never met his goon. But as the Troopers continued to stop me I kept a close eye out for anything unusual.

On one occasion the Trooper who pulled me over looked meaner than most. On reaching my window he spotted my Walther resting on the seat beside me.

"What's that for?" he snapped.

I calmly replied, "No particular reason, but I'll blow your fuckin' head off if you reach into my car."

With that he became more cordial. "Mike, just let me see your license and registration, please."

I obliged pleasantly. After all, we were both State officers, weren't we?

10 "Shoot 'Im, Steve"

Even though the payless paydays walkout had nothing to do with everyday prison matters, it further increased tension between officers and inmates. The inmates had now been locked up for extended periods on three separate occasions within three months. They saw this as an outrageous invasion of their world and as graphic proof that we were winning our fight to exert influence over prison operations.

Angry and eager to thwart us, they initiated open warfare. Within a three week period they inflicted thirty officer injuries. Even though the majority of these required hospitalization, management showed us little sympathy. On the contrary, some of the injured officers had to fight disciplinary action, then face inmate lawsuits.

The violence exploded suddenly. Max-blocks Two and Four had been set aside to house Walpole's most rebellious inmates next to those in Block Ten. Over time a process of natural selection brought forth leaders and aligned the rest behind them in powerful cliques. We had been watching the gang in Block Two for some time with an eye toward breaking it up. But as yet we had received no support from management.

Regulations prohibited moving inmates to different permanent living quarters purely at an officer's discretion. To initiate such a move a supervisor had to receive permission from the Superintendent, pending a decision by the Disciplinary Board. In an emergency a supervisor could move an inmate, but he would later need a damn good explanation.

On the night of August sixth, Officer John Scandia sat at his desk in Block Two watching the inmates grudgingly enter their cells for the overnight lockup. After they'd all disappeared inside a succession of loud clicks told him that the officer in the gallery had locked all the cell doors. Only then did he rise from his desk and began making his ten o'clock count.

He didn't anticipate trouble. It had been a quiet evening considering the mayhem that so often took place in Block Two. Even Connie Mancuso, *The Man* in the Max-section, hadn't appeared outside his cell since dinner. Scandia wondered how he should take that. Often when the kingpins laid low, trouble was on the way.

No one ever liked walking the tiers to make counts, but the presence of the gallery officer above gave Scandia a little extra feeling of security as he headed for the stairwell. He quickly mounted the twisting staircase so that he would be hidden from view for as short a time as possible. Finally he emerged on the third tier and started down.

Immediately as he passed the first cell the inmate inside called out, "Six-Five!" This expression, peculiar to Walpole, told the other inmates that an officer was on the tiers.

A moment later Scandia heard the unmistakable voice of Tommy Swoboda call out, "Get ready! One, two, three!"

"Fuck you, Sir!" All the inmates chorused in unison.

This was a little game Swoboda had organized for B-2. Every officer who worked that block had heard it every day for weeks. They all thought it funny, as Scandia did now.

Swoboda, only twenty-four years old, was a despicable character bent on resisting all authority. He'd already spent several years behind bars and now served as Mancuso's ramrod in B-2.

Bulked up by weightlifting, even at 5′9″ Swoboda posed a serious physical threat whether armed or not. He tried to impress everyone that he was dangerous by dressing carelessly, remaining unshaven, and addressing everyone in language oozing with profanity. Walpole housed many like him, but years in prison usually wore them down.

Swoboda was young. He showed no inclination to conform to rules or modify his behavior. Rather, he seemed to have aspirations to eventually carve out his own prison kingdom.

Scandia continued along, counting until he reached the fifth cell. Then suddenly the smile on his face vanished and twisted into a mask of pain as a large container of boiling water was hurled into his face. Almost simultaneously another large quantity struck him from behind.

Through blurred vision he could barely make out the two arms that had reached out of separate cells to carry out the attack. He backed away and stumbled back down the tier toward the stairwell.

The gallery officer had seen the attack and called control. He had identified the attackers so Lahoud dispatched a small team of officers to subdue and remove them to Block Ten. As they rushed down the corridor they passed the stricken Scandia being assisted toward the hospital.

By the time the team reached Block Two, pandemonium had broken out. The inmates were shouting to each other and pouring large quantities of water out on the walkways to make them slippery. Upon seeing the officers they shouted, "You're not taking them! To take them you'll have to take us all!"

Bracing themselves, the officers started in. In response, dozens of arms reached out through the bars unleashing a barrage of wet wadded toilet paper, canned goods, and boiling water. Twice the officers started forward, only to be forced back, arms covering head and face. Finally amidst hoots of derision, they retreated back into the corridor and called for help.

The inmates left us no choice. The only way to restore order was to enter the block in force and remove all the troublemakers. Had we chosen to back off, the overnight shift would have faced the same ugly situation with only half the officers. Even worse, we would have encouraged similar inmate rebellions in the future.

Roger Lahoud gathered some forty of us outside Block Two to carry out the transfer. As we shared glances of resignation, I sensed some tension but no unusual anxiety. Most of us had experienced situations like these in Walpole many times before. With the inmates locked in their cells, it certainly didn't qualify as a riot. We just saw it as another tough, dirty job—one that we had been trained to perform.

Lahoud pressed his way through the group and took charge in his usual professional manner. As he stood in the doorway, peering inside, the yelling increased.

"Motherfuckers, you're not taking them!"

"Come and get us, screws!"

Suddenly we heard Swoboda's voice above the rest, shouting an order.

"All right, guys, arm yourselves!"

Apparently he had been appointed to lead this exercise and intended making a positive impression on his boss. Suddenly the air was rent by a series of sharp reports that sounded like small bombs. We all shook our heads, knowing that several inmates had broken their sinks and toilets and had armed themselves with sharp-edged pieces of porcelain.

Lahoud turned back to us and shrugged. In his usual, matter-of-fact tone he stated, "Well, fellas, I guess it's time to suit up."

We now faced moving even more inmates because we couldn't allow them to remain in their cells without toilet facilities. The task promised to be long and arduous as well as dangerous, for only one inmate at a time could be moved through the corridor.

Helmets, batons, and a shotgun were brought from the armory. We did not bring in gas because it had fallen out of favor with management. They felt that officers tended to view the use of gas too lightly and would fire it at inmates when lesser means might suffice. I saw their point, but also felt it would be better to overreact and gas a few extra inmates than to underreact and have officers injured—or killed.

As the helmets and batons were passed out, Lahoud gave us our assignments. He assigned the shotgun to Steve Adair, union secretary and member of my E-Board. The rest of us would work as teams at various cells. Those not actually removing an inmate would make sure the other inmates did not strike out.

Finally ready, Lahoud calmly told us, "Go and do your jobs."

Most of us would have walked through hell for Roger, so we immediately pushed forward and surged through the door. At the sight of the officers entering, Swoboda called out, "Ready on first tier! Ready on second! Ready on third! Now!"

Yells and screams again filled the air and arms reached out through the bars to cast a shower of porcelain fragments at us. With forty of us bunched together we found it difficult to dodge the projectiles. They shattered off the concrete floor and walls and turned into shrapnel-like pieces.

Finally we gained the shelter of the tier overhangs and the stairwell. From there we cautiously worked our way down the rows of cells, identifying who had broken their fixtures and posting officers outside to keep them under control until they could be moved.

All resisted, but to varying degrees. Their favorite weapon was boiling water. Each had pegged his cell.

In one case three officers were scalded trying to force the peg free with a crowbar. When they finally broke in, the inmate began hurling punches. The narrow configuration of his cell aided him. Bunk, tables, and fixtures forced officers to approach him single file.

The lead officer ducked his head trying to use his helmet to protect himself from the blows. He then was assaulted with wild kicks, many of which struck home. At the same time he swung his baton, trying to hit a vulnerable spot.

Blows at the head were useless. The inmate protected himself against these by holding his arms high. So the officer struck at the knees in what we called the Lemay method.

The officers behind tried to help by reaching over their brother, but they couldn't do much until the weight of their combined charge drove the inmate against the back wall. Then they just piled on, ending the struggle.

Once they had him handcuffed they wrestled him, yelling, cursing, and kicking, out of his cell across the slippery tier down the stairwell and out into the corridor. On the way he shouted back to his friends, "They can't hold me there for long! I'll see you guys soon!"

Once out of the Max-section and moving through the central segment of the corridor, he suddenly quieted down. He told the officers who'd been dragging him, "All right, let me up. I'll go peaceably." After gaining his feet he walked calmly all the way down to where the Minimum Section began. Then suddenly he laid down again and began kicking and yelling. He forced the officers to drag him those final feet past the Minimum cellblocks into Block Ten.

All this outrageous behavior had of course been staged for the benefit of the other inmates. Why get yourself roughed up when your peers couldn't see it happening? It wouldn't enhance your tough guy image.

Most of the others followed his example. A few, however, did force the officers to drag or carry them struggling all the way. These were the hard core—men controlled by anger and hatred beyond all reason.

Because we had identified Swoboda as the ringleader, we left him for last. When a team of us finally moved into position to take him, we found him barricaded in his cell like the others, but crouched in a corner. He held two ugly shanks, one in each hand, both pointed in our direction. He kept yelling, "Come on, you motherfuckers! I've got somethin' for ya!"

Up until this point the shotgun had played a minor role in removing other inmates. Steve Adair had always proven himself to be a steady hand who appreciated the responsibility that the shotgun represented. He had stood by to provide support while the other inmates were removed, but had kept the shotgun pointed at the ceiling all that time.

In situations such as this the shotgun was loaded with modi-pak, a special non-lethal shell that contained hollow plastic BB's. I'd seen them fired at point blank range into a cardboard box and barely leave marks. They would, however, sting badly enough to incapacitate someone struck by a full charge.

Any officer handling a shotgun in Walpole had to be very careful. Pointing it at an inmate, no matter what its load, could have serious consequences. Inmates would almost always later sue both the prison and the individual officer for inflicting mental cruelty—the anxiety of facing a loaded shotgun. Administration feared these claims of brutality and therefore placed tight restrictions on the use of shotguns in the prison.

I'm sure Adair had all this in mind as he took up position outside Swoboda's cell. At the sight of the nine inch long shanks he jumped and abruptly trained the muzzle of the shotgun through the bars. Initially, I'm sure he reacted instinctively to protect the team of officers who were about to force the door.

Even looking down the gaping hole in the shotgun barrel did not discourage Swoboda's tongue.

"Think I'm afraid of that fuckin' cannon? You ain't got the guts to pull the trigger, you chickenshit bastard!"

I stood beside Steve. Just to his left, officers strained with a crowbar to try to break loose the peg Swoboda had installed. Inside he remained in his corner, snarling, "Come on, you motherfuckers! I'll kill myself a screw!"

Beside me, Adair looked concerned but cool. "All right, Tommy," he ordered, "drop the shanks."

"You want 'em, come and get 'em! Go ahead! Cut the fuckin' bars! I'm here waitin' for ya!"

Adair tried coaxing. "Tommy, drop the shanks. Don't make me shoot."

Swoboda raised his voice as if crying out to the entire cellblock, "A screw's dyin' tonight!"

Drops of sweat now dripped down Adair's face. He began pleading, "Drop the shanks, Tommy! Drop the fuckin' shanks!"

I kept one eye on the exchange and one on the officers trying to force the door. Swoboda had done an effective job of pegging it so the task was taking longer than usual.

The situation looked deadly. Swoboda was 165 pounds of solid muscle poised to strike. He had honed his shanks needle sharp. The officers going in after him carried nothing but a baton. They wore no bodily protection. The first officer to reach Swoboda would find himself at a serious disadvantage. A stabbing looked imminent.

For a second I felt grateful that I had been left off that assault team. Then I noticed that the first man in would be Eddie Woodson, an officer even slighter in stature than myself. I felt sick, knowing he would have little chance against Swoboda's shanks.

All the while Adair and Swoboda had continued shouting at each other.

"I'll shoot, Tommy!"

"Go ahead, motherfucker, go ahead!"

I looked once more at Swoboda and Woodson. Then seeing that the officers had nearly forced the door open, I shouted at Adair.

"Steve, shoot 'im!"

Adair swallowed hard but still refrained from pulling the trigger. "I'll shoot, Tommy, I'll shoot!" he cried.

Swoboda continued frothing and gesturing threateningly with the shanks.

"Shoot 'im Steve!" I urged again.

But Adair could not overcome his adversity to discharging a weapon against a fellow human being. He was still pleading with Swoboda when the door opened and the officers led by Woodson rushed forward in single file. The weight of bodies drove Woodson into Swoboda.

Swoboda's arms flailed. I heard grunts of agony as his shanks tore into flesh. Batons swung and the bodies piled on. Swoboda emitted a few howls of pain but otherwise continued cursing throughout the struggle. True to form he made the officers drag him kicking and spitting all the way to Block Ten.

When the bodies finally untangled, we found an ashen-faced Woodson sprawled on the floor. We counted nine holes in him. Somehow Swoboda had missed a vital spot. With some help, Woodson struggled to his feet and shuffled down to the medics. Needless to say he'd been lucky. Any one of his wounds, had they been inflicted an inch or so to either side, could have killed him.

Besides Woodson, the casualty report read nine officers, including Steve Adair, scalded seriously and sent to an outside hospital. Four men with injured backs from the scuffling went also.

Inmates claimed injury as well, some saying they were beaten into unconsciousness; but none of them had suffered so seriously that they could not fight the officers all the way to Block Ten. Swoboda claimed leg injuries from the batons; they certainly hadn't kept him from kicking at the officers as they moved him down the corridor.

The next day Fred Butterworth held a meeting to determine the details of the skirmish. Already inmates were crying lawsuit over guard brutality. The most serious charges were directed against Steve Adair for having pointed the shotgun at Swoboda. Butterworth indicated that criminal charges might be forthcoming.

"Fred, Adair showed great restraint by not shooting Swoboda," I said. "It could have cost Woodson his life. If I had been holding the shotgun I would've shot Swoboda to protect Woodson."

Fred looked at me through narrowed eyes. "If you had fired, I'd have seen to it you were doing time right now."

"What? Fred, are you serious?"

"As far as I'm concerned, shooting an inmate under those conditions would qualify as cruel and unusual punishment."

"But Swoboda was trying to kill Woodson."

"By barging in with shotgun and helmets you incited those inmates. True, they overreacted, but it's your job to recognize the mental state they're in. You go charging in threatening them and they're going to defend themselves. As professionals, you could have found another way to restore order. Shotguns are an absolute last resort."

Furious, I place my hands on hips and turned a full 360 degrees on the spot, before responding. "That does it. On behalf of the union I demand a clear policy from you on the use of weapons in the prison."

"We've always had a policy."

"Yes, it allows us to bring in shotguns during an emergency. It doesn't tell us under what circumstance we can discharge them. We always assumed we could shoot to protect someone's life. Now, from what you're saying, I don't have any idea what we can and can't do. Fred, I want a clear written policy as to under what conditions we can discharge firearms."

"Don't try to bully me. The present directive is all you need."

Silence closed in for several long seconds as we locked stares.

Then I said, "What about Swoboda? You're thinking about punishing Adair. Are you going to file charges against Swoboda?"

"I don't believe I have grounds. I think he could prove the officers instigated the riot."

"What about the two shanks? They aren't kitchen tools he uses to break up icecubes at his cocktail parties. They're meant to kill. His having them shows a propensity to commit murder. He almost succeeded last night."

"With all the violence in this institution, I think he could convince a court that he intended using them for self defense."

"But they're against prison regulations."

"True, but that alone doesn't make him a killer."

"Fred, why was he brought to Walpole?"

"That has nothing to do with last night. Look, I'm not going to waste my time filing charges against Swoboda. Woodson's wounds have turned out to be superficial anyway."

"Yeah, but now he faces days of convalescence. And what about his IA money? Will you help him get it?"

"He'll go through the same process as everyone else."

"That's what I figured."

"Look, I'm happy no one got seriously hurt, but as far as I'm concerned you guys brought this on yourselves."

The meeting ended.

Considering past history, more likely than not Fred was right about not bothering to file charges against Swoboda. Inmate lawyers always seemed to have ways of presenting cases that would confound both prosecutors and judges.

Bob Furtado once tried to pursue assault charges against an inmate who had struck him with porcelain during a similar riot. In that situation he had seen which inmate had reached out through the bars and thrown the chunk of porcelain down at him. It glanced off the wall and struck Bob's leg, opening a cut that required seventeen stitches to close.

When the case reached court, the guilty inmate presented an unusual defense. He brought three inmates with him as witnesses. No, they didn't all try to deny that the accused had thrown porcelain. Instead, all four of them claimed to have done so. They all seemed to want credit for the felonious assault. In the end, since the prosecutor had nothing more than Bob's word as evidence, the judge threw the case as charged out of court.

Eventually all of us involved in the Block Two riot were served with brutality lawsuits by inmates. More than one inmate accused me of having stepped on his face. These were outright lies. Throughout the fracas I had remained an observer and never touched an inmate. But they needed someone to sue and my name was well known.

From the opposite point of view, the injured officers could not file lawsuits against the inmates because of a regulation in the Department which classified such "injuries" as part of the job. This prohibited us from dealing with inmate violence on a personal level.

After the riot I encouraged the guys to challenge this regulation by filing suits against inmates with the District Attorney. I know Delahunt received several, but to my knowledge none of them were ever pursued.

When Butterworth refused to give us satisfaction concerning a clear policy on the use of firearms, I issued a union directive to all members. It read:

"Under no circumstances will Walpole guards involve themselves in any movement of inmates from one section of the prison to another that could result in the need to bring in shotguns. If such a move becomes necessary the Department should bring in the State Police."

Copies went to both Hall and Butterworth. Within a matter of minutes after Fred received his, I received a call from the Commissioner's office in Boston.

Hall's secretary said, "The Commissioner is disturbed by this directive you've just sent out concerning moving inmates. He wants to see you and your E-Board in his office this afternoon."

"We'll be there," I replied.

This time we didn't need the OER to referee. But the meeting did draw a special guest, State Senator Jack Backman, Chairman of the Committee on Human Services. He had heard that the meeting would discuss the use of force in the prison system, a subject of great concern to him.

The meeting opened with my giving a complete report of the Block Two riot. When I'd finished, Butterworth brought up many of the same points he'd made with me in his office. Then Hall opened the floor to discussion.

"Gentlemen," I began, "Superintendent Butterworth distorts the picture when he makes it appear as if inmates are normally peaceful and only become violent when instigated. Most inmates act violently to impress their peers. It is part of the inmate social structure. They welcome confrontations with officers because it enhances their image.

"In the majority of cases, when we move an inmate we are placed in a potentially dangerous situation. They look upon the very act as a challenge.

"They see us as infringing upon their right to be where they wish. By forcing them to move we are demeaning them in the eyes of fellow inmates. Their only means of saving face is to strike out at us. We must use force in these cases both to protect ourselves and to maintain order in the prison.

"There are times when the resistance of an inmate or groups of inmates becomes so violent that the only way to subdue them is by threatening them with weapons. We don't do this often or take it lightly. But we need this alternative if we are to maintain control over the prison. And we need a specifically defined policy. Don't train us with firearms, tell us we can carry them, and then threaten to prosecute us if we discharge them in an emergency. Under these circumstances you cannot expect us to confront violent inmates. We refuse to put ourselves in that situation."

Hall pondered my words and then said, "I can see your point. It makes sense to have a specifically defined policy. At the same time, we can't be calling in the State Police every time we need to move an inmate. Officers must move inmates."

Senator Beckman jumped into the discussion. "Officer McLaughlin, I can't believe that inmates can't be moved without violence occurring. No matter what they've done, they're still human beings. I'm sure that if you look hard enough you'll find a way."

Hall concluded the meeting by promising to form another committee to investigate methods to move inmates. I did not back off from my directive.

I later learned that Senator Backman and I did agree on a few things. We both thought Fred Butterworth should be removed as Walpole Superintendent and we both considered Governor Dukakis ultimately responsible for the appalling conditions at the prison. Beyond that we seemed to be living on opposite sides of the planet.

While I abhorred the permissive treatment policy at the prison, Backman contended that the Walpole administration was not lenient enough. He charged that Butterworth authorized guards to brutalize inmates. He and his committee had been gathering evidence of this alleged brutality for several months and on August 24 he issued a document entitled "An Incomplete Chronology of the Walpole Horror Show in the Last Two Years."

A cover memo stated in part, "The constant threats and harassment by guards is present not only against prisoners, but against other guards, prison personnel, even against ordained religious clergy. In the meantime, traffic of contraband and violence continues at Walpole State Prison."

Much of the document was compiled from affidavits submitted by inmates describing alleged incidents of brutality by guards. Sprinkled throughout, in chronological order, were listings of the inmate murders. Although guards were not outwardly accused of the murders, in the context of the entire document, who else could be responsible? Names of surviving inmates were blacked out on the document, ostensibly to protect the "innocent" from further harassment. This kept the officers from identifying their accusers and other investigators from verifying the allegations.

Typical of the entries was the brief account describing the insurrection led by Swoboda. It read: "At approximately 9:30 p.m. correctional officers from the Maximum Security section of MCI Walpole entered Block 2, a medium security block. The officers allegedly entered the cells of ____, ____, ____, and ____, beat them (some to a state of unconsciousness), and brought them to Block Ten." The blanks represent the blacked-out names.

That was the entire description. No reference to the scaldings, the destruction of receptacles, the assaults with porcelain, or the stabbing of Woodson. It also incorrectly referred to Block Two as a Medium Security block. In reality, Block Two as well as Block Four housed the most incorrigible of the Max-section inmates.

One complaint in Backman's report that appears over and over is the use of blue rooms to punish inmates. Walpole did have two blue rooms, both located in Block Ten. These rooms were regular cells without bed, toilet, sink, chair, or desk. Each had a hole in the floor into which the occupant could urinate and defecate. They also had a solid steel door in addition to the normal grill door. Basically cold and featureless, they seemed like throwbacks to the Dark Ages.

Originally these cells had been designed to house individuals who posed serious threats to themselves as well as to others. But since 1972 they had been declared illegal for their original purpose. Now, on occasion, they were used as temporary holding cells for inmates showing mental instability and in the process of being transferred out of Block Ten to the Bridgewater mental facility.

I would never try to defend the use of blue rooms. Still, I believe the many claims by inmates that they'd been locked up in blue rooms deserve clarification. One did not come in contact with a blue room unless he reached Block Ten. One did not reach Block Ten unless he'd shown himself to be extremely dangerous to other inmates and officers.

Block Ten always remained filled to capacity, but we still had to periodically move more inmates there. When men act violently crazy you must restrain them somewhere. If the blue rooms were the only cells vacant, they would be used, but only for a short period.

I would have preferred to see the rooms renovated into the same configuration as the other Block Ten cells. But that decision had to come from the Commissioner. We officers worked with what we had.

The tenseness in the prison again exploded into violence a week after the Block Two riot. On Monday, two officers standing by a cell in Block Ten were stabbed through the bars by the inmate they were feeding. The weapon was a sharpened channel selector rod which the attacker had removed from his television set. The shank had penetrated the officers' rubber raincoats and inflicted serious punctures to the chest. Both officers survived.

On Tuesday an officer was escorting an inmate through the Max corridor to a counseling session when suddenly they exchanged words. In a flash, the powerfully built inmate turned and felled the officer with a punch to the jaw. Senior Officer Wayne Northrup was standing nearby and rushed to aid his fellow. In trying to grab the inmate he sustained several blows to the ribs. When order was restored, both officers had to be driven to Norwood hospital for treatment.

Immediately after this I went down to Butterworth's office and demanded a major shakedown of all cellblocks to sweep them clean of weapons and contraband.

"I don't see any reason to disrupt the entire facility over two isolated incidents," he replied. "We'll never get all the weapons. The attacks are regrettable but they're going to happen. This is a prison."

The following day, Thursday, Block Ten blew up again. Four officers, two each escorting an inmate down the corridor toward the exercise cages, were suddenly turned upon. Three suffered stab wounds before the inmates could be subdued. More officers ran to aid their fellows only to be struck with boiling water hurled from the nearby cells.

It took the entire Block Ten complement to put down the disturbance. When the smoke cleared, the hospital list read: three officers stabbed, three scalded, and one suffering from severely wrenched neck. Fortunately again, no deaths. But how much longer would our luck hold out?

I again stormed down to Butterworth's office and demanded a major shakedown. This time he gave his permission.

On Friday we closed the prison to visitors, locked the inmates in their cells, and set out to conduct a thorough shakedown the likes of which Walpole hadn't seen for three years. Enthusiastic officers went over each cell from top to bottom, tearing apart bedding, riffling through possessions, closely scrutinizing appliances, and poking through cell fixtures. In addition we thoroughly searched stairwells, utility closets, and any other potential hiding place. Upon finishing we had confiscated over 150 weapons.

The inmates stood by seething and barraging us with profanity, but they were helpless to interfere. Not only did they lose much of their arsenal, but they became subjects of dozens of D-reports as possessors of contraband.

Outraged, they managed to inflict five more serious guard injuries in the next few days even though they were temporarily weaponless. But at least we experienced no more stabbings.

By the end of that three-week period thirty guards had been injured by inmates. This amounted to over twelve per cent of our ranks. Army units in battle would consider that casuality rate high.

During this period I was interviewed by the press several times. I made clear the conditions we were facing. I blamed Commissioner Hall and the Department for not acting on the requests we'd made during a year's worth of safety meetings.

When the press went to Hall for his view, all he could say was, "It's been one of those months. Prison tension rises during the summer because of the heat. The overcrowding doesn't help matters either."

The violence finally subsided, but then another strike ensued. This time the inmates struck. Half of the prison population refused to go to work. They didn't report for work call but rather remained in their cellblocks.

In the process of locking them up for the day we asked their leaders what was behind this. They all mouthed the same line:

"The last month or so you guards have been harassing and brutalizing us. Prison conditions have gone to hell. This is the only way we have of voicing a protest."

Work in the shops slowed to a crawl. The Commonwealth faced a slowdown in the production of license plates, broomsticks, and manhole covers (not to mention shanks). The situation concerned Butterworth enough to meet with an elected inmate committee to discuss the inmate grievances. I was not invited, but I managed to get myself a copy of the meeting's minutes.

The committee immediately got off on the wrong foot with Fred by requesting media observers. It thereby revealed its true intention, to drum up public sympathy. Fred, of course, had faced enough bad press due to me. He said:

"I wouldn't be here if I didn't think we could square some things away. But no media. I could be on TV every day. I don't want to run you people down. There are a lot of good inmates and good officers."

Stymied, the inmates jumped to their first issue. "Now that we're talking, must the strikers be locked up? We promise no problems in the blocks."

Fred replied, "You know that it's policy for Minimum inmates. They don't work, they don't have freedom of the blocks. You don't think I'll have officers sweeping and cleaning when inmates are roaming free and not working."

(Bravo Fred!)

The inmates moved on. They wanted the D-reports written after the shakedown to be "knocked down." Larker agreed on a "moratorium."

They wanted better medical attention, including quicker treatment and specialists available on site. Butterworth explained that he had difficulty recruiting and retaining good doctors because they were often threatened.

They wanted a more "nutritious" diet, balking at the frequency of bologna, cheese, and jello. Butterworth agreed to look into hiring a nutritionist.

They wanted their visitors treated more politely. This provoked an interesting exchange between black inmate spokesman, Arnold Smith, and Butterworth.

Smith complained, "If inmates are being subjected to skin searches, why do visitors also have to be searched? People don't like that. Women have to remove panties, and are told to squat. This is wrong. There are metal detectors. A man is searched after a visit. You can guess, if he has drugs on him, where they came from."

Butterworth replied. "Let me run this down. Since last January we have picked up fifty people bringing drugs in. It's all been in bras and panties. People are doing it. The only time a skin search is done is when a Shift Commander, Associate Deputy, Deputy Superintendent, or Superintendent issues an order. If the individual refuses, they can't enter. Remember, a guy was killed last week over two Talwin."

Smith still was not convinced. "This is unnecessary harassment. They shake down elderly women. I hope my grandmother wouldn't bring me in drugs."

Andrew Larker responded, "We picked up an old woman with drugs from a pat shake."

(Bravo, Andrew!)

Finally the inmates got to an issue of real importance—a vending machine concession. They supposedly wanted the money to buy recreational equipment.

"No problem with lollipops," Fred said.

Smith asked, "What about cigarettes. We used to have a cigarette concession."

Another inmate asked, "What about a picture-taking concession?"

Suddenly the meeting sounded like a gathering of entrepreneurs. When Butterworth finally adjourned the meeting he agreed to meet with the committee again the next day. That second meeting lasted only thirty seconds. When Fred refused to allow them outside mediators, the inmates walked out.

While the strike had little impact within the prison, it did achieve its goal of focusing public attention on the inmate claims of guard brutality. Seemingly in response, Attorney General Bellotti and District Attorney Delahunt announced that they had employed a team of State Troopers to help them investigate alleged incidents of violence at Walpole.

This was to be the fifth investigation of guard brutality allegations within the past year. Previously the Civil Rights Office, the U.S. Attorney General's Office, the Department of Corrections Security Management Team, and the FBI had all conducted similar investigations. In all four instances we were cleared of all charges. Subsequently the findings became public knowledge by being published in the newspapers and announced on radio and television.

After all this scrutiny by experts, what did Bellotti and Delahunt possibly hope to find by sending in the State Troopers? While investigators were interviewing officers inside the prison, I conducted a news conference in the parking lot describing the entire exercise as a witch hunt.

Nevertheless, the investigation went ahead. Delahunt had found among us a guard willing to testify that he had personally witnessed inmates being beaten by officers in the Block Two riot. With this individual as his star witness, Delahunt brought twenty-three officers before a grand jury. He eventually had to drop his case. His witness had not even been in the prison during the altercation.

The grand jury cleared every single officer of all charges. Then it proceeded to hand down nine indictments against five inmates, including Swoboda. Unfortunately all were simply charged with assault and battery with a dangerous weapon.

In Swoboda's case this hardly seemed appropriate since that night he'd more than once voiced his intention to "kill a screw." But Delahunt's view of the riot prevailed. He told a Boston newspaper, "The gaurds sustained no serious injuries. One spent a few days in Norwood Hospital due to a puncture wound in the abdomen." I wondered what had happened to the other eight holes in Woodson.

The fact that Delahunt dropped his case didn't convince the inmates to drop their lawsuits against us. In my studies at Northeastern University I had read that inmates around the country had filed many lawsuits against guards.

The courts had begun recognizing inmates' rights under the Constitution's Fifth, Sixth, Seventh, and Fourteenth Amendments. Up until my presidency I don't believe any Walpole inmates won such a suit. Then early in 1978 a favorable decision was handed down on a six-year-old case concerning an inmate brutalized in Block Ten. This seemed to break the dam and we found ourselves frequently named in lawsuits.

My first personal experience occurred after our two work stoppages earlier that year. Ten inmates banded together and filed a one-million-dollar lawsuit against me, claiming that by organizing the strikes I had deprived them of their rights. By being locked up twenty-four hours a day during both strikes they had lost access to counseling, visits, recreation, and other regular programs.

I went to the union attorneys for help and they told me I could possibly lose the suit if the inmates could prove I planned, orchestrated and called the strikes all by myself. That I had called the strikes to protect the guards' rights would not be pertinent. That my action had not been directed against the inmates also had no bearing. The inmates simply had to prove I was the sole instigator.

Fortunately they couldn't.

During the months that followed, the Walpole guards experienced many other lawsuits, some even more outrageous. Inmates who acted violently—killing other inmates, attacking guards, or destroying state property—had to be moved to a secure area, usually Block Ten.

Seldom did they go peacefully. Usually we had to drag or carry them. Yet once you put your hand on an inmate, no matter how violent he might be, no matter if he'd stabbed or otherwise injured you, you ran the serious risk of being sued for brutality.

If a guard had attempted to break up a fight between two inmates and was stabbed several times in the process, those two inmates would almost certainly have tried to bring him into court. He could be in the hospital recovering from his wounds, yet still be sued.

Liberally inclined lawyers sympathetic to inmate causes, trying to make a big name for themselves or simply looking for work, stood ready to pounce on these cases.

We guards received no support from the Department of Correction, nor any from the Attorney General's office. The Attorney General was supposed to defend us against brutality lawsuits. Instead, he chose to make us find our own attorneys. Often we didn't have access to legal minds comparable to those representing the inmates so the Attorney General's policy put us in serious jeopardy.

If we were the monsters that the inmates claimed, and some government officials chose to believe, Steve Adair would certainly have shot Swoboda and perhaps several other rioters. All had utilized dangerous weapons to seriously injure us. Yet Adair still refused to fire his shotgun even though he had been scalded, even though one of his brother officers faced being stabbed. He displayed uncommon restraint, not an urge to indulge in brutality.

11 Tear the Place Down

The appalling chronicle of inmate violence at Walpole reached the public largely via my appearances on the media. These revelations put the Department of Correction and the politicians who supported its views on the spot. Until I came along, the public thought that Commissioner Hall had largely straightened out the prison system in Massachusetts.

The turmoil I kept revealing to the media demanded an explanation from officials. The issue polarized everyone interested in corrections into groups with dissenting views. The Department itself, along with Governor Dukakis's political supporters, formed one group. Inmates and politicians who advocated inmate causes constituted another. My union and budget-conscious politicians made up a third group.

Hall and Butterworth put forth an argument difficult to refute. Hall pointed to the fact that he had turned around all the other prisons in the system. They continued to run smoothly with a minimum of violence. His "steppingstone" program also seemed to be working. According to them, Walpole was just an aberration.

Hall and other experts claimed that the prison had been poorly designed, saying that its large size and poor configuration encouraged violence. Many politicians, especially those who supported Hall and Dukakis, agreed. In my opinion, they found blaming steel and concrete much less embarrassing than indicting themselves. They, therefore, issued a cry to tear the place down and build new and smaller facilities.

I took a completely opposite stance. I saw some design flaws, yes, but I felt certain that if the institution received proper management most violence would be eradicated. I did agree that Walpole posed an unusual problem. But that realization should have prodded Hall into initiating a specially designed program. He was trying to treat the Walpole heavyweights in the same manner he treated less hardened inmates in the rest of his system. It didn't work.

I made this point time and again and gained substantial support from the political community. Fiscally conscious politicians did not wish to burden the public with vast expenditures on prison construction unless absolutely necessary.

The second view came from figures like Senator Jack Backman. They felt that violence occurred as a backlash against the inmates' brutal treatment at the hands of the guards. They blamed management, yes, but not for mismanaging—rather for conspiring with the sadistic guards to make life miserable for the inmates.

Government officials often toured Walpole, sometimes by appointment, sometimes without notice. When a Department of Public Health official visited to investigate charges of major sanitation problems, I was in the party that escorted him around the facility. A stone-faced man carrying a notebook, he looked suspicious and had little to say other than to ask a few questions.

We didn't hide anything from him. His pen scribbled many notes, particularly as we walked the Max-section cellblocks. There he noted a profusion of paper plates, cups, and cigarette butts laying on the floor instead of being tossed into conveniently placed trash barrels. Turning over one plate with his foot, he watched an engorged cockroach race for cover.

"How often are these blocks swept?"

"Daily, but within a short time the floors again look like this."

His pen hastily scribbled and continued to do so when he spotted the broken light fixtures and painted light bulbs. He didn't bother asking about those. Instead his eyes were drawn to the gallery windows overhead. These were coated with film and sludge made up of various substances.

"Those are the windows of the gallery," we told him. "From up there we open and close Max-block celldoors and observe inmate activity."

"How can you observe anything with the windows in that condition?"

We glanced at each other. "It's not easy."

"Take me up there, please."

We led him up another stairway into the narrow attic corridors. When he looked down through the windows I thought I saw his stoic expresssion crack a little.

"What is all this on the glass?"

"Food, human waste, paint, all sorts of substances they purchase from the canteen. Didn't you see all the plastic containers and aerosol cans they had in their cells?"

More scribbling, then on we went.

He had less to write about in the Minimum Section and fewer questions. But then we took him into Block Ten. As usual the grapevine had worked well. The inmates knew that a tour was coming through so they were on their better behavior. They liked to impress government officials with their deportment while pointing out shortcomings of the facility.

Upon seeing the ankle-deep refuse in the corridors, the official's face sagged. He didn't have to kick through the debris to find roaches. They scurried everywhere.

Seeing his shock, the inmates played upon it.

"Hey," one asked. "When is somebody going to clean this place up? We'd do it, but they won't let us out."

The official cast us an inquiring glance without mouthing the question.

"That's not true," we told him. "None of them ever volunteers to clean this place up. Who do you think is responsible for all the littering? We'd be glad to let them do the job. We make mops, brooms, soaps, cleaners, and insect sprays available to any inmate who wishes to use them. Except in isolated cases, we get no takers. The job is left to the officers. We do it as often as time allows, but we're tired of cleaning up after these guys. What you see is just a few days' accumultion."

We went a little further and suddenly an inmate reached out through the bars. The official jumped back. The inmate was holding by the tail the carcass of a dead rat. As it dangled before us, he said: "You've got to do something. My cell is infested with these things."

"Believe it or not, sir," the Block Ten Supervisor explained, "he's been raising those things as pets. Every time we take one away from him he manages to catch another somewhere. If we searched his cell

I think we could find a cage with a wheel inside that he built for his rats to run on."

"Now you're not going to believe that screwy story, are you?" the inmate protested. "Who would raise a rat for a pet? I tell you, this place is infested."

Wide-eyed, the official stared from him to us but said nothing. He had little more to say on the rest of the tour.

Later this official spoke before a legislative committee. I sat in the back listening as he presented a grave, yet accurate, picture of the conditions at Walpole. He ended his testimony by saying: "Portions of the prison are unfit for human habitation. And yet while it is our view that the facility is badly designed, we do not think it beyond reclamation."

Several of the committee members, of course, did not agree. Some of these visited the prison in a group a short time after.

Again these State senators and representatives received the full tour, this time with Larker leading. As they passed through the main living areas Larker's detailed explanations seemed to satisfy them. Most remained jovial and exchanged banter. Then they requested to be taken into Block Ten.

As usual the inmates had learned of this tour in advance and heaped even more trash in the corridors. Tommy Swoboda had become a resident here and he prepared an even bigger surprise.

As the appalled legislators tried to tiptoe through the garbage down the tier of cells, Swoboda came forward to the door of his cell and waved at them.

"Hey c'mere, look at this. My cell is so badly infested with bugs that they're constantly attacking me."

Exchanging alarmed looks, they approached him. He pressed his head sideways against the bars so that his left ear stuck through. Reaching out with his left arm, he pointed to the ear.

"Look at that," he complained.

All of the legislators crowded up close and gasped. They could see an ugly dark insect protruding out of the channel of his ear.

He whined, "This cockroach crawled into my ear three days ago and died. Now it's stuck in there and I can't get it out. I need a doctor to help me but the administration won't allow me medical attention."

The legislators' shock turned to outrage. They immediately turned around and marched Larker out of earshot to blast him for not seeing to better treatment of the inmates.

I can't completely blame the State Reps and Senators for swallowing Swoboda's story. It's inconceivable to the average person that any human being would kill a disgusting bug and then jam it in his ear just to get attention.

Block Ten wasn't the only place where we ran into this strange affection for cockroaches. One day Mel Varney and I arrived at the Maximum Security cell of one of Walpole's most celebrated inmate lawyers.

"All right, Arch, out of your cell, please." I said.

He'd always been docile, and had been confined to a wheelchair since his recovery from a shootout with police during an armed robbery. We didn't anticipate any trouble, but Mel still stood at his side.

"What's going on?" Arch asked.

"Just a routine cell search for contraband."

"Hey, man, I don't have anything in there I shouldn't. Don't go messing up everything. I've got all my papers in order."

He had plenty of papers all right. Also law books—dozens of them stacked in piles in a corner. I didn't really expect to find anything, but I had a job to do.

Quickly I sifted through his possessions, being careful not to disturb the order of his papers when I shuffled through them. Then I turned to the law books. Something could have been stashed inside one or several of them so I decided to given them at least a perfunctory examination.

I no sooner picked up the first book when something dark brown darted out of the binding and ran across my hand. My flesh crawling, I shook my hand violently and the damn roach dropped to the floor. Angrily I stamped on it.

"Hey, take it easy!" Arch protested.

"Just a damn cockroach," I shot back.

"Maybe to you."

I picked up the second book on the stack, and this time two roaches jumped out of the binding. Out of reflex I dropped the book so the little bastards couldn't get on me. Then I bent over and eyeballed the rest of the stack.

Roaches were crawling in and out of the bindings of all of them.

"Arch, do you realize that roaches are all over your books?"

"So what?"

I gaped at him and then said, "Mel, go get some insect spray."

"You can't do that!" Arch shouted. I'd never seen him so upset. "They belong to me; I've been raising them!"

"Raising them? You mean like pets?"

"What's wrong with that?"

I looked at the ceiling and shook my head. "Well I'm sorry, Arch, but prison regulations say no pets. Get the spray, Mel."

"You sonofabitch!" he screamed at me. "I won't let you do it! They're all I've got!"

Varney had to grab him as he swung his wheelchair toward me. This was an educated man with no record of violence since coming to Walpole. He was willing to risk serious disciplinary action over a few cockroaches.

At Walpole we weren't dealing with the average person's mentality. We were dealing with men who placed guns to someone's head and coldly pulled the triggers; who sprayed a crowd of onlookers with machine gun bullets during a bank robbery; who raped and maimed without second thoughts; who indulged in sexual activity in full view of dozens of people; who threw their own feces against walls outside their cells, knowing it would hang there for days staring back at them, fouling the air they breathed.

Elected officials should have remembered some of these things when evaluating what they saw. They should have found out that prison life, especially in a maximum security prison, does not in any way resemble life as you and I know it. There, rules of common, decent behavior are suspended.

Closing Walpole and opening one or more new institutions could not eliminate these hygienic problems. They are motivated by hostility and anger. Inmates like Swoboda will turn a new prison into a place unfit for human habitation within days.

I would never claim that Walpole was perfectly designed. I agreed in part with administration's claim that the prison had too many blind areas. However, I saw that we had other measures at our disposal that were simpler and cheaper than building new prisons.

Common sense would seem to tell anyone that the practical solution to the blind area problem would be to increase the number of officers on patrol. Bring more eyes into the areas through which the inmates circulated. Any area becomes a "blind area" when no officer is around to observe it.

Sometimes the legislators brought us to them. I spoke on a number of occasions before legislative committees. I appreciated the opportunity, for it gave me credibility and a chance to air some carefully thought out views.

One of my more memorable appearances came before a Joint Committee on Human Services chaired by Senator Jack Backman and Representative David Mofenson. For the first and only time I took Karen with me to give her a firsthand view of the Legislature's workings.

If I had not been a scheduled speaker, I would not have been able to squeeze her into the Committee Room. Several hundred spectators had filled the seats and stood pressed against the walls, partially blocking the walkways. Many belonged to a group called Families and Friends of Inmates.

The twenty-one senators and representatives sat behind a curved table, the two chairmen occupying the middle two seats. I felt surrounded.

I was the ninth out of sixteen scheduled speakers, so by the time I took the chair, I had some idea of what I would be facing. As I sat down, members of the press set up several microphones and turned on their TV camcorders. I was to be featured during the evening news programs. Looking around, I spoke with conviction:

"The single most serious threat to safe operation at Walpole is drugs. Unless you are willing to feed the inmates' habits on a daily basis, you must take positive steps to prevent drugs from entering the institution. Do not think for a moment that officers or other staff are lugging drugs in, for such peer pressure exists that they fear the consequences of doing so. The problem centers around screening visitors.

"The visiting room at Walpole offers the best opportunity for the introduction of drugs. Over the course of 1978 alone, 36 visitors were arrested for attempting to introduce contraband. This number is only the tip of the iceberg. The metal detector is inadequate in screening out syringes and will not detect drugs or paper currency. Even some types of ammunition may escape detection.

"How can we stop this? We do so by ending contact visits . . ."

Suddenly hissing and booing broke out behind me. Backman struck the gavel. The crowd quieted, but I could now sense heightened animosity at my back.

". . . A wall of plexiglass should separate the visitor from the inmate, allowing absolutely no contact between the two. As it is now, kissing and petting allow the transfer of drugs in balloons. These can be swallowed, carried inside by the inmate, and recovered through induced vomiting or bowel movements.

"Pursuant to this, we must begin to prosecute those who attempt to smuggle in contraband. If there is a delay in bringing the case to court, that person should still be denied entrance to the prison. We should also stop allowing ex-felons as visitors. We can't discourage the smuggling of contraband unless we deny entrance to those who have been involved in the past."

More booing and hissing erupted. Backman rapped the gavel again:

"Additionally, we must utilize a drug-sniffing dog. This will not stop the influx of paper currency, but will screen out the drugs themselves. Fears that the dog will bite are unfounded. These are highly trained animals.

"Another area to examine is the large number of programs available to inmates which serve little or no purpose in the scheme of rehabilitation; yet take away much needed security staff from trouble areas . . ."

I could hear murmuring behind me beginning to build.

". . . We must recognize that Walpole is undermanned. This keeps us from properly keeping the inmates' activities under observation. In a Minimum cellblock, one C.O. is responsible for the care, control, and supervision of seventy-two inmates. He must answer the phone; check inmates in and out of his block; answer inmates' questions; and, all too frequently, leave his cellblock to rush to the aid of brother officers in trouble. There is no way this officer can offer effective protection to inmates in his block.

"The only solution to this problem is to cut back the programs, free up the officers that supervise them, and assign these officers into the cellblock areas . . ."

These words were barely out when shouting and a violent scuffle broke out behind me. I looked over my shoulder and spotted two men wrestling with court officers trying to break free and rush towards me.

"You don't care about the inmates!" one shouted. "You'd rather see them dead!"

The room echoed with more boos as the court officers dragged the men out of the room. Backman again used his gavel.

"Another disturbance like this and I'll have to clear the room."

I continued. "One last area I'd like to comment on before taking your questions. Not enough people understand or appreciate the prison environment. I believe they mean well when they address some of the problems; but they do not perceive what we as officers must go through on a daily basis.

"One of the biggest detriments to our doing our jobs effectively is the fear of being sued for brutality. A crisis arises in a particular block; the officer in charge takes action to regain control; and next, a heavy lawsuit comes down for overzealousness. How can we be expected to interdict violent activity when we invariably face legal action as a result?

"These are my views, shared by those who have entrusted to me an awesome responsibility, that of promoting their safety in a system which appears not to care about them. I don't know what your true intentions are for holding these hearings, but regardless of your motives, my union and I will continue to pursue our goal of achieving safe working conditions. I'm ready to take your questions."

My last comment, in particular, annoyed most of the legislators. Many directed hostile remarks at me, but asked no questions. Feeling more defiant than ever when it was over, I walked to the back of the room and took my place beside Karen. We could have left then, but in spite of the hostile stares I received from the spectators, I decided to remain long enough to show everyone I wasn't afraid.

When attention finally shifted away from us, Karen asked in a low shaking voice, "Do you go through this every time you speak?"

I could only shrug in response.

Knowing they had been successful in drawing official attention to themselves, the inmates decided to stir up even more by engineering one of their "hunger strikes." News of these always leaked out to the press.

This time, as usual, we didn't get any advance warning. The only hint of trouble occurred the day before when most of the inmates put in larger orders than usual for food from the canteen. Even then, no one said a word about an action so the kitchen went ahead and prepared a full breakfast for some seven hundred inmates. This included some fourteen hundred eggs, bacon slices and toast, and several hundred potatoes.

The morning of the hunger strike my fellow block officers in the Minimum Section and I went down the tiers opening the cells. To our surprise, no one stepped out.

"Hey, chow time," I said to each inmate.

By the time I reached the end of the tier and saw no one heading toward the kitchen, I knew something was going down. As I retraced my steps, I looked closer and saw that many of them were busy over their hotplates, boiling water and heating up various canned foods.

Soon the odor of fried spam and hot spaghetti sauce penetrated the far corners of the block. Still they gave not one word of explanation.

I retreated to the corridor where I found the other block officers giving the same report. Larker had already heard and had come down to see for himself.

"Another hunger strike, fellas," he said disgustedly. "Follow the Superintendent's directive."

Butterworth had standing instructions that any organized action by the inmates against prison routine was to be met by an immediate lockup. One never knew when the inmates might have a second, more aggressive step planned.

"Andrew," I offered, "why don't we turn this into a real hunger strike by taking away their canned goods?"

He cast me a sour look. "McLaughlin, go do your job."

I reentered my block and immediately called out, "All right guys, you've got two minutes to come out or I'm locking you up for the day."

No one responded, so I went along and relocked the cells.

The strike only lasted a few days until they ran out of canned food. But in the meantime the story reached the press and we were again accused of guard brutality. The public, of course, envisioned inmates confined to their cells, exercising enormous will power to reject food in pursuit of principle.

However, no one told the public about the canned goods, loaves of bread, and potato chips stashed in each cell. Nor did they hear about the seven hundred portions of food discarded after each meal and sent to the state farm at Bridgewater to feed the pigs. The cooks had to prepare that food for every scheduled meal just in case the inmates decided to eat.

How could such a well-orchestrated action take place throughout the prison? Why did all inmates conform? Didn't any disagree?

After two and a half years at Walpole I came to believe that fully 85 percent of the inmates would have preferred doing their time, gradually passing through the system without causing trouble. In order to survive, however, they had to follow the instructions of the kingpins, who had organized the remaining 15 percent into gangs. These gangs would kill or maim anyone who didn't promptly follow orders.

Having seen this frequently demonstrated, the 85 percent were prepared to obey like automatons. If the order called for killing another, most would carry it out without hesitation even if they had nothing against the intended victim. How could a man surrender control of himself in such a fashion? Remember, the 85 percent had already committed crimes outside the walls and had showed little moral conscience.

In one classic case an inmate with barely a month left on his lengthy sentence piped another to death and got caught. At the time I couldn't understand why the guy would do such a crazy thing with so little time facing him, so I went to visit him in Block Ten.

I had to be careful to meet him in a corridor where none of the other inmates could see we were talking. If he thought someone could overhear us he would have completely clammed up.

"Why in hell did you do it?" I asked. "You didn't know that kid. Now there's a good chance you'll have another twenty years or so tacked on to your sentence."

"Look," he replied, "I didn't want to do it, but I got the word. You know what I mean? From *The Man.*"

I immediately took this to mean Mancuso.

"But with only a month, couldn't you have found some way to avoid Mancuso's thugs? Even filed for Protective Custody status?"

"Avoid Mancuso's hit men? In here? Man, you've been around long enough to know better than that. And P.C. status? Hey, I'm not crazy enough to brand myself for life."

"But you'd have been out in another month. P.C. status means nothing on the outside."

He grimaced. "You talk like a dumb asshole. Mancuso's got plenty of connections on the outside. Besides, I've never been able to stay outside for long. After a few months I'll be back here again. Then what do I do?" His defiant expression transformed into one of sad resignation.

I had nothing else to say.

His fear of talking reflected another circumstance that instigated violence in the prison. Each and every inmate was paranoid about being branded a "rat." Being considered an informer meant sudden death, especially if it was suspected the individual knew something important.

Rumors ran rampant among inmates and officers that Butterworth had his own "rat patrol"—a network of informers that reported directly to him. I never saw specific evidence of it, but my hunch is that there was truth to the rumor. In any case, it created enormous tension between inmates, discouraging them from passing along useful information to officers.

I remember having a casual conversation with an inmate about the Boston Red Sox baseball team. I sat at my desk; he stood on the flats perhaps twenty feet away. The distance forced us to raise our voices and this carried them to the far corners of the block. I found the discussion entertaining, but my voice started to suffer, so I rose from my chair and approached him. I had no sooner modulated my voice down when he threw up his arms and backed away into his cell. In a loud voice that everyone could hear he complained, "What're you trying to do, get me fuckin' killed?"

Another time I was strip-searching an inmate in the main trap when he said, "I don't know why you spend so much time searching us. The guards are bringing in most of the drugs."

I backed up a step to let him dress. "If that's true, give me a name or names."

He smirked. "You know who's doing it."

"If I did know I'd take action to stop it. You want to be of help, give me some names."

He cast me a long glance as if realizing I was sincere. Then he shook his head. "How long do you think I'd last inside if it came out I'd ratted on some guards."

"I'll protect you against the guards."

"I'm not worrying about the guards. The other inmates would hear I'd ratted and would figure I was doing it on them too."

I couldn't argue with him. Whether or not he did know something about officers bringing in drugs, unfortunately, I never found out.

The vast majority of the officers shared the opinion that to reduce violence we had to identify and then isolate the "controlling" inmates in a separate block or blocks where they could not affect the 85 percent who leaned toward cooperation. We spent many hours discussing the prison population, and finally compiled a list.

On August 20, 1978 I personally took this list to Fred Butterworth. It bore the names of thirty-five Minimum inmates who had heavily involved themselves in behind the scenes activity that disrupted the Minimum Section.

"What do you expect me to do with this?" he asked.

"We recommend that these heavies be reclassified and sent to the Max-section. At the same time you can transfer several conforming Max-inmates to Minimum. I understand there are a number who have amassed clean records."

"Many of the men on this list also have clean records."

"That may be so, but we've watched them for months. We're

absolutely certain they make up the core of all the trouble in the Minimum Section."

"So on the word of you and your officers you expect me to change a man's status, take away many of his privileges and put him among the incorrigibles? How do I justify that to the Department and the inmate's counsel? He'll be screaming discrimination."

"Fred, you've been around here a lot longer than I have. You know these guys and what they're capable of doing. It's time to quit worrying about protocol and start taking action to stop them."

"I repeat, how do I justify that? I just can't act without regard to rules and regulations. You never seem to understand that."

"The Department has been given certain discretionary latitude. Look at the Interstate Compact. If you can transfer inmates out of state, you certainly should be able to move them from one section of Walpole to another."

The Interstate Compact had been authorized a few years before. It allowed the Department to "trade" inmates with another state. It ran on the theory that if a powerful, troublemaking inmate is transferred to a prison where no one knows him, he becomes like everyone else until he can build a reputation and gather another private army. Even if he succeeds, it will take him months or years. The Federal Bureau of Prisons had been successfully diffusing their heavy duty inmates for decades using this technique.

I'd suggested this at previous safety meetings but Fred always turned a deaf ear. Now he cast me a sardonic smile.

"Back on that again, are you? Look, even if this list is accurate, I don't want to put all the most dangerous inmates in the same block. That block would become a serious threat to the security of the prison. The disturbances that would result could be cataclysmic. I don't want riots again like we experienced in the early 1970's."

I responded, "But the way things are, the entire prison is a battleground. If we isolated the heavies together we'd know what to expect. We could beef up security and be ready for anything. Now we're trying to put down disturbances everywhere."

"The answer is no."

Tragically, our list was not acted on. At the time we compiled it one of the listed individuals had already received three major D-reports within ten days of arriving in Minimum. Yet he maintained his Minimum status until five months later when he was indicted for killing another Minimum inmate. Had the list received serious attention, one inmate might have escaped being placed on the list of the murdered.

As run at that time, Walpole was a pitiful, tragic place. I remember a mother coming to me just after her young son had been committed. She'd heard of Walpole's terrible reputation and knew of me from my appearances on television. She asked me, "How does my son survive in a jungle like Walpole? What would you do?"

I hesitated to reply. I thought of the homosexuals who would pounce on him. I thought of the kingpins who would take his money and obligate him. Many times in the past I had indeed pondered what I would do if suddenly thrust in the place of such a young man. I had devised only one possible strategy to preserve my dignity and sanity. But I dared not voice it to his mother.

My words would've been: "I'd learn who the kingpin inmate of my cellblock was. Then I'd find a bed leg, a heavy stick, or a pipe of some kind. At an opportune moment I'd sneak up behind him and try to cave in his skull. Hopefully I'd kill him and be sent to Block Ten where I could be safe for a few months. If things went as planned, I'd come out with a reputation for being dangerously crazy. That would keep most of the inmates away. Naturally I would have to watch for the payback, but if inmates thought you were crazy, they'd usually leave you alone."

If this was the best advice one could give, what did it say for the way the institution was run?

12 Just Another Day at the Office

When someone immerses himself in violence over an extended period, he's likely to lose sight of what it's like to live normally. This was certainly true in my case. I might never have realized how extreme my lifestyle had become if Karen had not been there to remind me.

In the midst of building her own life, she found herself in the cross fire of mine. We still cared about each other deeply. We still lived together and took our marriage seriously. We still tried to carry on the normal activities that most couples experience. But Walpole kept interfering.

I accept the blame for much of this. During my time as union president I seemed to carry the job with me every waking hour. I allowed the responsibility to draw me away from home more and more. Karen told me that at times she had only known I'd stopped home by seeing me on television in a fresh change of clothes.

When I did spend time with her I would often spoil things by rambling on about the prison, but I couldn't help myself. I should've been more considerate, but my interest in Walpole was all-consuming.

Karen loved company. If we'd have visitors I'd make an effort to control myself, but often they'd draw the stories out of me. One night I remember coming home tired from work shortly after midnight. Approaching the house I heard voices inside and guessed that Karen was enjoying one of her parties. As I slipped off my work boots, which

Karen always made me leave outside so I wouldn't carry in Walpole's roaches and feces, I realized I was in no mood to socialize. Still, I couldn't be rude, so I walked quietly in and stopped by the entrance to the living room, hoping to excuse myself after a brief exchange of pleasantries.

Attention immediately shifted to me. I felt terribly awkward, standing there in my filthy uniform and stocking feet, but they didn't seem to notice.

"What's going on at Walpole, Mike?" one of the men immediately asked.

I glanced at Karen and saw her eyes roll toward the ceiling so I tried to brush off the question.

"Oh, not much."

"Don't give us that," he persisted. "I just saw you on television a couple of days ago, bitching about safety and talking about going on strike."

I still tried to dodge. "That's old news now . . ."

"Come on Mike," they chorused. "Give us the dope."

I caught Karen's eye and with a trace of a smile she shrugged. So I began to explain and soon found the adrenalin flowing. I always seemed to possess a hidden reserve of energy when talking about Walpole. For the next few hours, in spite of needing a shower and sleep, I stood there spinning my tales. Everyone in the room sat listening, eyes agape, mesmerized.

The funny thing is, Karen herself got caught up in the story. At one point one of her girlfriends interrupted.

"Mike, are you sure you're not stretching the truth just a little?"

Before I could defend myself Karen jumped in. "Are you kidding? Believe me, this man is not exaggerating!"

Later she pointed out to me that a major reason why we maintained our steady flow of visitors was that people considered me colorful. Their regular lives revolved around spouses, children, pets, and house payments—generally pretty routine stuff. They found it a stimulating change of pace to have a friend who lived on the edge. Anytime they felt like some excitement they could pop over to see the McLaughlins and hear a few blood-curdling tales.

The publicity and media attention did help offset the negative aspects of the job, even for Karen. She couldn't help but feel proud of me and find it exciting to be in frequent contact with news celebrities. I did many interviews on my lawn and front porch. After a time it became common for her to take phone calls from major newscasters and chat with them on the phone like old friends.

Unfortunately, not all of the attention I drew to her was of a positive nature. With Walpole inmates having access to pay telephones, she often received obscene or threatening calls. I would see her pick up the receiver and then after a few seconds turn white and hold it away from her ear. She didn't have to tell me who was on the other end. My heart would tumble and I'd feel enormously guilty.

Had it been your average pervert she might have lambasted him. But what could she say to this hardened creep? He would feed off knowing he frightened or angered her. After a time she learned to hang up without speaking, and go about her business.

The first few times it happened I stormed down to the prison, determined to find the guilty party and see him punished. But I soon learned I could do nothing to stop these calls as long as Walpole's policy toward phone use remained lax. All inmates had access to phones and it was virtually impossible to determine whom they called. To make things worse, I couldn't change my phone number with so many people needing to reach me.

Even more disquieting than the calls were the times when Arlington town police were assigned to guard her against possible assault. When an inmate who had threatened my life either escaped or secured his release, Karen would have to spend a number of evenings sitting in the dark with two officers, waiting for me to get home. I can be thankful that no one ever tried to get at me by physically attacking her. And I'm grateful to the Arlington police for looking after her.

It took some time, but I convinced Karen to take a tour of Walpole. I did so proudly, like any husband who wants to show off his place of work to his wife. I also hoped it would give her a better understanding of my dedication to the job.

I had her come during the early evening while the entire prison was locked up waiting for programs to begin. I met her in the administration building and sensed a little nervousness. This seemed to deepen as she was put through the routine pat search and then ushered into the trap. I saw her flinch when the heavy metal door slid closed with a clang.

At that moment I really felt proud of her. Over the past few years I'd bombarded her with grisly stories and yet here she was, looking cool, dignified, and very attractive.

As we stepped out into the neatly landscaped prison yard, surprise appeared on her face.

"Michael, I had no idea it was so nice. Do the inmates do the gardening?"

"Yes. That's one of the work programs."

"It shows sensitivity."

"Yes," I smiled weakly, glad that none of them were in sight to express their "sensitivity" to her.

We walked down the sidewalk to the visiting room, which was now temporarily vacant. After a brief look I led her through the inner trap into the main corridor.

She'd met many of the officers previously, but I still felt grateful to see so many come forward to warmly welcome her. I also noticed several strategically placed in the corridor to see that nothing interfered with us. I immediately sensed this put Karen more at ease.

I started to the right and walked her to the main grille that sealed off the Max-Section. There I stopped.

"We won't go any further," I explained in a low voice. "They're all locked up, but if they see you some might get uncouth. Most Max-inmates are rebellious and would love the chance to embarrass me. No use encouraging a scene."

From where we stood I pointed out various facilities and described the Max-section layout. Then I turned, retraced a few steps, and walked her through the dining area. From there I took her to the hospital, law library and the counseling rooms. She had few questions. Seeing her pale tone, I guessed she was a little nervous.

We passed through the grille into the Minimum Section and I stopped just outside the A-2 gate.

Looking worried she whispered, "Won't the inmates see me here?"

"They may, but they're locked in their cells. These guys are better behaved. I don't think they'll cause a problem."

Just then the A-1 gate opened and out walked Ollie Axelson, a large inmate with a face of coarse features that looked like they'd been rearranged more than once in some dark alley. Ollie had no love for me, so I immediately tensed. Karen did too. Then she blushed as he slowly raked her from head to toe with an appraising stare.

Not taking his eyes off her, he paused and asked me, "Who's the fox?"

I began boiling at the implications of his words and replied sharply, "My wife."

He smirked, casting me a look as if he wondered what she saw in me. Then this big, dangerous looking con suddenly turned very polite. "How do ya do, Mrs. McLaughlin. Don't take no offense at my description of ya. I meant it as a compliment."

Karen nodded and smiled weakly. Then Ollie went on his way, leaving Karen with a surprised, almost bewildered look on her face.

I realized what had taken place and explained, "Most inmates treat women with respect. Many of them have wives and children of their own and tend to hate rapists and child molesters. They fear that while they're in here their families might become victims of such attacks. They're particularly sensitive because they have firsthand knowledge of the type of men who do molest women and children."

As we turned our attention back to the inmate living quarters she commented softly, "It looks pretty much like what I've seen in movies and on television except for the possessions. Why are these guys allowed so many things?"

I chuckled, "I've been trying to get an answer to that question for two years."

"They've got more bottles and junk than I keep in our bathroom. Can't they use some of that to hurt you guards?"

"Can and do."

"And I know they're men, but don't you have some regulations about order and cleanliness?"

I could only shrug. I had her wait where she was while I entered A-2 and used the desk phone. I called into Block Ten and reached Officer Kline.

"Dick, what about it? I'd like to bring in Karen."

"Sure," he replied. "Give me a few minutes. They'll all be locked up then."

We took our time and had no sooner reached the Block Ten grille when Dick peered out through a bulletproof window in the solid door beyond. Identifying us, he smiled, nodded, and swung the door open, then unlocked the grille.

Once inside, he quickly secured the gate and door behind us. Then he knocked on the inner door. An officer, who had been peering at us through another glass window, immediately opened the door.

I never could get accustomed to the foul air in Block Ten, but that day with Karen along, the blast that struck us seemed particularly strong. It smelled like I was escorting my wife into an overused outhouse. From her color and look of dismay I knew she was experiencing similar thoughts. Still, she did not try to back out.

As Dick led us down the short flight of stairs to the first level, he said in a low voice, "I can't let you stay too long, Mrs. McLaughlin. A visit is due and two inmates are scheduled to go to the law library. I don't want to let anyone get a glimpse of you. If they know you're here they'll make a fuss, so keep your voice down."

Karen and I followed him down short corridors, pausing as he opened and closed heavy grilles that sealed them off from each other. A main corridor accessed the two lower cellblock tiers. Dick led us to a far end where a longer, narrower corridor ran along the cells. He raised a finger to his lips and pointed through the grille with his other hand.

Karen took one look and appeared ready to vomit. One sight dominated that corridor. Garbage! Everywhere! Paper cups, plates, and wrappers, metal cans—I can't begin to describe what else made up that mess, or crawled through it calling it home. As usual it lay several inches deep.

I half-expected Karen to involuntarily scream or utter some outrage, but she heeded Dick's warning and endured the sight with a hand covering her mouth. After a few seconds she just shook her head and motioned vigorously that she had seen enough.

Another of my guided tours did not run as smoothly. My uncle Ed, a priest who naturally has an interest in steering lost sheep back onto the path to salvation, expressed an interest in visiting Walpole. I was pleased to oblige. Any extra representation of God we could introduce into the institution could only help matters.

Father Ed had heard me recount a number of my harrowing experiences and, as we entered the facility, I could sense his nervousness. To reassure him I said, "Father Ed, don't worry about anyone trying to cause us serious trouble. There are really only eight men in this place that want to see me dead and they're locked up in Ten-block. We're not going to Ten-block so don't worry about them. I'll show you everything else. The rest of the inmates may horse around or yell out things, but don't pay any attention. It's all talk. The only inmates who could really cause a problem are locked away."

Father Ed wore his collar and habit and, like Karen, did not receive as much as a harsh word from the inmates. As the tour proceeded through the cellblock areas I could feel him loosening up. He began asking questions and even exchanged kind words with some of the inmates. We moved on to the service areas, again without incident, until we reached the locked door of the law library.

I knocked to draw the attention of the officer posted inside.

Seeing it was me, he spoke through the door, "Mike, you can't come in here."

I thought he was objecting to my bringing in a visitor. I responded, "This is my uncle. I've got permission to tour the prison. I just want to give him a quick look at the library. Then we'll leave."

"Mike," he insisted, "I'm telling you you can't come in here."

His attitude annoyed me so my voice took on an authoritative tone. "Look, he's only going to be here a short time. We won't interfere with the inmates. Now let me in."

Recognizing my determined look, he nodded, unlocked the door, and let us in. Curiously, he stepped outside and locked the door behind him.

A wall separated the doorway from the main portion of the library. When we rounded it I found sitting at a table directly before me the very eight inmates I had described to my uncle. Since they were not dangerous to each other, all had been given passes at the same time out of Block Ten to use the library to work on their cases.

"You motherfucker!" one of them shouted.

A scramble ensued with them vaulting over the table and jumping over chairs to surround me. A few picked up chairs as if to hit me with them. Loud curses and threats sounded:

"I'll cut your heart out! I'll tear your throat out! I'll cut your head off!" The favorite threats of Walpole inmates always seemed to involve cutting something off.

Somehow in the confusion Father Ed managed to sneak back around the corner. There he stood, shaking. I remained standing where I was, knowing I couldn't get away. I didn't know what I could do, but as always, when threatened, I placed my hands on my hips. Then I listened to them rave.

"You're torturing us! You're trying to kill us! We're gonna kill you before you kill us!" On and on. Some looked ready to carry out their threats. I couldn't help but be scared, but I maintained my outward composure.

I remembered the macho reasoning that drove them. In the presence of each other they had to act out their hatred. Yet because they had not expected to encounter me, they were probably not prepared to kill me in that moment. Had I thought I was about to die, I might have fallen to pieces. But sensing that they were acting out a role gave me the strength to act out my own.

I didn't try to interrupt their bluster. Instead I encouraged them to continue and expel all their frustration.

"Yeah, go ahead. You've got me. Don't stop now. What else is bothering you? What about you? What've you got to say?"

I gave them several minutes to yell and scream and threaten my life. Gradually the tension lessened and we finally zeroed in on the issues really bothering them.

First, it became clear they didn't want me as badly as they made out. The fact that I had been the one primarily responsible for getting them transferred to Block Ten forced them to vow revenge. But actually other issues bothered them more.

One of them said, "You put us in Block Ten. We're trying to make the best of it—get settled in—and now we hear you want to turn the place upside down and make it even tougher on us."

"Yeah," complained a second. "We hardly ever get out of our cells. All we got there is a few possessions. Now we hear you want to take them away too."

"And visits." said a third. "You want to separate us from our women."

"Not only on visits," said a fourth. "You don't want us to have furloughs."

Others chimed in with even more complaints. As I heard them out I looked each one in the eye as he spoke to let him know I was listening.

Finally I said, "Look, fellas. I won't deny there's some truth in all of the things you've said. But let me explain what's behind it. Walpole is like a battlefield. You won't deny that."

I had their complete attention. Taking a deep breath, I plunged on, "I can't believe you or anyone else really likes to live under these conditions—you can't close your eyes at night and know you'll be alive in the morning. We've got to stop the violence. Like it or not, you guys are going to be here for years. Wouldn't you rather serve your time in peace?"

The question made them think, but one quickly responded, "What good's peace if you take everything away from us?"

"Yeah," several growled.

"I'm only pushing to take away privileges from those who commit violence. Block Ten is supposed to be a place to isolate wrongdoers. The threat of being sent there should discourage violence."

I swept my eyes over the group, making eye contact with all of them. "But as it is now, with the privileges enjoyed in Ten, inmates purposely attack each other or officers just to get sent there. That isn't right. It encourages you guys to feed off each other. You compete to see who can be the most violent. In the end nobody's safe. I know you're all tough guys, but how many of you really felt safe when you were in Population? You feel safer in Ten Block."

I saw their anger-hardened faces begin to soften.

"You may have a point," one of them said, "but what about our visits? We need contact with our women and kids."

"I have no desire to eliminate visits. I just want them more closely supervised. It's not fair for inmates to be having sex in clear view of others who are trying to visit with their mothers or kids. That's caused numerous fights and stabbings. I know it hurts to be separated from your visitors by a screen, but it's only fair. Block Ten is not supposed to be a country club. The idea is to work your way out of Ten by good behavior so you can enjoy better privileges back in Population."

"I don't like it," one said.

"Yeah," said another, "but he's right about feeding off each other. Man, something should be done around here. I'm gettin' a little tired of protecting my fuckin' back from young punks trying to make a reputation."

"What else you got in mind?" a third asked.

Amazingly they listened and engaged me in a constructive debate that lasted about a half hour. Then they sat back down at the table and again directed their attention to the law books.

Relieved, I turned and walked toward the door. When I rounded the corner on my way out, I found Father Ed still rooted to the spot, as white as a sheet. Later, outside the prison, I asked him, "Well, what did you think of the place?"

In an unsteady voice he replied, "It's going to take a couple of weeks just to settle down and put all this in perspective. I guess the only question I have now is, how can you work there? What's wrong with you?"

A number of people who knew me also wanted to know the answer to that question.

Father Bob Doherty, the Catholic chaplain, became my confessor during my most difficult days at Walpole. I was so aware of being a target that I hit on him with a confession at least once, and sometimes two and three times, a week. I did so to keep my conscience clear, in constant readiness to meet my Maker. Thank God that Father Doherty was there to provide support, not only to me, but to inmates seeking spiritual guidance.

The Father recognized his role, performing his service without interfering in security matters or the operation of the prison. He understood the necessity of isolating these men. I particularly admired his work because he tirelessly tended to the spiritual needs of the inmates while under constant harassment by management.

I once heard a deputy superitendent say, "The only reason Father Doherty has been assigned here is that he's a loser as a priest and couldn't function in a regular parish."

The statement still outrages me. I had seen Father Doherty help many of the inmates in areas where management and civilian counseling had failed. In contrast, the inattentiveness of that deputy had permitted more than one inmate murder and led to numerous guard injuries.

As the months passed the inmates continued to give me good reason to seek Father Doherty. The kingpins had come to recognize that my power in the prison now rivaled Fred Butterworth's. With Fred, however, they could bargain. I appeared uncompromising. The only way to remove the threat I posed to their kingdoms would be to get me out of the way once and for all.

Various segments of the prison population had their own specific method for accomplishing this. The Max-section inmates believed in direct action. However, they had a problem of limited access to me. I only occasionally worked Max-cellblocks and those assignments were spasmodic, with no advance notice of my arrival. Without working out a plan beforehand, they could not effectively organize an action to take me. I was too alert to fall victim to anything haphazard.

On one occasion the procedure broke down and nearly cost me my life. I had gone through a period of some eight months without working overtime; I'd always spent extra hours at the prison, but only on union business.

Finally I caught up on my union work and decided to put in some overtime to generate extra income for a planned vacation. I contacted the supervisor of the dayshift and told him I wanted to work.

My request caused some heat and, I suspect, drew some undesirable attention. The supervisor claimed he was booked up. He did not add me to the overtime list until called by Andrew Larker and ordered to do so. Larker had not suddenly gained any affection for me; he was simply responding to the union contract, which allowed me to work a specific amount of overtime. Management either permitted me to come in and work, or paid me to stay home.

When I arrived at the prison shortly after seven the following morning, the supervisor approached me. He acted cordially and showed me the roster sheet. Roll call had already taken place so all assignments had been made. He pointed out where my name had first been written, then erased and written in elsewhere.

"Mac," he said, "I want you to know I had you down for Block Four. But you're the president, you don't belong in that block. I'm sending you on a transportation trip instead. Go down and have a coffee and I'll call you at eight or eight-thirty when I'm ready."

This was standard procedure for taking inmates on court trips. The escorting officers would relax while the morning count took place and breakfast was served. Then they would pick up their inmate and head for court.

"I want you to know," I told him, "I'm quite willing to work Block Four."

"Yeah, but you don't belong there. Go get some coffee and I'll call you when I need you."

I didn't object any further. Transportation was usually easy duty. In the meantime I had an hour or so to relax.

By the time I reached the kitchen it was 7:15 and the day's routine had begun. I filled my cup and started chatting with the other officers. Our conversation lasted precisely until 7:25. Then, BANG! BANG! BANG! The unmistakable alarm echoed throughout the prison. It always sent shivers through me.

We rushed out into the main corridor near Control. The officers inside pointed down to the Max-end, so off we went at a full run. Upon arriving we found the problem was in Block Four. Inmates had crowded up against the grille, yelling and gesturing through the bars. When they saw me they went even more berserk.

The officer who had replaced me there now stood in the corridor, pale with fright, shaking.

"Jesus Christ!" he gasped, "I just managed to get my ass out of there. When the gallery unlocked the cells all forty-five of them came charging out like a fuckin' herd of buffalo. Mac, they were screaming your name. They must've thought you were gonna be in there."

I turned to the supervisor who had made the assignments.

"Any sign of trouble overnight?"

"None reported to me."

"If they expected me to show up here this morning, someone had to tell them last night to give them time to plan their action. Someone with access to the roster sheets."

He turned red under my accusing glare. “Mac, I don’t know how it could have happened. We’re always careful about things like that.”

“Yeah, sure.”

I was just about to rip into him further when Shift Commander O’Rourke put his hand on my shoulder.

“I think it’s best if you make yourself scarce. Your presence is inciting these bastards even more.”

I glanced at the grille and saw dozens of the inmates straining against the bars cursing me and yelling threats at the other officers. O’Rourke would have to put them down by force. Since I could only be a detriment to that effort, I turned and stormed back down to the kitchen.

I never learned who was responsible for the break in security or whether it had been intentional.

Minimum inmates didn’t need to take drastic action to get me. Freedom of movement gave them easy access to me whenever I was posted there. Lyle Kramer and his henchmen in the “Execution Squad” cooked up one particularly memorable scheme.

The first hint of potential trouble came in the form of rumors. Several officers had heard inmates mumbling about not going to work that particular morning. We could not verify the rumor, nor did we have any idea how extensive the action might be. Therefore, we took no unusual precautions. If the inmates decided to strike, we’d simply lock them in their cells and go about our business.

I had been posted to the Minimum corridor. Earlier, minimum inmates had filed down to the dining hall for breakfast, leaving corridor and cellblocks vacant. It seemed like a good time for the Minimum officers to take a coffee break. Suddenly I found myself alone with all the keys to the Minimum end.

Before the officers returned, the inmates began drifting back from breakfast. They returned singly or in small groups, hanging out in the corridor, waiting for work call. With the rumors of the stoppage on my mind, I was curious to see whether they’d carry it out. Within a short time I was standing alone amidst over 200 inmates.

I felt nothing unusual about this. I often mingled with large groups of inmates, although usually with other officers nearby. Still, I felt no particular alarm until one of the inmates muttered under his breath, “Cover your ass.”

The words told me clearly that not only was the work stoppage about to take place, but that the inmates intended taking me hostage in the process.

Several inmates stood between me and the corridor grille. I could never hope to escape by running for it. In the opposite direction stood the solidly locked door leading to Block Ten. I would find no help in that direction either. For the moment the best thing to do was to determine the extent of the conspiracy and which inmates were responsible. If I couldn't escape, maybe I could develop a strategy to talk my way out.

I casually maneuvered myself into a position where I stood in the corridor between the entrances to Blocks A-2 and A-3. I knew that the leaders of this exercise would never become directly involved. Instead they would place themselves on the perimeter with a clear view of the action.

Sure enough, when I glanced into A-2 I spotted Kramer sitting in a chair on the second tier, legs balanced on the railing staring out at me. I saw this as clear proof of his involvement. He lived on the far end of the third tier, but could not see out into the corridor from there. He had moved to the second tier to observe.

When I glanced in the opposite direction into A-3, I saw Arnold Smith, the gang leader of the blacks, positioned in a similar location on that block's second tier. No one besides Kramer and Smith occupied their respective blocks, a sure indication that both were controlling an operation. Further down another inmate leader sat in the officer's chair peeking around the corner from A-1. I also spotted Chuck Small, Kramer's most trusted lieutenant, circulating on the fringe.

By the time I finished my quick appraisal I had identified five leaders controlling groups of inmates. Obviously the entire Minimum Section was involved.

My mind raced, searching for a way out. I had vowed never to be taken hostage, but I couldn't physically hold off two hundred men. If I resisted too violently the order might be given to put an end to me on the spot. I would rather that than face torture, but I would not have to face that choice until they actually moved against me. That would likely not happen until work call at 7:50. I still had a few minutes.

One last assessment told me that all escape routes had been closed. So, accepting that the inmates had me in their power, I decided to follow my instincts and play their game. I moved even deeper into the gathering and began exchanging jive talk to give the appearance I wasn't alarmed.

"Well, it's almost time for work, guys," I announced in a loud voice.

"Yeah, sure, McLaughlin," they responded, obviously convinced they weren't going anywhere.'

"Hey you don't want to strike," I bantered back. "You don't want to be locked in today. It's going to be a great day out there."

"Yeah, right."

My words meant little. By now I was scared to death but still determined not to show it. Through my actions I hoped I was saying, "I'm not worried. You want me for a hostage? You want me dead? So what? I'm ready to die. Are you?"

I continued my act for a few agonizingly long minutes until 7:50 was almost upon us. Then suddenly I heard whistling from down the corridor. Turning to look, I spotted Jim Knight cheerfully approaching. Jim was a civilian worker and member of our union. Everyone knew that he also doubled as my business manager on union matters, so no one saw anything unusual in his coming to see me.

Working his way through the gathering, Jim walked up to me and said, "How's it going, Mike? Any hot issues you're working on?"

I had to play along until I could warn him. "No, Jim. Union business is pretty quiet these days. I can use the rest."

All the while I maneuvered him to a spot that I thought afforded us enough space to exchange undetected whispers. When I thought those nearby had focused their attention elsewhere, I risked it.

"Get the hell out of here. I'm going to be taken hostage."

He whispered back, "What the fuck do you think I'm doing here? Take a look."

Out of the corner of my eye I glanced back down the corridor just in time to spot a helmeted head peeking around a corner. My heart leapt. I wasn't alone after all.

"Nice to know, Jim," I mumbled, feeling much better.

"We're ready for 'em," he softly singsonged.

I knew then that the inmates would have to take me immediately or not at all, because the corridor would soon be filled with guards.

The decision lay with Kramer. From my position I could just see him. Did he know what he would be facing? Did he want me that badly?

Then, seconds before the 7:50 call came, he suddenly gave a hand signal, picked up his chair, and walked down the tier out of sight. Glancing into A-3 I saw Smith do the same thing. I could feel the tension lift. When the horn went off a second later, all the inmates turned and began filing through the grille gate. Just like that, everyone went to work as if nothing had happened.

Once everyone had gone I made my way down toward the control room on a pair of unsteady legs. In a side corridor adjacent to the schoolhouse I found some fifty guards waiting in full riot gear—helmets, batons, shotguns, and tear gas. They had been tipped by an inmate. Just how Kramer had learned of their presence I can only guess.

Twice within a period of five months I received a tip that a particular inmate had taken out contracts on my life. A bank robber/murderer, he now did his time in Block Ten. Knowing he had connections, I took the tip seriously and went to see him.

"Look," I told him, "I heard about this contract of yours. I hope you realize that if I die, you're going to face some very angry officers."

He folded his arms and smirked. "McLaughlin, you can't prove a fuckin' thing."

"I don't have to prove anything, buddy. I've already fingered you. The guards are going to assume you're responsible. Who knows what could happen to you?"

His smirk disappeared.

Within an hour I learned through the grapevine that he had pulled the contract. This surprised both inmates and guards, because he had built a reputation for being fearless.

Apparently his courage returned five months later, and he decided to come after me a second time. Again, I acted on the tip and visited him.

"You know," I told him, "you're becoming a real pain in the ass. I warned you before about this contract crap. I'm ready to die, are you?"

His alarm showed clearly on his face. "Now wait a minute, McLaughlin . . ."

"No, you wait a minute," I pointed at him. "Watch yourself." Before he could utter another word I turned and walked away.

My words served their purpose and, as before, within an hour or so he cancelled the contract. I never had that problem with him again.

Whether the guards would have carried out my inferred threat I don't know. Basically, as a group, they behaved themselves well, especially considering the frequent tormenting they received at the hands of the inmates. There may have been others, but I personally witnessed only one incident of guard brutality. This occurred when a notorious rapist/murderer arrived to begin his sentence.

His victim had been a young girl. The gruesome crime had received enormous publicity and the trial generated red-hot emotion throughout the state. Some of the guards found themselves swept up in the vigilante atmosphere that had surrounded the case.

In the process of escorting him inside, the officers held him in the trap and threatened him with terrifying reprisals, all the while shoving him violently back and forth. I resented that man as much as they and almost found myself caught up in their frenzy. But I managed to maintain control and finally calmed them down by reminding them of their responsibility as officers.

Unless you understand the inmates' unwritten code, their behavior toward me might seem inconsistent and irrational. Even some men who hated me and wanted me dead would stand up for me, if they thought other inmates were treating me unfairly. They did this because they wanted to settle their own scores with me directly. They knew how it felt to receive a raw deal. They wanted me to receive a fair shake, which to them meant telling me face-to-face why they were stabbing me before they rammed the shank home.

This peculiar morality was evident once in the dining hall during a meal for Minimum inmates. Some two hundred sat at tables, with several officers, including myself, standing along the walls observing. Everyone seemed relaxed.

Then I spotted a plume of cigarette smoke rising in the center of the room. This put me on the alert, because regulations stipulated no smoking in the dining room for inmates or officers. The culprit was a young black inmate who hadn't been long in the Minimum Section.

I felt like someone who had been enjoying a beautiful outing only to have a surprise shower dampen everything. You wish it would go away, but you can see it's going to hang around for awhile.

I glanced at the other officers, many of whom were standing much closer to the offending inmate. All appeared oblivious to the infraction. I knew this couldn't be the case. They simply didn't want to take on the distasteful task of confronting the fellow in front of so many of his friends. To save face, the inmate might attack you. The other two hundred might jump to his defense, setting off a riot. Was it worth the risk to enforce this nit-picky rule?

To the others I guess not. But I remembered the old axiom—bend one rule and they'll have you bending them all. Even though I was union president, I still took my guard job seriously and did not try to avoid dirty tasks. The inmate had stepped out of line. To maintain proper order he had to be called on it.

Gathering myself, I pushed away from the wall and weaved my way between tables until I stood beside him.

"There's no smoking in the dining room," I told him. "Either put the cigarette out or leave." Then, to relieve some of the pressure, I turned around and started walking away, assuming he'd obey my instruction.

He didn't. When I glanced back and saw him still puffing away, I turned and approached him again.

"Okay," I said, "you'll have to leave the dining room."

He finally saw I meant business and replied, "I'll put it out."

"Too late. Leave the dining room and smoke it out in the corridor."

Hatred flashed in his eyes. I could sense him coiling like a spring. In typical inmate fashion he stood up and faced me. Like many of them, he towered over me and sported the usual array of bulging muscles.

"You mother-fuckin' racist," he growled. "You're always picking on the blacks. I oughta cut your fuckin' heart out. You got no business telling me to do anything. If I want to smoke the fuckin' cigarette I'll smoke it."

I stood there with hands on hips, prepared to defend myself, but also wondering how I could get the guy out of there without triggering an explosion from the rest of the inmates. His accusation concerning racism was particularly unsettling. I was not in the least a racist. To be classified a racist in a prison can cause you very serious problems. I had enough problems already without that one. Still, I couldn't stand there and debate the issue with him.

Then suddenly two of the more influential inmates, one black and one white, stepped between us. The black one said, "McLaughlin's a lot of things, but he's no racist."

He needed to say no more. Not wanting any trouble with these guys, the troublemaker turned and walked out without another word. The two peacemakers took their seats without saying anything to me. I returned to my position against the wall as if nothing had happened.

The two inmates who'd intervened had no love for me. They would've been happy to see me removed. But not for the unjust accusation of being a racist. It might not make sense to the average person, but it made sense to them.

In general, I probably got along better with minorities in Walpole than with the whites, many of whom were controlled by the Italian and Irish mafias. Even within the prison the Italians were highly organized, had a lot of money and, therefore, a lot of power. The Irish were poorer and lower in the pecking order, but they still operated in tightly-knit gangs that thrived on violence. Between them, these two factions caused most of the serious trouble in the prison.

On the other hand, the Hispanics and blacks had little money and poor organization. Most of them were pawns being preyed upon by those with power. In their helpless state the vast majority recognized that I was trying to help them by emasculating the gangs. I sensed they respected me and, therefore, I felt more comfortable around them.

The complexity of my relationship to the inmates was easily misunderstood by those on the periphery. I could appear tough, uncompromising and unfeeling, when all the while my actions served the best interests of the majority of the inmates. Inmate advocate groups, in particular, fed off this misperception and cast a lot of heat in my direction. They wanted to believe the worst and chose me, president of the guards' union, as the target of their wildest charges. During one meeting in this period, the group, Friends and Families of Inmates, invited Senator Backman and the heads of the unions to speak to them about brutality in prisons. Hearing that the others had accepted, I saw this as a good opportunity to defend the guards against the wild charges I knew would be flying. I decided to attend, over the objections of Council 93, who feared that I would embarrass the union.

The meeting place was a church in Boston. On arrival I learned that the other scheduled speakers had cancelled and sent underlings to take their places. None of these substitutes had firsthand experience with prison activity, leaving me the only person who could speak authoritatively on the topic. Circumstances had set me up as the only target for this hostile audience.

A minister served as the moderator and drew questions for me from the audience. After I had answered several of the sharp, pointed variety, an elderly lady stood up, tears streaming from her eyes. She identified herself as the mother of a Walpole inmate. When I heard her name I immediately remembered her son. He had recently drawn our attention by seeking to kill another inmate. The officers had intervened and removed him to Block Ten.

In a voice broken with emotion she accused, "My son told me you dragged him to Block Ten for no reason and on the way you personally kicked him in the face several times. You guards beat him and threw him down a flight of stairs. Then you strip-searched him and shut him up in a blue room without even a toilet in it. And you wouldn't feed him all day—" The tears began flowing so heavily she couldn't continue.

The crowd grumbled angrily in support. I felt like Lucifer appearing before a Baptist prayer meeting.

I didn't want to hurt this lady, but a point had to be made, both to defend us against an untruth and to enlighten everyone there concerning the realities of Block Ten.

"Ma'am," I responded, "I'm very aware of your son's transfer. I read the report the next day. You see, I had a day off and wasn't at the prison during the incident. So your son is mistaken when he says I kicked him in the face.

"Now, not having been there, I can't say how physical the guards became when moving him. I did hear he put up quite a struggle, so I wouldn't be surprised if they had to be rough with him. However, I don't believe he was roughed up nearly to the extent he claims.

"Be that as it may, let me offer you this. If you want him out of Block Ten, I can accomplish that for you. I would be perfectly happy to go back and recommend that he be put back in Population. But consider this—all of you."

I glanced around at the audience to make sure I had their attention. "If her son returns to Population, one of your sons will likely die. You see, her son was sent to Block Ten for trying to kill one of your sons."

I let that fact sink in before I continued, "I stand here awaiting your advice. All of you as a group, tell me what you want me to do."

As suddenly as that woman had stood up, she sat down, shock showing plainly on her face through her tears. I waited. Not one person in that audience suggested we release her son from Block Ten.

Some of the inmates' relatives did get the message that we were trying to accomplish something positive. One day an inmate's mother and grandmother approached me in the lobby of the prison. The grandmother said, "Somebody in here has to care about the drug flow. We appreciate what you're trying to do."

The mother added, "Thank you. Keep up the fight."

Praise like that helped our morale tremendously. Unfortunately, none of us got very much of it.

13 Dump The Duke

During the summer of 1978 another election campaign for Governor of Massachusetts had begun and I watched it closely, considering the outcome crucial to our union's cause. Frank Hall would probably remain Commissioner of Corrections and Fred Butterworth would be Superintendent at Walpole as long as Dukakis was Governor.

The prospects for beating Dukakis didn't look good. He was a reasonably popular incumbent representing the dominant party in the state. None of his Democratic challengers showed particular strength. He had a substantial lead in the polls.

Although I hadn't vigorously opposed Dukakis's election as Governor in 1975, I had reservations about him. In some areas I thought him too liberal. In others I felt he was making promises that he couldn't fulfill. He had run as the reform candidate, pledging to restore integrity to state government by dismantling the ancient system of political patronage. He also promised, without reservation, "no new taxes."

Dukakis had to break that past promise during his first year. His predecessor, Governor Sargent, had generated such an enormous deficit that Dukakis wasn't able to cut spending enough to avoid more taxes. By Massachusetts law, the Governor must submit a balanced budget.

I didn't scrutinize his position on law enforcement and corrections closely until I became union president in 1977. Even then I believed Dukakis had properly delegated authority, only to have his subordinates keep him in the dark.

But as I took part in negotiations with his corrections people, watching the simplest items go unresolved, I began to think differently. Someone was responsible. Hall bore his share, yes, but who had endorsed Hall and retained him in the position of Commissioner? As Governor, Dukakis had a duty to keep watch on his subordinates.

I felt Dukakis showed his indifference by failing to dismantle the patronage system in corrections. He had made the elimination of patronage a cornerstone of his original campaign for the governorship. Yet three and a half years into his term, corrections people faced the same "good old boy" system they always had. My frustrated career was a prime example. Most of my fellow officers faced similar bleak prospects for their own. If Dukakis had indeed ended the patronage system in Massachusetts, why were corrections people still victims of it?

I also opposed his public stance on crime issues, particularly his failure to address Walpole's problems. He strongly opposed the death penalty, having vetoed a bill in 1975 that would have reinstated it. I don't support the "eye for an eye" approach to punishment, but I do see the death penalty as a useful tool in the corrections process. It has value as a deterrent on the streets and can also deter murders within the prison system itself.

As things stood at Walpole, inmates serving life sentences had little to lose by killing guards or other inmates. Banishment to Block Ten represented the most severe punishment they could get. So how do you dissuade an angry killer from killing again when punishment is minimal? Had an electric chair been waiting outside Block Ten, inmates would have thought twice about stabbing guards.

Another issue beginning to rear its ugly head was furloughs for first-degree murderers. Governor Sargent had instituted the program in 1972, making it relatively new when Dukakis took office.

In theory the furlough program gave inmates incentive to behave. It provided opportunities to gradually orient themselves to the outside world before being granted permanent release. For those who had displayed excellent behavior over many years, a furlough of up to forty-eight hours might be granted. Some prisoners would be eligible for as many as fourteen furlough days per year.

Dukakis had supported the program, pocket-vetoing a bill that would have banned them. He explained, "The bill would have cut the heart out of efforts at inmate rehabilitation."

I didn't oppose the furlough program as conceived, but I certainly had reservations over its implementation. The talk I'd heard about including Walpole inmates in the furlough program alarmed me.

Officers had no wish to hold back inmates who demonstrated a sincere change in attitude. We rooted for the better ones to make it. But I felt furloughs should be administered in accordance with Hall's stepping-stone concept. Only inmates who had worked their way via good behavior to lesser security prisons should be eligible. The problem with that, of course, was the tendency of the Department to move the bad apples through the system. With that happening, furloughs threatened to become a real problem.

State prison officials and outside experts have claimed the Massachusetts furlough program shows a good record. A House committee found that since 1972, first degree murderers have been granted over 5500 furloughs. These have resulted in eleven inmates escaping, only two of whom are still at large. Five, however, did commit serious crimes before being recaptured.

Furlough advocates like to point to the low percentage of escapes in comparison to the number of furloughs. However, this percentage does not represent the true picture. Many inmates receive numerous furloughs, therefore considerably less than 5500 murderers have been furloughed. When the number of inmates who participated is considered rather than the number of furloughs given, the percentage rate of failure increases dramatically.

So, has the program really worked with an inmate who returns from his first nine furloughs, only to escape on his tenth? The Department of Corrections would like to claim only a 10 percent failure rate in this case. I consider it 100 percent.

Moreover, the escape rate represents a price we citizens pay for the furlough program. What are we gaining from this painful investment? Do the murderers who return from their furloughs gain enough from the program to justify the public enduring the crimes subsequently committed by those who escape?

If the furlough system is retained, the leaks must be plugged to protect the lives of the public. The Department needs to be considerably more discriminating not only about who gets the furloughs, but also who decides who should get them.

Dukakis didn't face a major problem with the electorate over furloughs. No spectacular cases of furlough violation had yet occurred. The issue that finally convinced me to oppose him was his record on unions in general. Like so many politicians, he claimed to be a friend of labor, but in the previous few months he had ignored the pleas of AFSCME during the payless paydays controversy, brought in Ira Cobb, a union buster from New York, to reinforce the Office of Employee Relations and had strongly supported a union contract that I viewed as being grossly inadequate for our needs.

With all this in mind, I determined to support another gubernatorial candidate. Edward King, also a Democrat, looked good. My father, during his years attending Boston College, had known of King through the football program.

Recently King had served as the Executive Director of the Massachusetts Port Authority, a position that also placed him in charge of Logan International Airport. I had heard that he had done positive things for union people; so I went to his campaign headquarters in Boston.

King was a big, raw-boned guy, at least 6′2″ and well over 200 lbs. He had been a football star at Boston College and later had played a few years professionally with the Baltimore Colts in the 1950's. Even at his age he looked in top physical shape. His assistant introduced me as the President of the guard's union at Walpole, and his hand dwarfed mine as we exchanged a handshake.

"So you're Ed King, the famous B.C. football star," I bantered.

"I don't know how famous," he said, smiling.

"My father said you were famous as the 'Boston Strong Boy' a few years back when you guys were in college."

His smile widened. "Who's your father?"

"Bernie McLaughlin. You might not remember him. You weren't in the same class."

"Sure, I remember Bernie. He was an upperclassman, wasn't he?"

"Yeah, he's a little older than you."

For a few minutes the conversation remained at the pleasantry level. Then I got to the point. His union.

"Well, Ed, have you heard about what's happening at Walpole these days?"

He looked puzzled. "Can't say I have."

"It's been on the news, Ed, and in the papers. Walpole's in trouble. We have a lot of rioting, and I'm constantly going on strike to protect my members against poor management practices. I need some help.

I'm not getting it from the current Governor. I'd like to see him replaced."

King nodded encouragingly. I went on, "I figure you might be the right guy. If you are, I think I can help you. But first I need to hear some answers to questions my union feels are very important to us."

He invited me to proceed. By the time I finished I felt we had many of the same views on both law enforcement and corrections. He definitely favored making security, rather than treatment, the focus in the state's prison system. Safety of the public came first. He supported capital punishment. He frowned on commuting sentences for first degree murderers. King believed in beefing up the ranks of the State Police and the Corrections Department. He convinced me that he was concerned about the guards' plight and would back us in our effort to improve safety conditions at Walpole. He also committed himself to supporting an important bill before the legislature which would put us under the Secretary of Public Safety rather than the Secretary of Human Services. He came across as being sincere.

I told him, "I'll give you all the help I can. I can't offer you campaign money—we're a poor local—but I can promise you manpower. And I'll work through my union to get other unions to support you."

He rose and again shook my hand. "If you can do that for me I'd appreciate it."

I knew I'd have no problem swinging my local behind the candidacy of Ed King. But three hundred votes wouldn't make much difference. In order to have a significant impact on the election, I needed to influence the statewide union with its 60,000-plus membership.

King was the underdog at the beginning of the campaign. The best his supporters were hoping for was a small margin of victory. We estimated that under a million votes would be cast in the primary. This meant that the AFSCME vote alone would amount to approximately six percent of the total. When one considers that each committed person usually controls two and a half votes, then our AFSCME endorsement would influence 150,000 votes, or just under twenty per cent! King could never win the election without the endorsement. Dukakis might, but it would be a close call.

Over 160 presidents represented the locals that made up AFSCME. Since we had been meeting once a month to discuss normal union matters, all of them had come to know me well. I felt comfortable calling them on the phone or approaching them before and after our meetings to drive home the necessity of supporting King. Many seemed receptive, but one major obstacle stood in the way. His name was Sam Frustaci.

In spite of the fact that most of the presidents were thinking people who had pledged to forcefully represent their own locals, virtually all had fallen under Frustaci's control. He held a powerful position in AFSCME and ruled the entire union with an iron fist. He should have taken orders from the elected Executive Board, but had gained so much power in the union that he was able to determine who got elected to the board.

Frustaci planned to steer the union behind Dukakis in the upcoming primary. To carry it out, he didn't feel he had to put a lot of pressure on the presidents. Apparently Sam felt that letting them know his preference would be sufficient. He was so confident he didn't schedule an endorsement meeting until two weeks before the election.

This gave me several weeks to try to wean the presidents away from him. I started to make phone calls. Most of the other presidents worked for different departments in the state, but we had one common bond—the contract that Dukakis had supported. I based my appeal to them on the contract's unfairness.

Once the word spread among the presidents that Mike McLaughlin supported King, they started calling me, making my task easier. They hadn't even considered that anyone in the union would seriously oppose Frustaci. Now, hearing that I was doing so, they started getting interested. Most of them felt the same way I did about the contract, but no one had offered an alternative. They hadn't perceived the governor's race as a chance to improve their lot as a union.

I found groups of interested listeners during recesses of our presidents' meetings. Most of them had heard me criticizing the contract before. Now I began emphasizing King's record on unions in comparison to Dukakis's.

The presidents began realizing that they did indeed have a choice, and that if they stuck together they could have an enormous impact on choosing a new governor. I felt I was making progress.

As the campaign heated up, someone in King's campaign came up with the slogan, "Dump the Duke." King had it printed on several hundred thousand bumper stickers. Naturally most of the Walpole guards plastered them on their cars. Shortly afterwards, the state issued an edict claiming that these stickers violated a law forbidding campaign slogans on state property. All cars bearing them were denied access to state parking facilities.

The Walpole administration immediately took steps to enforce this regulation in the Walpole parking lot. This set off another little scrap. I maintained that the law didn't apply to a general slogan like "Dump the Duke."

Management disagreed, threatening to have the cars cited and impounded and the employee owners disciplined. I told them we'd take them to court if they tried.

Hot words flew but nothing serious happened. A few of my guys caved in and removed the stickers, but generally, "Dump the Duke" could be seen all over the Walpole parking lot. And none of our cars were towed.

Throughout the campaign I never entered the area of King's political advisors, but I did attend strategy meetings and was often asked to solicit commitments from union people or to speak before key groups of ordinary citizens who had strong concerns over the law and order issue.

Since I wasn't viewed as a politician, my words often seemed to create more impact than those from members of his inner circle. That group, although quite experienced in state politics, did not have my personal relationship with many media people. On King's behalf I appeared at many forums to discuss corrections.

During one radio show appearance I made strong comments against the furlough program. Stating that I didn't oppose the program completely, I said: "No furloughs for Walpole inmates. Walpole houses maximum security inmates. That status alone should disqualify them from furlough eligibility."

The next morning I learned that my appearance had drawn more of an audience than I'd bargained for. Shortly after work call I was walking alone down Walpole's Minimum corridor when I began sensing something amiss. I passed only a few inmates, these either on their way to special programs or performing maintenance work. Normally I would receive passing comments or nods, but today they remained silent, expressionless, and avoided making eye contact. This put me on alert, but I didn't suspect the deep trouble awaiting me. It struck me as I approached the corridor leading to the yard.

Suddenly about fifty inmates swept out of that passage and other hiding places and within the blink of an eye surrounded me. I immediately recognized them as some of the most dangerous men in the prison. All had committed serious armed robberies or murders. Now I could see that they were armed with knives, shanks, and pipes.

Even more frightening, their eyes were cold and resigned, staring through me as if they perceived me as an object, not a person. I cast another quick glance around, looking for help, but duties had momentarily drawn all other officers out of the corridor. This gang had planned well.

Once the circle had formed, the ringleader stepped into the middle with me. "McLaughlin, we heard you on the radio last night. We want you to explain your furlough position to our faces."

I knew how important the promise of furloughs was to these men. I also sensed that they had already made up their minds what they intended doing. They knew my position. Only the inmate code held them back. They wanted to see how I'd react to their challenge. They expected me to modify what I'd said and try to lie my way out of this spot.

I'd faced many serious threats at Walpole in the past, but now I sensed my time had come. Everything pointed to their having planned to kill me. Their tense postures and impatient gestures told me that bravado would not get me out of this spot.

In the instant before I spoke, only two things occurred to me. First, I cleared my conscience by uttering a silent prayer. Then I reminded myself to tell the complete truth. Double talking or lying would instantly get me killed. I was likely going to die anyway, so it might as well be with the truth on my lips.

Somehow my voice remained steady, "Fellas, I'm not going to try to back out of what you heard me say. I don't believe Walpole inmates should be furloughed. You're here because you're considered the most dangerous inmates in the state. It doesn't make sense to furlough you until you prove you're ready to deal with society. You do that by first working your way to a lesser security prison and then doing good time there."

I immediately heard feet shuffling in agitation and voices grunting and groaning with displeasure. The ringleader looked me straight in the eye, disappointed at what I'd said. Now circumstances were about to force him to do something he preferred not to.

Finally he asked me, "What about those of us who don't want to leave Walpole and go to another prison? We put in our time too. Why shouldn't we be able to earn furloughs?"

In a very deliberate voice, looking directly at him, I replied, "Any inmate who wants to stay in this crazy place must be sick and should be denied furlough privileges on that basis alone."

The foot shuffling increased and the groans grew louder. There was nothing more for me to say. I sensed my time was short. My fate lay in their leader's hands. One word from him and they would all pounce on me. They had little to lose. A court could never determine whether it was the first or the twentieth blow that killed me. And without that determination, no inmate could be convicted of murder.

The ringleader suddenly seemed torn by conflict. He continued standing there, turning his body from side to side, looking at the others as if about to give a signal. Seconds seemed like hours. Then finally he looked at me and said, "McLaughlin, we don't agree with you, but we respect your honesty."

Even as I heard his words I still thought I was dead. I tensed as I saw him give a signal. Then, as quickly as they had surrounded me, the inmates disappeared! I can't recall seeing them walk away. It happened that fast.

Slouching for a moment against the wall, I breathed a sigh of relief. The inmate code had saved me. So many people, including officers and managers, had lied so often in Walpole that the inmates respected someone telling the truth—even if that truth hurt. Many guards had been stabbed for not being direct and forthright in their answers.

During the campaign, I had spoken with King concerning the prison.

"Ed, You can't really get a true feeling for the problems and dangers we face at Walpole without seeing the place for yourself. Why don't you let me personally take you on a tour?"

He looked at me doubtfully. "Can you guarantee my safety while I'm there?"

"Ed, I can't even guarantee my own safety."

Looking a little embarrassed he said, "Then I think I'll have to pass on the tour for now."

I thought it amusing that this burly, tough talking ex-football star would decline my invitation to spend a few hours in the prison when smaller, less macho, common guys reported for work there every day. King never entered Walpole. I guess my descriptions of the danger there had sunk in.

I know for certain he appreciated my views on prison and law enforcement issues, because he had me help draft his strategy papers on those subjects. The papers helped him talk toughly and authoritatively while avoiding needless controversy. His opponent hesitated to attack him on these positions, because the people obviously agreed with them.

While all my work for King was important, the key moment was to come at the meeting when AFSCME would decide who to endorse. Although I felt I had made inroads for King, I couldn't be sure of just how strong a hold Frustaci still maintained. It was one thing for a president to give me a verbal commitment when we met off by ourselves; quite another for him to stand up before his peers and defy Frustaci.

With only two weeks left before the primary election, the race for the Democratic nomination for governor had tightened considerably. Some polls even showed King ahead. During that summer Dukakis hadn't campaigned hard or bothered to raise much money. Now he found himself in an unexpectedly tough dogfight. This made the AFSCME endorsement more important than ever.

I felt a heavy burden on my shoulders as I arrived for the meeting. This lifted somewhat when I received enthusiastic greetings and encouragement from several other presidents. With the hall beginning to fill, I placed myself in a position to greet as many of those attending as possible. By the time Frustaci called the meeting to order, I felt optimistic for King's chances, because nearly all the 160 local presidents were there.

After clearing away routine business, Frustaci made an impassioned plea.

"Because of our loyalty and solidarity, this union has gained in strength these past four years. In that time we've done much for our members—" He proceeded to rattle off a number of items that I considered unimportant.

"We have accomplished all this in the term of Governor Mike Dukakis. I don't claim that Dukakis has done all that he could have done for us, but neither has he interfered. We have flourished during his four years. Why should we change horses now? I say it makes more sense to support the devil we know over a devil we don't know.

"The major reason we came here is to endorse a candidate for Governor. Let's take care of it right away and unanimously endorse Mike Dukakis."

Despite my weeks of effort, his brief plea seemed to captivate the entire audience. The hall resounded with loud clapping and cheers. The audience appeared ready to endorse Dukakis by acclamation.

Riding high on this wave of approval, Frustaci asked, "Is there anyone else who has something to say before we put this to a vote?"

In spite of my disappointment, I raised my hand. Frustaci spotted me. He knew I'd been campaigning for King. After the enthusiastic response to his speech he must have felt confident that he had the other presidents in his pocket. If I wanted to butt my head against a brick wall by taking the microphone now, fine with him. I knew he hadn't forgotten or forgiven what I'd done to him at the Statehouse during the payless paydays demonstration. That was in front of a crowd of members who had no reason to fear him; this was an audience of union officials who had many reasons to fear Frustaci's power. He'd let me see the difference.

When I first took the microphone it might as well have been a viper for all the confidence I felt. I knew how difficult it was to sway the emotional momentum of a crowd.

"Brothers and sisters," I began. "It isn't easy to stand up here after all that applause and take issue with what Sam just said.

"But somehow I just don't see these last four years as gloriously as Sam paints them. Just in the past year my local has been forced by Dukakis's people to strike for everything we've achieved. Because of them nearly twenty-five percent of our number were injured in the past year alone.

"And, worse yet, because of dirty tricks played by the Dukakis administration, most of the injured guards don't get their Industrial Accident pay for months. There's more. The Governor's budgetary cutbacks have cut down on the most basic kinds of maintenance, adding to the hazards our members face. The same shortsighted financial squeeze prevented us from working overtime at a time when we were understaffed—putting us in even more danger.

"It comes down to one thing: our workplace is unsafe and the Governor's administration gives us absolutely no cooperation in making changes.

"The biggest obstacle to negotiating safe conditions at the prison is the same contract that hamstrings all of us. Dukakis's negotiators sold us a bad bill of goods. We can blame ourselves for that. But what kind of Governor offers you a contract that lowers your pay standards, dilutes your benefits, cuts back on safety standards in the work place, and takes the teeth out of the grievance process? Certainly not a Governor who respects unions or union people.

"Dukakis brags about removing patronage from his administration. Have you seen evidence of that in your work place? Can you honestly say that you have better opportunities for job advancement now than you did before? At Walpole, officers haven't seen Civil Service exams during Dukakis' term. Have you?

"When has the Governor gone to bat for us? Think back just a few months to the payless paydays fiasco. Did he care about us then? Not a bit. Instead he used us to pursue his own personal agenda. Dukakis chose to let us go without pay rather than back off from a stupid political fight with the Legislature. Many of us lay our lives on the line daily for that pay, little as it is. What kind of Governor ignores our basic needs for his own political gain? Not one I want back in office.

"As most of you already know, I support Ed King. In the course of coming to know Ed King intimately, I've scrutinized his record closely. As Executive Director of the Massachusetts Port Authority he has shown empathy for union people. I've questioned him at length and feel confident he will support our efforts to improve work conditions and our living standard. He will not leave us sucking air while he pursues his own personal ambitions.

"I believe that King is our friend. But even if he turned out to be a devil, as Sam suggested he might be, he couldn't possibly be any worse than the devil we've had for the past four years.

"This body represents over 60,000 union members. Together we can make a substantial impact on the outcome of this election. We need a change, and within this group lies the power to make it happen."

I received a standing ovation. Frustaci stood off to the side, beet red, looking defeated even before the vote was taken. This was the second time I had briefly wrested control of his union from him, but on this occasion I had struck at his power base.

The vote gave unanimous endorsement to King. I felt elated to have achieved a goal far beyond anything I'd dreamed of undertaking when I first set foot in King's office.

The last piece of business that evening was to authorize an immediate mailing to the 60,000 membership urging them to support King. The mailing went out, and I believe that virtually all of the membership who went to the polls voted for King. He shocked everyone in the state, winning the 1978 Democratic primary by nine per cent, or 76,000 votes. If it's really true that each person committed beforehand is worth 2.4 votes, then my swinging the AFSCME endorsement to King dealt a serious, if not mortal, blow to Dukakis's reelection effort.

Even though he'd defeated Dukakis, King still faced a stiff battle against Republican Frank Hatch in the general election. At the same time, I again had to face off with Frustaci before AFSCME to gain its endorsement for King.

This time Frustaci wanted us to remain neutral. He did have a case because Hatch's position on unions was similar to King's.

When my turn came to speak I carefully avoided attacking Frustaci's stance. Instead I concentrated on all the positive reasons to vote for King. I summed up by saying, "We don't want a Republican for Governor. We supported Ed King in the primary. Why should we jump ship now? King's the same guy he was two months ago."

Whether my speech wasn't as convincing as the one I'd given against Dukakis, or whether Frustaci had improved on his, I received no standing ovation this time. The vote was close. The final count showed that King had also won the second endorsement.

And in the general election he won the governorship.

King invited me to a private meeting at the Statehouse just a few days before he was to take the oath of office. I arrived on time for the early evening appointment and was directed by a police officer to a dark stairwell. After trying to feel my way down like a blind man, I finally lit my cigarette lighter. Only then was I able to make it to the bottom. There I found myself in a long, darkened corridor, barely illuminated by a lighted doorway at the far end.

The Governor-elect had been assigned a dreary office in the further reaches of the basement. King sat inside, alone, at the head of a long table, shirtsleeves rolled up and tie undone. The environment hadn't dampened his spirits.

After shaking hands I asked him, "Well, Ed, how does it feel to know that you're about to be Governor?"

He leaned back in his chair, swung his feet up on the table and replied, "Mike, it feels great. I feel like I'm ready to serve and carry out my campaign promises."

For a few moments we made small talk and touched on Walpole and my union work. Then he surprised me by asking with a smile, "So tell me, Mike, what do you want?" The inflection made it clear that he was asking what sort of reward I wanted for my services.

I had made the appointment as a courtesy call, one friend meeting another to offer congratulations. I intended asking how he specifically planned to address the Walpole problem and to implement some of his promises concerning the union. But I had no thought of asking for any personal favors.

"I don't want anything, Ed," I replied, "as long as I have the open door policy you promised. I want to be able to call you when I have a problem."

He looked puzzled. "You've already got that, no problem. But what do *you* want?"

Before thinking further I rattled off, "Gee, Ed, I don't want anything. I'm just trying to get the best for my guys. You know, open up their career paths for them; make Walpole safe—"

Suddenly the words backed up in my throat. As he sat there silently measuring me, I realized that he was offering me a job. This man, this friend, who was about to be sworn in as Governor of Massachusetts, was offering me a position. The gesture so overwhelmed me that I was unable to respond immediately.

Fortunately he gave me a few moments to gather my wits. Here was my chance to outflank the wall that Frank Hall had placed in my path.

"On second thought, Ed, since you mention it, there is something I would like. I'd love to be Department Spokesman. I think it's clear I know how to speak publicly and present policy. I'd love to work my way into a top job by speaking for the Department of Corrections. I'd have only one problem. I couldn't work under Frank Hall. He has to go."

As King paused to make a note, I could almost hear his wheels clicking. He said, "I've been told Hall's a pretty good guy. He's well liked around here."

"I don't know who likes him," I replied, "but I know the guards don't. The guy's done a lot of damage. If I'm going to join the Department of Corrections, Frank must go."

King sat there silently. Sensing an opportunity might be slipping away, I tried again.

"Ed, if it's a problem making me Department Spokesman, I've had this dream of someday being Superintendent at Walpole."

His eyebrows rose. "Fred Butterworth has some pretty strong backing. Everyone seems to like him too."

I almost choked. "Everyone likes Fred Butterworth and Frank Hall? Ed, how can you say that? Who's everybody? We guards don't like either of them! They've gotten a lot of people hurt!" I paused a moment to calm down.

"Look, Ed, I'd like to be Superintendent at Walpole, but if I can't be for now, I can work towards it. In the meantime, Department Spokesman would be fine. But Hall has to go."

King would not commit himself any further than to say he'd give it some thought. But I sensed something in his expression that told me my words had made an impact. As I rose to leave he made me promise that as long as his door remained open, no guard strikes would take place at Walpole. I told him if his door remained open we should have no need to strike. With that we parted, promising to keep in touch.

I left the Statehouse that night feeling like a moron. I should have anticipated that he might be prepared to offer me something. I should have gone to the appointment having outlined a full program for the Corrections Department. I should have asked to be Superintendent at Walpole or an Associate Commissioner with some authority under a Commissioner who knew what he was doing.

Department Spokesman? What an asinine choice! The position had no authority. Besides, who in his right mind would want to be a mouthpiece for someone they violently disagreed with?

Obviously those months of campaigning had still not taught me the subtleties of politics. By asking King, I could've easily had a position under Hall in the Department. Instead I risked sacrificing that leverage by demanding Hall's ouster.

On the morning of January 4, 1979, for the first time in four years, Michael Dukakis walked down the steps of the Statehouse as a common citizen. Reporters gathered around. One asked, "Governor, now that your term is over, do you feel a sense of failure in any areas?"

"Two," he replied, pain in his eyes. "Children's Services, and Walpole."

That evening Karen and I attended King's inaugural. Twice I formally shook the new Governor's hand and felt on top of the world.

In the following two weeks I appeared on two major television shows. Everywhere I turned I received positive response. The confidence it generated carried into the prison; I began to take an even stronger stance on safety issues. This angered the inmates more than ever but I didn't care. I felt I had momentum and I wanted to make full use of it.

Then, within two weeks after King's inauguration, I achieved one of the biggest goals I had set for myself as president. Ironically I was sitting in my living room quietly watching an evening newscast when I learned of it.

The announcer said, "Today the Governor's office announced that Frank Hall has resigned as Commissioner of Corrections. No reason was given for the resignation. Hall has held his position for the past six years and has been popular. His sudden decision took Statehouse insiders by surprise. Hall's assistant, Larry Meacham, has been named Interim Commissioner."

My first inclination was to do a jig, but the announcement of Meacham's appointment watered down my enthusiasm. I respected him even less than Hall.

The next day I called King and told him, "I'm gratified to hear of the Hall resignation, but under no circumstances will we accept Larry Meacham as permanent Commissioner. Interim, okay, but find somebody soon, please."

King assured me the appointment would officially last only forty-five days. By that time he expected to find a permanent replacement. He also carefully avoided any reference to the reason behind Hall's resignation.

Nevertheless, I could only feel that I had been the major factor in Hall's removal. Hall had no job awaiting him. And King had no one to replace him with. If everyone else liked Hall, as King had claimed, the only reason for Hall to leave would have been to placate me. I later heard inside word that King had not invited Hall to stay on.

That still left Fred Butterworth at Walpole, but I didn't expect anything to happen with him until a permanent Commissioner was appointed. I could wait, knowing that with the Governor behind me, Butterworth could not foil me much longer.

My path crossed Dukakis's three or four times in the next year. He had taken a teaching job and made guest speaking appearances at luncheons I attended. Since I held no grudges, I tried approaching him to shake hands. He seemed to feel uncomfortable doing so and would usually manage to avoid me without appearing rude. Then, to my complete astonishment, in his talks he'd address segments directly toward me.

Usually the luncheons had union overtones, so his subject frequently touched on union/management relations. At the first one of these I attended he spent several minutes describing how he had alienated unions during his governorship. Then he looked directly at me and said, "Don't you agree, Mike, that it would have been much better had I occasionally attended your safety meetings personally and showed you that I was indeed concerned about your issues?" I could only nod in response, stunned.

During those early weeks of 1979 all sorts of opportunities were thrust upon me. One day I received an unexpected call from Richard Young of Northeastern University, Dean of the evening school programs for law enforcement, corrections, and security. I had previously taken his courses but had not talked to him in over three years. He had since, of course, heard much of me in relation to my union activities.

Now he wanted two things from me. First, he wanted me to sign a contract to teach for him. Second, he wanted me to join the Park Street Corporation, an organization that met weekly to discuss important issues concerning criminal justice.

The membership list of the Park Street Corporation read like a Who's Who of law enforcement and criminal justice in Massachusetts. Included were: Attorney General Bellotti, future U.S. Senator John Kerry, the Commissioner of Corrections, the judges of the Massachusetts Supreme Court, the Chief of the Boston Police Department, and so on. Anybody who was anybody in the field belonged. I looked upon this invitation as a great opportunity both to make important professional contacts and to gain deeper insights into penology.

When I went to my first meeting, I anticipated having some breakfast and being introduced to Dean Young's friends and colleagues. But when I arrived I was startled to learn I had been scheduled as the guest speaker! They wanted me to speak for an hour or more on the situation at Walpole.

In spite of coming unprepared, I found the task easy until halfway through, when District Attorney Delahunt walked in. Delahunt and I had recently tangled over brutality charges he'd filed against several of my guys. He'd put up a tough, dirty fight before a grand jury, but all the officers were finally fully exonerated. Now I found that he too was a member of the Park Street Corporation.

Shaking off the surprise, I continued my talk successfully, filling nearly two hours. The question and answer session afterward proved fruitful in clearing up areas of misunderstanding. The members led me to believe that I had been one of the more dynamic, interesting speakers to appear, and invited me back the following week to report on progress I might have made.

Delahunt attended this second session. Before my talk has progressed very far, he and I exchanged heated words. He apparently exercised clout with the group for I was not invited back again.

After that, my momentum seemed to falter.

Two months after the Hall resignation, I still had no word from King concerning a job in the Department. I still held out hope, because a special investigator from the Statehouse had contacted me. He told me I had cleared an exhaustive check on my background and would be recommended for employment at any level of State Government. Nice words, but why the delay?

Meanwhile, we still had Larry Meacham as Commissioner. This particularly concerned me, because tension in Block Ten had reached crisis proportions. We needed leadership from the Department and access to someone who could make constructive decisions.

I spent a lot of time thinking about these delays. I knew that forces not particularly friendly to me also had King's ear and were aware that he had checked out my background. I specifically remembered the police official who had threatened my life.

I also sensed that my sudden rise had alienated a number of longtime King supporters who saw me sharing the influence they had previously held exclusively. It seemed increasingly difficult to make contact with the Governor. I began to fear that I had enemies around King who were intent on driving a wedge between King and me.

My promotion and getting a new Commissioner could wait, but not the Block Ten situation at Walpole. Considering the number of injuries taking place, two months of inattention was too long. Meacham would never move on his own. He needed a kick from above. It took perseverance, but I finally did get through to King and convinced him to order his Secretary of Human Services, Chick Mahoney, to convene a meeting with me and the Department over the grave situation in Block Ten.

14 A Perfect Ten

Cell Block 10—dark, stinking, dangerous. The walls facing the cells were foully coated with several months' accumulation of food and human wastes. Whether out of blind rage, the urge to damage the prison, or plain insanity, Ten's inmates had themselves hurled this putrid material out through the bars. There it remained to decay and release a noxious stench that penetrated to the farthest corners of the block.

What didn't stick to the walls ended up on the floor, a vast quantity of garbage that sometimes reached ankle depth. Rats and regiments of roaches roamed at will. Instead of trying to exterminate them, some inmates coaxed the vermin into their cells and made pets of them.

It would take a battery of psychologists to explain why human beings would deliberately and thoroughly defile the place where they ate, slept and spent their days. I only know that those were the everyday conditions in the Departmental Segregation Unit, sometimes called DSU—but better known as Block Ten.

The defiant, volatile nature of the Block Ten inmates dictated that they be subjected to a special routine. Normally they were kept locked in their cells twenty-three hours a day. In the remaining hour, guards would escort them either outside to specially constructed exercise cages or to showers at the block's end nearest the corridor.

Regulations stated that they should be let out one at a time, but crowded conditions demanded that this rule be relaxed. Often two inmates would share an exercise cage or pass each other in the corridor—under close escort, of course. It was imperative that officers recognized which inmates hated each other and not allow them out at the same time.

Unlike the population cellblocks, Ten was divided into two separate floors. Each had two tiers of cells built back to back.

Block Tenners couldn't see much from their cells. The only windows sat high on the opposite wall. They could look up and down their corridor only by holding a hand mirror out through the bars.

Since they couldn't see each other, they eased their isolation by carrying on loud conversations that reverberated off the concrete walls. Some were friendly; others carried threats of murder. Dozens of radios and TVs blared constantly. Typewriters clicked relentlessly as inmates wrote books or appeals on their cases.

A spine-tingling scream occasionally cut through this din. The screams came from inmates who could no longer handle being penned up in this purgatory. If one of them was too far gone, he was escorted to a blue room and held there until transportation could be arranged to Bridgewater State Hospital. In many ways, Block Ten had more in common with a 19th century insane asylum than with a contemporary prison.

There were, however, two major differences: Most of its fifty-eight residents retained their twisted rationality. And most of them were armed.

Although administered by Walpole's Superintendent, Block Ten remained under the direct supervision of the Commissioner of Corrections. Thus, Meacham in Boston, not Butterworth at Walpole, set the rules here. This policy existed because the block had been set aside to house incorrigibles from the entire system, not just Walpole.

As I mentioned earlier, the circumstances facing these men were not as miserable as they might have seemed. DSU status still allowed them the same possessions as the inmates in Population. Add to this increased physical safety, twice-a-week showers, better meal service, daily access to telephones, the privilege of visiting the law library whenever they wanted, no restrictions on receiving medication, and no limit on the number of visits—and suddenly their circumstance looked much better.

The last two items in particular made Block Ten especially attractive. Many inmates sought to space out as a means of handling their miserable situations. A place where they could receive medication virtually at their own discretion must have looked like the Garden of Eden. Management felt it was worth the risk of turning them into addicts if drugs would help keep them under control. The guards strongly felt that it only encouraged inmates to commit violent acts that would get them sent to Block Ten.

The Block Ten visiting program provided another powerful incentive. Ten had its own two visiting rooms. They each accommodated two inmates and their visitors at the same time. Originally both inmates were supposed to sit on one side of a table; their visitors on the other. A screen extending from tabletop to ceiling separated them. An officer kept watch. Then, typical of Walpole, the policy relaxed. Inmates suddenly began entertaining their visitors on the same side of the table.

I heard about the consequences secondhand, since Block Ten officers worked isolated from the rest of us and always handled DSU trouble by themselves.

One night Officer Dick Kline related to me over a beer after work:

"Mike, no matter how many times I see it, I'll never understand how any man can bang his wife right in front of someone else."

"You've seen that in Ten-block too?"

"Every goddamn day. Hell, we've got ourselves a conjugal visit program even though it's not supposed to be allowed in Walpole. Today three female visitors show up at the same time. The inmates involved were Frazier, Vance, and Smith. Smith has his mother; Frazier his girlfriend; Vance his wife. You know Smith—we don't want him near the others. So we give him and his mother one visiting room to themselves. We put the other two couples together and I have to watch them. Naturally, each couple sits on the same side of the screen . . ."

I interrupted. "How long has that been going on, Dick? What the hell is the screen for?"

"It just started happening some months back. The inmates started bitching and, like in everything else, got their way."

Kline took a deep pull on his beer. "So anyway, I'm standing there, observing for awhile and everything's fine. They're hugging and petting, but nothing heavy. Then I get called outside. That constantly happens. We're shorthanded just like you guys, so we often have to leave visits by themselves and go take care of something else. When I get back, there's Frazier with his old lady on the table, banging away."

"What about Vance and his wife?"

"They're sitting there three feet away, trying to act like nothing's happening. But his wife is wasted. She's so damn red in the face I thought she would have a stroke. And Vance, he's pissed, but he can't confront Frazier with his wife there."

I shook my head. "It's beyond me how a state institution can create a situation where immoral behavior like that can take place."

"I gave up trying to figure that out," Kline said. "But there's the question of what Vance is going to do about it. He's not in Ten because he's a choirboy. I'm betting the first chance he gets he's going to stick Frazier—just another case where leniency leads to violence."

I nodded. "No wonder drugs are getting into Ten. With contact visits like that, there's no way to stop visitors from passing the stuff."

"Tell me about it. And it's going to get worse." He smiled grimly. "Used to take a little ingenuity for them to get the stuff. Give you an example. One day I'm walking around the outside of the building doing a routine check. I round the corner on the A-3 side and spot an inmate knelt down beneath our windows. He spots me and takes off. I yell, but after a few steps let him go. When I look over at where he'd been, I see this tin can being slowly reeled in by a string through one of the broken windows. I run over, grab the thing and yank it free. It's loaded with Talwin. Suddenly from inside, Frazier starts screaming, threatening to kill whoever 'stole his stuff.' When I identify myself he still doesn't stop. Says it doesn't matter that I'm a guard, he'll still kill me."

Kline's story was typical. The situation in Ten got worse. Eventually even the screen came down, removing all possibility of controlling contact during visits. Naturally, drugs began freely flowing in, special delivery.

Drugs and women—and all inmates had to do to get them was stab someone. Of course, once in Ten they had to continue acting violently or face being replaced by someone from Population who also wanted in on "conjugal" visits and unlimited drugs.

The around-the-clock Block Ten nightmare was supervised by twenty-five guards, divided into the usual three shifts. These officers considered themselves the prison's elite—hand-picked for the "Commissioner's Block." The honor was a dubious one. Block Ten offered the most degrading and dangerous duty at Walpole.

The guards, wearing heavy, calf-length raincoats made their counts and fed the prisoners. The raincoats shielded their uniforms from the urine, feces, food, and boiling water thrown at them. They also gave some protection against stabbings; the heavy rubber was difficult to penetrate with a shank or a sharpened TV antenna.

To make things worse, the officers had to operate in appalling lighting conditions. A Block Ten steward, Terry Erskine, finally brought up the problem at a union meeting.

"Mike, we've got a miserable lighting situation in Ten. It's so bad that when an officer makes his rounds at night you can't see him from the lobby once he moves ten feet or so down the corridor."

"Ten feet! Is it breakage?"

"Mostly. We have 160 fixtures in there, but only about ten per cent work. We're down to fifteen or twenty working bulbs."

"In the entire building?"

"It's nothing new, man. Lighting's been that way for as long as I've been there. Lights get busted, but they don't seem to get fixed."

"Terry, why haven't you made an issue of this before? I've been fighting the safety issue for almost two years now, but you guys in Ten have always turned a deaf ear."

"I know, man, but you know them. They like to take care of things themselves."

"Yeah, I know," I replied bitterly. "And where has it gotten them? We've had thirty-seven inmate-inflicted guard injuries in Ten during the last four months alone!"

Erskine shrugged disconsolately. "I know."

I persisted. "I've been trying to make Ten a major union safety issue, but at every meeting you guys stonewall me. You tell me to lay off, it's your business. I'll get the inmates mad and make them worse. Hell, that's management's line!"

We stared at each other for an instant before I went on, "How much worse can the inmates get? You guys are too caught up in acting macho, and I'm fed up with it. This isn't just your problem. Every time one of you gets hurt management pulls a Population officer to replace him. Eventually we all face duty in Ten."

"Well," Erskine replied, "I think the guys are finally ready to listen. Hell, we're all tired of running a gauntlet every night to make our counts. The corridors are only five feet wide and every one of those bastards is armed."

"Are you saying your guys will support me if I make Ten an issue?"

"I can't guarantee it, but let me talk to them. They are coming around."

I calmed down. "All right, at least let's address the lighting problem. What have you done so far?"

"I've talked to Larker. He says maintenance will get to it when they can."

"Same old crap. Next time put it in writing and copy me in. That might inspire Larker to act."

During the next three months Erskine wrote Larker six memos asking for the lights to be fixed. Terry handed me a copy of the seventh one day as I stood in the main corridor.

He explained, "I just saw Larker and handed him this memo. When he saw it he screamed at me, 'Those fuckin' lights were fixed!' "

"Were they?"

"Would I be writing this if they were? When I told Larker they were still out he said the inmates must have already busted the new ones. Hey man, we're not idiots. No one in Ten has seen lights put in." He threw up his arms, turned, and walked toward the Block Ten grille.

I watched him go, reflecting that in the past seven months the toll had risen to seventy-six guards seriously injured by inmates in Block Ten. Thirty-nine of these injuries had been inflicted since the first of the year—in less than three months!

Larker's attitude typified the response of management. It saw the situation as tolerable. After all, these were the most vicious criminals incarcerated in Massachusetts. What else could you expect from them? Besides, the officers working Ten weren't complaining. Why should I?

Considering its function, the Department of Corrections was sending strange signals to ruthless criminals, many of whom would someday walk the streets as free men—perhaps in their neighborhoods.

As the number of guard injuries in Block Ten continued to mount, I continued struggling against the majority of my members to build the situation into an issue. Even Population officers were inclined to lay off Block Ten. They figured we had enough issues to address in the rest of the prison without stirring up a beehive over the DSU.

Initially their resistance limited me to background dog work. I filed Block Ten grievances on behalf of the union as a whole, since the individual guards from Block Ten would not come to me and file. These grievances addressed such things as the poor lighting, the broken windows, and the lack of thorough visitor searches.

The violence against guards in Ten by itself generated a huge amount of paperwork that I worked on with a growing sense of outrage. I could almost experience the acts themselves from the graphic reports. One hit particularly hard.

One night Officer Augie Kafka donned his raincoat and let himself into the upper right corridor to make his count. It was after midnight. He immediately switched on his flashlight since only two ceiling bulbs were operating and these illuminated only a few feet of the 120 foot long corridor. As he worked his way along, the only sounds were the low murmur of a TV, his feet swishing through the garbage, and an occasional snore.

He turned his light upon each individual inmate, looking for skin and some indication that they were still breathing. As he continued on he found each man on his bunk, even the guy watching TV. Then he got to cell #14, the second to the last. The bunk was empty.

Suddenly, out of the corner of his eye, he saw something move. An instant later he felt a heavy blow to his side followed by searing pain. He managed to train his flashlight and saw inmate Frazier reaching out through the bars with a broomstick. Its sharpened end now dripped blood—Kafka's!

Already weakened by the blow, Kafka managed to stumble backward against the far security door, cringing there, barely out of reach of the deadly broom. An incensed Frazier kept reaching out as far as he could, jabbing away, trying to inflict more wounds. All the while he continued mumbling curses under his breath, trying to further terrorize Kafka without alerting other officers.

Badly injured, Kafka managed to cry out weakly. He would have tried to crawl out had the way not led past Frazier's cell. All he could do was cower against the wall, trying to fend off the spear, hoping his feeble cries would be heard down at the far end before he bled to death.

Fortunately an alert officer heard him and came to the rescue. Kafka survived and eventually returned to work. And Frazier? He was punished—sort of. They took away his possessions and exercise time—for a while.

Seventy-six of these reports, many just as shocking, landed in my lap in that seven-month period. The total complement of Block Ten officers numbered twenty-five. This was an annual casualty rate that exceeded five hundred percent! It meant that each officer, had he been able to remain on the job for a full year, would suffer five serious injuries! To any thinking person, these figures would have been intolerable. But no one would act until I finally used my influence with Governor King to set up a March 21 meeting with his Human Services Secretary, Chick Mahoney.

We met in the Commissioner's office in Boston with the usual cast of characters from the Department and Council 93. I took the floor first.

"Gentlemen," I began, "Until now I have not made Block Ten a major union issue. But my membership can no longer ignore the fact that seventy-six of us have been injured by inmate attack in the last seven months.

"Many of these injuries could have been avoided if just a few simple precautions had been taken. We want to push for these precautions now to prevent further injuries.

"At this point I'm not talking about anything major. First, lighting. We need lightbulbs replaced. As of now, over ninety per cent of the bulbs are broken. At night our men do their rounds virtually in the dark. It's difficult to even see an attack coming under those conditions.

"Second, we want the broken windows replaced. The broken windows encourage the passage of drugs from the outside. Drug-addicted inmates become extremely violent when their supply is interdicted. We've had officers attacked because they've intercepted tin cans filled with drugs that were being pulled in by fish line through broken windows. Fixing those windows would prevent officers from being placed in that position.

"Third, we want management to look into the possibility of installing a master antenna system. All TV sets now use rabbit ear antennas that can easily be removed and sharpened into shanks. With a master system we could remove the rabbit ears and eliminate a major source of weapons—"

I went on to describe other weapon sources and suggested a major shakedown and equipment inspection to locate weapons now in existence.

Meacham proceeded to calmly take a position I had heard many times before. "Obviously Officer McLaughlin does not have to concern himself with the Corrections Department's budget.

"Fixing lighting and windows, and installing an antenna system would take capital expenditure and additional manpower because the maintenance budget is already strained.

"As far as capital outlays, an antenna system for the DSU is of low priority when compared to other equipment needed in the prison system."

"Commissioner," I protested, "lightbulbs aren't a capital expense. And in terms of manpower, the officers would be happy to replace the bulbs themselves. But we can't even get those."

"I've been told that the lightbulbs are constantly replaced but inmates just break them again. We'll always have a problem with some lights not working."

"We're talking more than ninety per cent. The officers can't be expected to work in the dark."

"Aren't you exaggerating, Officer McLaughlin?"

"The facts speak for themselves."

What more could I say? The issues had been presented in a few minutes. They were so basic they left nothing to argue.

Mahoney had remained silent, watching all this. Finally he turned to me and said, "Mike, you paint a stark picture of Block Ten. If it's true, we obviously want to take steps to correct the problems. Just what specific steps are called for will take some study. I intend to assign members of my staff to work with the Commissioner's office on this matter. Give us a little time and I assure you we'll straighten the situation out to your satisfaction."

I didn't like something in his tone, but I couldn't quarrel with his proposal. He had committed the Department to action on Block Ten.

"Thank you," I replied. "All of us appreciate your concern and look forward to working with you on cleaning up the DSU."

I left the meeting gratified that I now had progress to report to my membership. I could show the guards that I exercised a degree of control over the issue. At that moment I never dreamed that the Block Ten situation had reached its meltdown point.

The first jolt hit just two days later. Shortly after 3 p.m. I received a call at home from one of my stewards. His excited voice said, "Mike, just after the 3–11 guys took their posts, three more officers were stabbed in Ten-block." He rattled off their names.

I felt like I'd been kicked in the stomach. "How bad are they?"

"They'll be out awhile, but none of the wounds looked too serious."

I breathed a sigh of relief. "Thank God for that. How're the guys taking it?"

"They're pissed, but what can we do?"

"How's Butterworth dealing with it?"

"He hasn't done anything yet, but then it only happened a few minutes ago. You know, I don't get it. The guys were just making their counts and the bastards stuck 'em. What the hell did they gain out of that?"

"Has anything ever made sense in Ten? Don't let it get to you. You'll probably conduct a shakedown in a little while. Do a thorough one."

"We'll get those fuckin' shanks, you can bet on that."

After he hung up it registered on me that we had just sustained guard injuries numbered 77, 78 and 79 in Block Ten.

While upset that three more officers had fallen victim, I restrained my temper, reminding myself that Chick Mahoney needed time to work through the Commissioner and develop a program to solve Ten's problems.

All I wanted at that point was to make sure Butterworth acted promptly and in the spirit of the safety meeting conducted by Mahoney. This meant at the least an immediate shakedown of Block Ten for the weapons used in the latest assaults—certainly a reasonable, commonsense response.

I had already put in a hard day on union business but I nevertheless grabbed my briefcase, gave Karen a weak apology, kissed her, and then hurried to my car. As I drove rapidly to the prison I anticipated supporting Butterworth in the shakedown effort by keeping my guys under control. I didn't want tempers to run wild. The last thing we needed was a charge of guard brutality.

As I turned into the prison driveway a feeling of foreboding descended. Considering the emergency, the lot was strangely empty. After parking, I walked briskly inside. Everything looked routine so I went immediately to the outer control room. Inside was Officer Grove.

"What's happening in Ten-block?" I asked him.

He held out his hands, palms up. "Nothing."

"No shakedown?"

"Nope. Doesn't look like there's going to be one either. The 7–3 shift hung around waiting to take part, but Butterworth sent them home."

Outraged, I spun on my heel and stormed down to Fred's office. I marched right past his secretary through his open door.

"Fred, what's this about no shakedown for Ten-block?"

My sudden appearance startled him, but he quickly recovered. "We'll shake it down in the morning when we have enough officers."

"In the morning? What about the shanks they've got in there

now. Do you expect my guys to walk those corridors when they know the inmates are ready to stab them?"

"I told you, I don't have the officers!"

"You damn well had the officers a little while ago! The 7–3 shift was waiting around to do the shakedown! Why didn't you use them?"

He cast me a defiant look. "I don't have to explain my reasons to you."

I pointed a finger at him. "Fred, on behalf of the union I'm demanding an immediate shakedown of Ten-block. If you don't have enough officers, call back the 7–3 shift. They'll gladly come back in to shake the place down."

"Look, McLaughlin, we're not conducting a shakedown until morning. That's final."

Apparently the meeting with Mahoney had made no impact upon Fred. He preferred ignoring a serious safety hazard over yielding to union pressure. He expected the guards to reestablish normal Block Ten routine even while weapons still wet with their comrades' blood remained in the hands of inmates bent on murder.

I had come to the prison that night with no intention of turning this incident into a confrontation. In fact, I had been prepared to applaud and praise Fred for initiating a prompt shakedown.

This seemed an ideal opportunity for him to demonstrate concern for the officers' safety. Instead he chose to make it clear that he could run the prison any way he wanted.

Faced with Fred's pigheadedness, I immediately called a meeting of my Executive Board. When we convened early that evening, everyone was upset and disappointed. All of us had thought we'd made real progress at the previous Wednesday's meeting. Now during the first subsequent safety crisis we found the Superintendent still stubbornly defying what we felt were reasonable requests. During the meeting I got a call from Terry Erskine in Block Ten.

"Mike, what should we do? With three guys out because of stab wounds we're really shorthanded here. Everybody knows the bastards have shanks and are itching to use them again. The goddamn lights still aren't fixed. If we walk down the corridors now, no telling what might happen. Yet we can't just disobey orders. We're supposed to do our jobs."

"Terry, until we resolve the issue of a shakedown, stay away from the inmates. Don't feed them. Don't give them medication. Don't make counts. Don't walk the corridors. No more contact with the inmates in Ten-block."

"The bastards will start climbing the walls."

"They can kill themselves for all I care. My primary concern is that no more guards get injured."

Erskine passed along my instructions and the Block Ten officers obeyed. Within minutes Fred Butterworth heard about it and called.

"McLaughlin, you have no right to tell them that! I'm going to start suspending people!"

"Go ahead and suspend them," I told him. "They're not going near the inmates until the block is shaken down. You're not putting any more guards in the hospital tonight."

Butterworth called Boston. Within a few hours Randy Deegan and Mike Fair arrived from the Commissioner's office. Rather than back down, Fred had called for heavy reinforcements. He obviously intended to force a full-fledged confrontation rather than budge one inch.

I wasn't happy to see Deegan. He was in his last week as Deputy Commissioner, about to move into a prominent job in Civil Service. He had nothing to lose by slugging it out with us. I considered Fair a more reasonable guy, but he wouldn't be calling the shots.

The Executive Board and I concurred that if management intended putting up such a tremendous fight over a basic procedure like a shakedown, the time had come to throw the entire Block Ten issue on the table.

No longer would we be satisfied with a routine shakedown—a quick sifting through an inmate's possessions for easily identifiable weapons. We'd demand the complete inspection of all possessions from which weapons were regularly made. This would also allow us to perform a thorough sweep for drugs. To properly carry this out we needed to remove everything from the cells so that all containers, appliances, and machines could be taken apart and thoroughly searched. Only after we had determined that an item was contraband-free would we return it.

Our attitude had become, enough is enough. Let's do the shakedown properly or not at all.

Early that evening we went into talks with Deegan, Butterworth and Larker in the Superintendent's office. From the outset, Deegan demanded, "Block Ten officers must resume their full duties at once."

I replied, "No. The next time officers approach DSU inmates will be to perform a major shakedown."

"McLaughlin, even you admit there are always weapons in Block Ten. Because of the type of inmate housed there a guard always faces extra danger. They know that when they take the assignment. They don't face any more danger tonight than they usually do."

"If that's true then you make my point for me. Officers shouldn't work that block at any time until it's cleaned up."

Deegan wouldn't budge. "No shakedown until morning."

He did stop short of ordering the guards into the corridors, and this concession kept us talking. Had he issued that order, we would have refused to obey. This would have forced him to suspend people on the spot, thus triggering a major walkout. At this point no one wanted a strike.

When the 11–7 shift arrived I took aside those that worked Block Ten and repeated my orders.

"Don't go near the inmates. I don't care what they do to the cellblock or to themselves." Locked in as they were, they couldn't harm each other.

It was well past midnight when Deegan adjourned the meeting. He still stood firm. "A shakedown will proceed tomorrow at 8 a.m. It will be conducted my way. That means a routine search for shanks only. Officers will leave everything else alone. Any officer refusing to participate will be suspended."

Deegan's words did not intimidate us. The guys were not afraid to strike. I felt confident that I still had the Governor behind me, and that if I asked him to attend a meeting personally, he would try to be there.

Shortly after 2 a.m. I decided that circumstances demanded I call King on his private number in spite of the hour. I had an apology all prepared, but the voice that answered abruptly made apologizing unnecessary.

"I'm sorry, but Governor King is attending a special conference in Washington."

I felt a thud in my stomach. Now I knew why Randy Deegan felt so powerful. He thought he had me cut off from King.

Just how deeply did this conspiracy run? Did I have any other allies in the government who would help me reach King? I first tried Chick Mahoney.

"Chick, we've got a mess at Walpole. We've had three more guards stabbed in Block Ten, but still the Department won't allow us to conduct a thorough shakedown. My guys are mad. I don't know how much longer I can control them. I think it's going to take the Governor's word to break the stalemate. I need his number in Washington."

"Mike I can appreciate your situation, but I'm not authorized to give out his number. He's asked not to be disturbed. I'll be glad to give the Governor a message in the morning."

"Chick, maybe you don't understand. The Governor promised that I could call him when I had a serious problem. He doesn't want any strikes at Walpole. I promised there wouldn't be any. But now I need his help. If we don't resolve this thing by 8 a.m. tomorrow, I very likely will be forced into a job action I don't want. If that happens I will have broken my promise to King. I don't want that."

"Mike, I'd like to help you but I can't. I promise to give him your message in the morning as soon as I can."

I sensed he was putting me off, so I tried two more cabinet members, both of whom told me to call someone else. Then I called the Secretary of Public Safety.

"I'm not going to call King for you," he declared. "You got yourself into this mess, let's see you get yourself out. Just remember, I'll be ready with the State Police for anything you want to try in the morning."

"This told me that further calls to government officials would be fruitless. They had all allied themselves against me in spite of us working together to get King elected. I now suspected that they intended using the Block Ten incident to force me to strike and thereby destroy my relationship with King.

My last hope was to randomly call hotels in Washington. I tried this for nearly an hour before finally giving up at 4 a.m. More than twenty-four hours had passed since I'd slept, but a solution to the crisis—and getting some rest—seemed as far away as ever.

At 8 a.m. Management ordered a routine shakedown of Block Ten. I promptly defied them with a counterorder. Within minutes the entire prison started to rumble with gossip and rumors.

For the next few hours I went from meeting to meeting with different groups of officers, keeping them posted. Throughout, we maintained absolute unity. Not a single officer agreed to participate in the sham shakedown. We presented such a solid front that management didn't dare carry out its threat and suspend anyone.

The remainder of Saturday was consumed by meetings in Boston between the Union and the Office of Employee Relations. In the meantime no shakedown occurred and the Block Ten inmates still weren't fed or given their medications. I wasn't too concerned. If they hadn't thrown it all at the guards, the inmates should have an ample supply of canned food. And I was sure they also had enough spare drugs hidden in their cells to sustain the especially needy.

The meetings with the OER ended without agreement. Ira Cobb told us, "You've got until 8 a.m. Sunday morning to conduct a shakedown as per Randy Deegan's instructions. If you don't comply I'll authorize the Department to bring in the State Police to do your jobs for you. If that happens, you'll see firings instead of suspensions."

By Sunday morning I was suffering from extreme exhaustion. I had gone forty-eight hours without sleep and still saw no prospects for rest.

Yet I felt inspired. The guys remained unified behind me. As I walked through the corridor officers offered words of encouragement, shook my hand, and patted me on the back. Some with thirty years service told me, "Enough's enough. We've got to bring this thing to a head sometime. Might as well be now."

These guys, many of them close to retirement, had a lot on the line, starting with their pensions. I really felt concerned for them, because I wasn't sure we could win. Our cause was righteous, but virtually everyone in government seemed to be mobilized against us.

We had one last meeting in Butterworth's office before the nine o'clock deadline. Neither side budged. Randy Deegan stated, very cockily: "This is the way it's going to be. I'm not going to court to fight the inmates in front of television cameras over a silly issue like you're presenting."

Seventy-nine guard injuries in one block within a seven month period—that was silly to him? Maybe because it wasn't his blood, his pain, his life that had been, and would be, at risk.

I tried reasoning with him one last time. "Randy, give us the tools to do the job. If we take the TVs and radios and a judge later orders us to give them back, no problem. But in the meantime we'll have Ten-block cleaned up."

Wasted breath. It didn't matter anyway. My plea had come too late. No sooner had the meeting concluded than I got a call from one of the men working Block Ten.

"Mike, Officer Bill Esposito has just been injured by an inmate."

My stomach heaved. "How the hell did that happen? You guys were supposed to stay away from those bastards!"

"Well, the inmates hadn't been fed in thirty-six hours. We decided it'd be okay to give 'em breakfast. Esposito was pouring coffee for one of them when the fucker threw some chemical shit in his face. Now he can't see. His eyes look like hell. I think it's real serious."

"Goddammit, I told you guys to stay out of the corridors!"

"We shoulda listened to you, man. I'm sorry."

I quickly regained control of myself. "All right, it's happened. Let's just make sure we get fast medical treatment for Esposito."

"He's on his way to the medic right now."

I hung up and tried to gather my thoughts. What now?

It couldn't have been more than ten minutes later when I phoned into the Minimum Section to see how the officers there had reacted. I was surprised when Assistant Deputy Tinker answered.

"Stanley, what are you doing picking up this line?"

"You tell me. You called the strike. Everybody gave me their keys and walked out."

His words struck me speechless. The guys had walked out on their own?

I hung up the phone wondering how extensive this action was. No one had exited through the administration building. If they had walked out it could only be through the vehicle trap at the side of the prison.

I hurried out front and looked to the left along the prison wall. Sure enough, moments later they came marching around the corner in four lines like a military unit—the entire shift of eighty-two officers including those from Block Ten. The sight sent chills of admiration through me.

I hadn't wanted the strike to commence without some sort of official declaration, but I couldn't worry about that now. As I took charge of setting up the picket lines, I kept thinking about my no-strike promise to Governor King.

How could I explain the circumstances to him before others poisoned his mind against me? Governor King was the only influential friend I'd made in government and now, however unintentionally, I had broken my word to him.

I never saw a more aroused, aggressive group of guys on a picket line. The officers were so angry that if members of management had approached them, I believe a punch-out would have resulted. Events had me upset too, especially the Esposito injury, but I didn't really snap until he was brought back from the hospital.

His face looked a mess. Bandages covered one eye. The other, watering and bloodshot, had nearly swollen shut. The prognosis wasn't good—he might partially lose his sight. Eye injuries always sickened me.

When I saw a TV camera crew boring in on Esposito, I blew my top. I shouted abuse at the cameramen, then blasted the two officers who had brought Esposito back. Control was rapidly slipping away and physical exhaustion stood in the way of me restoring it.

At that point a mature woman onlooker foolishly asked me, "What happened, did his eye get scratched with a fingernail?"

I couldn't even pass off that harmless question.

"You fucking slut!" I shouted. "That man may be blind the rest of his fucking life!"

The woman stared at me, dumfounded. I didn't apologize then, but I hope she reads these lines and will accept my apology now. I was totally out of line to call her that.

Suddenly I felt rotten. I had insulted a harmless woman. I had broken my vow never to use foul language in public. I was slipping over the edge. The mind-numbing fatigue brought on by fifty hours of continuous confrontation without sleep had finally caught up with me.

To regain my composure I left the picket line and walked down the highway several hundred yards. Finding a small piece of seclusion between the parked cars, I broke down.

As I bent over crying uncontrollably, thinking I was out of sight, I suddenly felt a hand on my shoulder. I glanced up to find Steve Adair bending over me.

"Mike," he said, "get it together. The TV cameras are filming you. We need you to keep up your image for us."

His words were like cold water in my face. Embarrassed, I took a deep breath, wiped my eyes, and returned to the picket line, ready to do battle.

During the next hours I received some encouragement. Media exposure had defined the issues and swung the people to our side. They were outraged to hear that inmates controlled Walpole. Those driving by the prison saluted us with their horns and waved to show that they sympathized. In addition, word of our dilemma spread through the Department of Corrections and a contingent of twenty guards from MCI Concord arrived to lend support.

Meanwhile, management had not sat still. At 4 p.m. a deputy sheriff served me with a temporary court injunction ordering us back to work. He also handed me an order to appear before the Suffolk Superior Court at noon the next day.

I planned to make the court appearance, but my men ignored the injunction. No one left the picket line.

Shortly after, another deputy sheriff arrived. Someone directed him to me and, as he approached, the Concord guards dropped in behind.

"Mike McLaughlin?" he asked.

"That's right."

"I have a warrant here for your arrest from the Norfolk County District Attorney." He showed me the document.

All the guards began grumbling. I didn't know what to say. I couldn't very well resist arrest.

Then, before the deputy could take me into custody, the Concord guards surrounded me, forming a barrier with their bodies. Their spokesman stepped before the deputy.

"If I were you I'd leave now. We're not going to stand by and let you arrest him. If you do, we'll spread this strike and disrupt the traffic flow into and out of Dedham Center" (where I would've been arrigned).

This threatened to bring enormous confusion to a major metropolitan area and generate even more publicity for our cause. The bewildered deputy left and did not return.

Throughout Sunday afternoon and late into Sunday evening I attended a series of meetings with the Office of Employee Relations and the Department of Corrections. We met on the same spacious floor where a half-dozen conference rooms sat side-by-side. In one, all the familiar faces had gathered. Cobb of the OER; Meacham, Deegan, Fair, Butterworth, and Larker from Corrections. Chick Mahoney sat in to represent the governor's office. Spataro and Frustaci had arrived to counsel me and my Executive Board. Each faction had a supporting cast of minor characters. So important was the issue, and the possible sanctions that could result, that the presidents from all Department of Corrections facilities also attended.

Before entering that first meeting I decided to call Karen to tell her she should not expect me home that evening. When I did not find her home I called my parents to have them pass the message on to her later. Just hearing the friendly voice of my mother choked me up.

She knew me well and could sense when I was hurt or in trouble. She had also seen the news and knew we were on strike again.

I could hear her shout, "Bernie! Mike's crying! Pick up the phone!"

With both parents now on the phone, I lost all composure and the tears flowed freely.

"Do you want us to come down?" she entreated, a hint of panic in her own voice.

"No way!" I insisted.

Since a child I had avoided any behavior that might make me look like a "momma's boy." No way would I allow her to "come to my rescue" now, during my biggest test.

As all the players of both sides walked past the phone booth, I sensed that those whose views I represented were seeing my softer side for the first time. This I didn't mind. What did concern me was that management people were also seeing this vulnerable side of me. I feared that they might take this as encouragement to hit me even harder in the meetings.

One more time I gathered my composure. I hung up the phone, took a deep breath, reaffirmed my determination, and willed myself to be strong for the guys. I entered the meeting room with renewed purpose ready for all consequences. I would not let my local down. We were right. Therefore, whatever I had to do, I could feel at peace with myself.

The Department made it clear from the opening gavel that they did not intend to compromise. "Corrections Officers do not have the right to decide prison policy."

"We're not trying to determine prison policy," I countered. "We're trying to get management to abide by the regulations in the union contract, specifically those concerning safety. The DSU does not meet the description 'safe, clean, wholesome surrounding,' as stated in the contract. How could any reasonable person argue that it is, when eighty officers have been seriously injured there in the past seven months alone?"

Meacham responded, "Officers have accepted assignment to the DSU on a voluntary basis. They know what they face when they take the job. We're not saying that the DSU is what we'd like it to be, but we must be realistic. There we deal with the most difficult inmates in the state. There's bound to be some violence."

"Some violence? Eighty injuries in seven months?"

"That's far too many, I know, but what you want us to do would only increase the violence. Decisions concerning the DSU need to be made by qualified penologists."

"We've been waiting years for these people to make them. Obviously they haven't made the right ones. The Walpole officers know what needs to be done. We don't want to meddle in making prison policy. All we want is to be able to work in reasonably safe conditions. These can easily be brought about by implementing the various points I am about to present. If you refuse us, do not expect us to return to work."

Everyone knew I faced a court appearance the next day. I could see from their arrogant looks that management fully expected the judge to break the back of the strike.

And so I started presenting my issues. The first concerned classifying DSU inmates. We wanted to isolate the worst of the worst on the lower floor, allowing those upstairs more privileges. Those downstairs would lose virtually everything. It would be restored only after they showed improvement in their behavior over a period of time. At that point they'd be moved upstairs to the more privileged area.

Management would not discuss this with us openly. They immediately called for the first of what was to be many caucuses. As the night proceeded I brought up issues such as lighting, panic buttons, removal of electronic equipment for thorough inspection, confiscation of rabbit ear antennas, and so on.

They wouldn't talk about more than one or two of the issues without calling for one of these private powwows. Then they'd stroll out of the room with the allegedly impartial Cobb and Mahoney in tow. Each caucus would drag out for more than an hour. Then they'd return with the same old story:

"We can't give you that. Let's get on to the next issue."

In the meantime our guys had sat there figuring the meeting would resume in ten or fifteen minutes. After all, we were working guys who punched a clock. Time meant something to us.

Even during meal breaks we'd send out for food, hoping to expedite the resumption of the talks. Management refused to follow our example. They went out to eat every time, and didn't limit their meals to an hour. Considering the gravity of the situation, this didn't seem right. It only added to our frustration and resentment.

Sunday had been rough, but I faced an even more hectic schedule on Monday. The talks broke off after midnight and resumed early the next morning. At 10:30 a.m. I managed to break away from the OER meeting to attend a Public Service Committee hearing at the Statehouse. This was a combined conference of the Massachusetts legislature, attended by both state senators and representatives.

I particularly wanted to attend this conference because I'd been invited to speak upon the bill in question. It proposed to remove the Department of Corrections from the Human Services Department and place it under the Department of Public Safety. This would change the focus of Corrections from treatment to security orientation, something the union and I wanted badly.

When my turn to speak came, the frustration of the past two days heavily salted my words. I delivered a graphic, impassioned description of the guards' predicament.

I described the daily terror we faced, the actual guard injuries, personal tragedies caused by the withholding of IA monies during convalescence, and the absence of any opportunity for job advancement. By the time I finished, the eyes of many panel members had turned moist. Depression had settled over the room. Clearly everyone now favored the bill's passage.

Then, just as I concluded, the phone rang. A clerk passed it to the panel's chairman, who listened to the brief message and said, "I understand."

Upon hanging up the receiver he announced, "The Governor has suggested that this bill ought not to pass. We will, therefore, allow it to go into study."

This action effectively killed the bill. Everything I had just said no longer had pertinence because the bill would not be up for vote for some time—if ever.

I knew that King had returned from Washington just a few hours before. When reporters had asked him if he knew about the Walpole strike he replied, "I heard." Then he angrily stalked away.

This told me that I had indeed seriously damaged our friendship, but I never dreamed that he would allow the incident to alter his stance on Corrections. He had always favored tougher security in prisons. He had also supported passage of this bill. Abandoning it now could only be his way of telling me, "I was willing to give you my support before you broke your no-strike commitment to me—now you can fend for yourself."

I felt a dull ache in the pit of my stomach. King had cast us out on our own; my job no longer had meaning. Without the governor's support my avenue into management had again closed. Sure, I'd stick it out as union president through this crisis. I'd fight management to the end, because I owed it to my members. But I didn't see any way to win.

Reaching down deep inside, I tapped into my old stubborness. I resolved to go down fighting. They could fire me, throw me in jail—

whatever. But I would not back down. We had made our demands. Either they'd be met or I wouldn't agree to go back to work.

Before going to court I had a few minutes to meet with Chick Mahoney and Governor King's chief secretary. The latter told me.

"The Governor refuses to get involved in the Walpole guards' strike. He expects you to deal directly with Corrections and Human Services."

"The Corrections people are the ones who've caused our safety problems. How can we resolve anything talking to them?" I turned to Mahoney. "You're the Secretary of Human Services. Can't we talk to you?"

Jaw set, he shook his head from side to side. "Not about your demands, until you return to work."

"The issues are clear," I said. "We're not going back to work until you talk to us."

End of meeting.

I didn't have time to sulk about it. Spataro and I rushed out of the building and hurried the half-block to the Suffolk County Courthouse. I had been here numerous times escorting inmates. Now suddenly the old colonial brick structure no longer looked friendly. I was convinced I had no way to avoid the wrath of the judge and felt certain I'd be in jail that afternoon and subject to the ten-thousand-dollars-a-day fine levied upon union members who struck against the Commonwealth.

In the lobby dozens of reporters had gathered. They now pressed forward, flashbulbs popping, microphones extended, seeking my comments. I had to ignore them for I'd barely arrived in time. We rushed into the courtroom to take our places.

On previous occasions I'd admired the rustic oak wall paneling and the long colonial windows decked out in blinds. This day the courtroom looked like any other I'd seen, including those in movies—cold, sterile, forbidding. Even the elderly judge with his white hair contrasted against his dark robe, reminded me of so many others I'd seen.

I could read nothing in the judge's expression. He stated concisely the question before the court—whether we had defied the injunction issued yesterday. Joe Spataro had accompanied members of my E-Board and me, and he proceeded to give a dissertation in defense of the action we had taken. The judge abruptly stopped him.

"Mr. Spataro, the Court recognizes that there are serious problems at Walpole. Guards are being injured. They certainly appear to have reason to be concerned for their safety. We sympathize with them. But their safety is not the issue before this court. The only issue before this court—the only one I can examine—is whether or not employees of the Commonwealth are on strike. Is your union on strike or is it not on strike?"

The direct question caught Spataro at a loss for words. Telling the truth would certainly incriminate us. I stood there, just plain scared. No one had to tell me what going to jail would be like.

After a tense, silent moment the judge, sensing our dilemma, turned to the attorneys representing the OER. "Do you have any evidence that Commonwealth employees are on strike at Walpole?"

They replied confidently, "Indeed we do. We have newspaper accounts and video tapes, your Honor. It's been all over the news for the past two days that the Walpole guards are on strike."

I could see no defense against that but, like the Lone Ranger, the judge came to our rescue.

"I can't take newspaper accounts or video tapes as evidence. What other evidence do you have?"

"Well, Your Honor, we don't have anything else except these photos from the newspapers showing the guards walking a picket line."

The judge shot a hard look at them. "Do your homework. Produce incontrovertible evidence that the union is on strike or don't take up my time. You have until 10 a.m. tomorrow to do that or I'll throw the case out of court."

I felt like a lamb who had just slipped out of the lion's jaws. Of all people, the judge had helped us. We'd found a friend we'd never expected. This turn of events injected me with a badly needed dose of optimism.

Outside the courtoom Spataro pulled me aside. "You heard the judge, right?"

"I sure did."

"You know what to do?"

"Consider it done."

I hurried to my car, drove straight to Walpole, and ordered the picket line dissolved. I told the men to go home and play sick. Now let the OER prove we were on strike.

That skirmish won, we went back to meetings with the OER in Boston. These dragged into the wee hours without result. Management kept its heels dug in expecting us to crack.

Ironically, late during the last meeting of the day Cobb admitted to me in front of everyone: "Mike, in my estimation, everything you've presented here is both right, and good correctional policy.

"But its implementation is a management prerogative. As long as management refused to budge I have to stand behind them. Article Twenty does not apply here. I suggest you give in to keep yourself out of jail. You may be right, but you're going to lose."

Cobb's statement made Meacham flush. Yet he still managed to maintain his smug look, as if he still felt certain the Department would finally win one against me.

As we were leaving OER headquarters, Spataro continued to counsel me. On Tuesday morning we would have one last OER meeting, then a hearing before the State Labor Relations Board, before our scheduled return to court.

Spataro told me, "Tomorrow bring every document on safety you've got. Then take the floor at the Labor Relations Board and make as long a presentation as you can. I might just get the judge to delay the court hearing if he knows we're still talking to the LRB."

If he wanted a show I could give him one. I could talk at length on every one of the eight attacks on Block Ten officers. But if this weak play was all we had left, what were our chances of winning?

When morning finally came I kissed Karen goodby for God only knew how long. In my mind I figured I had three stops to make: first the meeting with the OER where our demands would be rejected for the final time; second, a stop before the Labor Relations Board where I would present our safety concerns—probably fruitlessly; and third, an appearance in court where I would be sentenced for contempt and hauled off to jail. It promised to be quite a day.

I carried with me a large suitcase holding some fifty pounds of papers. People who recognized me from my TV appearances probably thought I was fleeing town or was already on my way to jail.

After parking in a nearby garage, I began the ten minute walk up Beacon Hill toward the Statehouse. All along the way, people honked their horns at me and yelled out encouragement. Even with jail facing me, I felt I had achieved the most important goal of all. I had informed the public of Walpole's troubles and aroused their concern. We might lose the battle, but I felt confident of winning the war.

I'd been told the Department of Corrections had prepared the elephant pens at the Boston Garden for us. Generally used only when the circus came to town, these enclosures were now to become our

Walpole. Officers from the Suffolk House of Correction had already been assigned to stand guard over us. Of all the sick ironies.

As the crucial meeting assembled in that same conference room at OER headquarters, I noticed that Council 93 looked defeated and my E-Board very worried. 93's people faced fines. My E-Board might be sent to jail with me, as might guards from across the state if they carried out their threat to expand the strike in response to my jailing. At that moment I didn't feel particularly inclined to carry on a filibuster.

Then the opposition's key figures walked in. When I saw a wide smile plastered on Cobb's face I angrily directed my eyes down at the table.

"Good morning," he began. "I hope you all had a good night's rest."

Say what you have to say, I thought, but spare me this bullshit. Get it over with and let's move on. I'm ready to see the judge and take the consequences.

When Cobb finally got down to business, I almost choked on his first words. "Gentlemen, I'm pleased to inform you that you've won. Every issue you've presented over this table in the past three days has been agreed to, one hundred percent."

I felt like I'd been hit with a sucker punch. "What do you mean we've won?" I asked. "What have we won?" I began naming issues.

Cobb waved a hand. "You've won them all—every issue you've presented here. A document is being draw up now and will be signed by the governor's office, Commissioner Meacham, and you, Mike, as union president. It will have teeth and will guarantee you redress if there's any breakdown in the future."

When I glanced at Meacham I knew I had heard correctly. I saw no smile on his face, only discouragement and defeat.

Still hardly believing this sudden turn of events, I said as evenly as I could, "Thank you. We'll look at the document when it's ready and go from there."

After management left the room I turned to my guys. Some of them had started mumbling that I'd sold out.

"Hey," I said, "We all heard Ira Cobb say we'll have a document before us in a few minutes. Hold your accusations until we look at it. You owe me that much."

When we received the document, the realization finally hit that we had indeed won. All the issues I had advanced over the past seven months were listed.

Inmates were to be classified by tier, the better behaved placed on the upper tiers and given more privileges.

Panic buttons would be installed. Lighting would be improved. TVs and radios of all inmates would be inspected.

A master antenna system would be installed to eliminte the individual antennas so often turned into weapons. Unruly behavior would be punished by loss of TV and radio. TVs on the lower tiers would be suspended outside the cells, beyond the inmates' reach.

Contact visits would end and a new plexiglass screen would be installed to separate inmates from visitors. Only one inmate would be allowed out of a cell at a time, and he would be handcuffed and escorted by two officers.

Upon returning to work, the officers would conduct a thorough shakedown of Block Ten. Other items clarified those main points.

The document consisted of two simple typewritten pages. To me it looked better than Leonardo da Vinci's Mona Lisa. At last Ten-block would be safety oriented.

While I rushed off to organize a union meeting, Spataro headed for court to get a continuance. That afternoon the membership greeted me and my E-Board with cheers, then unanimously ratified the agreement in time for the 3–11 shift to return to work.

I was standing in the administration building lobby watching them file into the prison when Randy Deegan came up and offered me his hand. I just glared at him. I don't think the guy had ever even seen an inmate before last year. I had no use for him.

"I'm not going to shake your hand," I told him. "I don't like you. You didn't have to put us on strike. You nearly caused all these guys to lose their jobs—and what would you have gained?" Then I turned and walked out to a news conference set up on the front steps.

Thinking about it later I realized that Governor King had intervened. Everybody, including his closest advisers, had stonewalled us. The one person who had expressed empathy with us was Ira Cobb.

Under ordinary circumstances Cobb probably would've taken a hard line position against the inmates and supported the guards. I sensed this from the sympathetic slant of his questioning and his curious stares at the Corrections people when they took issue with the simplest of safety measures. Reflecting on what must have happened, I suspect he went to the governor to break the stalemate.

The day after the settlement, the shakedown of Block Ten began. I had managed to get some rest and was back on the day shift. By afternoon I found time to wander down to see how the exercise was going. Officer Dick Kline greeted me warmly at the Block Ten grille then ushered me inside. We walked past the guard station and stopped at the head of the corridor that led along the lower right tier.

The shakedown had already progressed about three quarters of the way down. The officers dealt with two cells at a time. They shackled the resident inmates with both wrist and leg irons, then held them in the visiting rooms where two guards were posted.

All the officers still worked in their raincoats since we could never disarm the inmates of their sputum, urine and feces. Even in the face of this wet barrage, the officers enjoyed the shakedown, savoring their great victory.

As could be expected in Block Ten, the inmates yelled threats and obscenities. All of them were pressing forward against their grille doors, many reaching through making obscene gestures. At this stage the flipoff, never a very sharp weapon, was immensely pathetic—as though some degenerate con's raised middle finger could mean anything to us now.

They had lost everything. Even pictures were taken off their walls and packed in boxes to be shipped home. Had I not known what led to this action I might have felt sorry for them.

Standing at the far end of the block, overseeing the shakedown in his own raincoat, was Andrew Larker. When he caught sight of me, he called, "Hey, McLaughlin, c'mere."

The last thing I wanted to do was walk down that corridor. The inmates were already raving like madmen. They hadn't seen me since the settlement. They would certainly blame me for everything, and use this opportunity to express themselves.

I'd spend the last five days battling management. Just when I thought I'd won and could relax, did I have to be exposed to a barrage of recycled potatoes and beans? In all my time at Walpole I'd only been pissed on once. Never had I been hit with anything solid, whether eaten first or not. Was it going to happen now? I wasn't even wearing a raincoat—no small consideration at a time like this. I wasn't eager to wear what they'd throw.

Dick Kline sensed my apprehension and said, "C'mon, Mac. I've got to go down there anyway."

In another example of how my fellow officers tried to protect me, Kline escorted me along the line of cells, placing himself nearest the inmates and shielding me with his body. As it turned out, this wasn't necessary.

Strangely, as each inmate caught sight of me, he abruptly stopped his antics and backed away to the rear of the cell. From there he stared at me with expressionless eyes, motionless and silent, until I passed out of view. All except one displayed this same curious reaction.

The exception, Peter DiLauro, occupied the fifth cell. True to form, Peter reached through the bars like King Kong, trying to grab me.

"You punk bastard motherfucker," he roared. "You had no right to do this to us! I'll kill you! If I get my hands on you I'll tear your throat out!"

Ignoring Peter, I continued down the corridor until I stood face to face with Larker.

"What did you want to see me about, Andrew?"

"Nothing," he answered with a smartass grin. "Just wanted to see if you had the balls to come down here."

I gave him a sour look. "Satisfied? Come on, Dick, let's get out of here."

Kline and I started back, and, as before, all the inmates except DiLauro remained silently at the rear of their cells. Peter continued bellowing threats and curses, using considerably more vehemence than originality, all the while straining through the bars to grab me. Apparently he had no more concept of the futility of trying to get at me than would a caged animal.

I stopped in front of his cell and looked straight into his rage-distorted face. The bars holding him back suddenly looked flimsy; Peter appeared strong enough to tear them apart.

"Why did you do this?" he screamed. "Why? You didn't have to take everything! We're people! We gotta have something!"

"No, Peter," I told him calmly, carefully staying just out of reach of his meathook hands. "You don't deserve anything. Behave yourself. Work your way out of Ten-block. That's how the system is meant to be."

When I returned to the head of the corridor, Fred Butterworth was waiting. Looking worried and resigned, he said in a low, defeated voice, "Mac, do me a favor and stay out of Ten-block for a while. Let it calm down. There's too much heat in here right now."

"Fred," I replied, "Andrew called me down there."

"Yeah, Mac, I know he did. But stay out of Ten-block for the time being."

I only entered Block Ten one more time during my service at

Walpole. A few days after the shakedown I looked in to inspect the place. I remained standing alone at the end of the corridor staring down one of the lower tiers. For once the inmates were quiet.

I'd made no sound but suddenly an arm reached out of a cell three-quarters of the way down. A small hand-mirror faced in my direction.

A moment later I recognized the voice of an inmate named O'Dea. An Irish kid from Boston, he based his claim to toughness on being able to chew glass and make his mouth bleed. He had killed another inmate and thus ended up here, although he had never admitted the crime.

"Hey, McLaughlin. You took our TVs. You took our radios. You took our typewriters. You took everything. Nothin' else you can take from us now. We're gonna kill a screw."

I heaved a big sigh and shook my head. These guys never gave up, never learned.

"You're wrong O'Dea. You got one thing we didn't take—your life. Be happy about that." Then I walked out.

I proved Fred Butterworth wrong about something too. He anticipated a lot of heat in Ten, but on the contrary, my reforms stood the test of time. After the carnage of the previous seven months, the entire following year passed without a single serious inmate-caused injury in the DSU.

15 A Man Called Peter

The Block Ten settlement represented a major crossroads for me. I had never intended to stay on at Walpole as an officer. My relationship with King had promised to lead me into higher management. After the strike, however, I couldn't be sure where I stood.

I knew King respected my abilities. Otherwise he would not have run the extensive background check on me. He had also mentioned to certain of my friends after the strike how much I had impressed him. This gave me hope that the breach between us could somehow be mended.

If all failed with King, I did have one attractive option. The election for Sheriff of Middlesex County was scheduled to occur in 1980. Politics had always interested me and with my corrections background and my newly-won prominence in the media, I stood a decent chance of winning.

I definitely needed to effect some change in my career. My position as union president generated a great deal of work without providing remuneration. I still remained a common corrections officer, facing the same dangers at the same low pay scale. I had neglected domestic goals that Karen and I had set together.

In addition, the danger I faced had increased. After seeing what I'd accomplished in Block Ten the inmates showed increased hostility toward me. Stark evidence of this was finding my address and phone number spray painted on all the block walls.

And yet, I still had trouble committing myself to leaving Walpole. I had never been one to abandon a job only partially finished. We had won in Block Ten, yes, but the remainder of the prison continued to slip. The Department of Corrections seemed to have girded itself to resist us on every level. Larry Meacham remained on as Commissioner and Butterworth looked as deeply entrenched as ever.

At the same time District Attorney Delahunt kept nipping at our heels like an angry hound. His next scheme directed against us entailed injecting observers into the prison to monitor inmates and officers. Naturally these "objective observers" would be chosen from an inmate advocate group he had selected.

What more can one say about that? Who did the guy represent, the people of Norfolk County, or those who had committed crimes against them? I managed to get the proposal shot down on the state level.

Shortly afterwards, I had another collision with Butterworth. This time the circumstances involved an escape—the only time while I worked there that an inmate got away from inside the prison.

Butterworth's investigation claimed that Billy Freeman had hid himself in a false compartment built secretly by inmates in the trunk of the Protestant chaplain's car. The car received regular maintenance in the auto shop.

The chaplain had no idea the inmates had tampered with his car. He unwittingly drove Freeman undetected through the vehicle trap to freedom. Procedure demanded that all vehicles be searched thoroughly before leaving the prison, so Butterworth blamed the guards for the escape.

When I talked to the officer responsible he told me, "Mike, I thoroughly searched the Reverend's car. I know all about false compartments. I'm certain there were none in that car when I searched it."

"Then how did he get out?"

"You know Freeman. Maybe he just walked out."

If it had been another inmate, the suggestion would have been absurd. But everyone knew that Billy Freeman had a talent that could have provided him the means of escape.

Freeman had gained a reputation as a convincing female impersonator. Word had it that when dressed up, he could look downright foxy. He only needed the clothing and makeup, and I knew several female counselors close enough to inmates to bring him what he requested. He may have convinced them that he wanted the items for a party or variety show.

At twenty-two, Freeman was the innocent-looking type that women consider cute. This usually made them overlook the fact that he was doing 25–35 for an armed robbery that involved opening fire on a crowd in suburban Boston with a machine gun.

After the escape I demanded a shakedown and thorough search to help substantiate either Butterworth's explanation or my hypothesis. Need I say it? Butterworth refused. Shakedowns disrupted prison routine.

Later, on the front steps of the prison, I met with newsmen covering the story. "A dangerous felon has escaped and still the Superintendent refuses to order a shakedown, lockup, or thorough search. Who is to say that other inmates might not take the same route out? Unfortunately, here the inmates' feelings always come first. Security always comes second. For that reason we are calling for the removal of Fred Butterworth."

My demand made the newspapers. But I didn't get Fred's resignation, or the shakedown, or any concessions toward straightening out the rest of the prison.

The only thing I got from the Freeman escape was hassle. Freeman had threatened to kill me several times, so the Arlington police had to spend more time with Karen.

And inside the prison the inmates taunted me. "Big bad Mike McLaughlin is gonna get his from some beautiful broad he stops to flirt with on the street."

Again, I took the threat seriously, and for months kept a close eye on unfamiliar attractive ladies approaching me. The police didn't catch Freeman for seven years.

All attempts to mend relations with King failed. Whatever his reason, he would not see me. The avenue into corrections remained as closed to me as ever. That left me with my aspiration to become sheriff. The election lay a year in the future. Since I saw many reforms to work toward at Walpole, and the guys still wanted me, in June 1979 I stood unopposed for my third term as president.

A month later Walpole blew up on Butterworth and almost blew me away too.

Sunday, July 29th, began as a beautiful morning. Rain was in the forecast for later in the day, but, as I drove into the prison's parking lot, I could only think enviously of Karen enjoying the day at our beach cottage.

My assignment that day, the Visitors' Room, suited me fine. Being the weekend we'd be busy, but I'd have the opportunity to spend time outdoors and could avoid the tension that built in the block areas on hot days. My days of seeking the most hazardous assignments were behind me.

I'd been assigned to work with C.O. Ron Zachary under Senior Officer Vern Warstler.

At about 11 a.m. two female visitors arrived to see inmate Curt Javery in Block Nine. After they signed in, I instructed them to proceed along a designated walkway to Block Nine's exercise yard.

Because I knew the lock on the B-9 yard gate didn't work, I emphasized that they should wait outside until an officer came to escort them to the B-9 visiting room. The gate's lock had been broken for two months and, typically, despite our repeated requests, management hadn't seen to its fixing.

Being Maximum Protective Custody made Block Nine an especially sensitive area. To allow visitors to wander around in the B-9 yard without supervision would have been a serious breach in security.

I'd no sooner phoned Block Nine to announce the arrival of the ladies when I saw them open the gate and enter the yard. One of them, Javery's mother, had visited Walpole many times and certainly knew the authority inherent in an officer's instructions. She'd simply decided to do what she wanted.

"Vern," I commented, "the Javery visitors just entered the Block Nine yard without an escort. Shouldn't we do something about it?"

"Did you instruct them to wait at the gate for an escort?" Warstler asked.

"Sure did."

Warstler immediately picked up the phone and called Wayne Northrup, the officer in charge of Block Nine.

"Wayne, terminate the Javery visit. Send those ladies back here at once."

Within moments we watched the ladies retrace their steps. On the way the inmates shouted down to them from the open windows. "Hey, where ya goin'?"

The ladies called back, "The screws have kicked us out. I guess they don't want us to see you."

They reentered the visitors' room complaining loudly.

"Hey what is this? We drove over an hour through the heat to get here. Now you throw us out."

Warstler replied, "Officer McLaughlin told you to wait by the gate. You didn't listen. You broke the rules, so you lose the privilege of this visit. If you want you can come back for the afternoon session."

They left in a huff, still bitching loudly.

By one o'clock I'd almost forgotten the Javery incident. I had just stepped back into the yard after escorting visitors to the A-6 visiting room when I heard Block Nine's solid yard door slam shut. Any door slamming in Walpole meant trouble.

I saw one of the new officers running toward Nine's door; so I dashed along the chainlink fence separating A-6 from Block Nine and entered the yard the same way the visitors had. When I reached him he was still pounding on the locked door seeking entrance.

"What's going on?" I asked.

"I can't get back in. I was preparing the yard for recreation period when somebody locked me out."

Moments later several other officers arrived. I sent one to the control room to secure a spare key. Just as he started off, a voice boomed from a second tier window above us.

"Stay the fuck away, McLaughlin. We've got your four screws. You try breaking in, we'll chop off a head and throw it out to you."

Immediate recogniton sent my stomach tumbling. I looked up to see Peter DiLauro's enraged face staring down at me.

Just three weeks before, DiLauro had been transferred here from Block Ten. What in hell had prompted Butterworth to authorize such a transfer I couldn't begin to imagine. DiLauro had been petitioning for months to get out of Block Ten, but I'd heard that the Commissioner's office had denied him. Now here he was.

Naturally I remembered the shakedown after the Block Ten strike, when Peter had threatened to tear me limb from limb.

Block Nine had been set aside for inmates who needed protection from people like DiLauro. He'd just spent over two years in Block Ten and deserved every minute of it. Transferring him here to Block Nine amounted to lodging a wolf in the henhouse.

When I thought of the hostages I remembered that Peter had been awaiting execution for killing a police officer at the time the state's capital punishment law got struck down. I also remembered the medics he'd taken hostage some years back. He had now served sixteen years of a life term.

"All right, Peter," I said. "Don't go off half-cocked and do things you'll regret."

"You screws are gonna be doin' the regrettin' unless we get what we want. We're ready to die if we have to."

I could hear the inmates yelling at each other and ordering the officers into cells. Threats spilled out the window. "Screws are gonna bleed! Screws are gonna die!"

Supervisor Ben Randall and Vern Warstler arrived. I quickly filled them in while DiLauro, soon joined by inmate Rudy Palmero, continued to stare down at us. Randall immediately took charge.

"What do you want, Peter?"

"Ben, get Butterworth and Larker over here right away or we're gonna kill these motherfuckers."

"All right, but before I do anything, I want to know the condition of my men."

"Northrup is cut over the eye," Palmero said. "The others are okay."

"I want to see Northrup. Bring him to the window."

"You're not giving the orders now!" Palmero shouted. "We're in charge—"

"Shut up and bring Northrup," DiLauro growled, nodding toward the interior of the block.

Within seconds they shoved Northrup's face against a window grate where the glass had been broken. We could see blood over his right eye and around his mouth.

He'd obviously been roughed up more than Palmero wanted to let on. We later learned that in the process of being taken, he'd been hit over the head with a chair, beaten with a broom handle, and punched on the jaw.

"You all right, Wayne?" Randall called up.

"My head and chest hurt, but I'm okay, Ben. Everybody's all right so far. They've got us locked up in a cell." He gulped down a breath. "They've got shanks, Ben. They mean business. Give 'em what they want and get us the hell out of here."

These words had barely escaped his mouth when Palmero yanked him away from the window. We heard the cell door slam shut, presumably locking Northrup up again.

"All right, Peter," Randall called up. "We'll try to reach Butterworth and Larker. They're not in the prison so it'll take a little time."

"Don't give me any shit, Randall, or we'll kill these fuckers for sure."

"Nobody's giving you any shit. You want Butterworth and Larker here, we'll get them here. Just give us a little time."

"That's not all we want. We've got other demands."

During this conversation Assistant Deputy Tinker reached the scene. Tinker had consistently shown himself to be a yes-man who wouldn't go to the bathroom without checking with Butterworth; so I wasn't too happy to have him poke his nose into the proceedings.

"Why don't you put together a list, Peter?" Tinker suggested. "It might save time if we had one in our hands when the Superintendent arrives."

This seemed to make sense to DiLauro. He left the window and we could hear him calling his confederates together. A few minutes later the slow clicking of a typewriter could be heard from the otherwise silent second floor. Yes-man or not, Tinker had bought us fifteen, maybe twenty, precious minutes.

So far the situation had been handled intelligently. But I still felt on edge. The decisive moment for some really tough decisions was racing at us, and I had no confidence in Tinker's ability to make them in time. Randall knew what to do but had to defer to Tinker. I had to defer to them both, but I held a trump card.

As president of the union, I had a big say when my members were in jeopardy. Good old Article Twenty. No one could order me away now.

For the time being I contented myself with standing by and observing. It certainly wouldn't help to bicker among ourselves. If the inmates picked up any conflict in our ranks, they would feel stronger and might increase their demands.

Finally the typewritten list floated down to the grass. I managed to get a glimpse of it over Tinker's shoulder. As I'd suspected, the major concern was not the handling of the Javery visitors, but rather the planned inmate transfer from Block Nine to Block Four.

A stupid rumor had been circulated by counselors in the past few weeks claiming that Block Four in the Max Section would be used to house overflow Protective Custody Inmates. In its present configuration, Block Four offered no special security to any inmate. Any Protective Custody Inmates placed there now would have a short life expectancy.

The rumor was just another example of counselors stirring up trouble over nothing. Management had discussed using Block Four for P.C. Inmates as a contingency plan for the future when B-9 and A-6 began to overflow. At that time Block Four would be evacuated of population inmates before P.C. inmates were moved in. As foolish as they sometimes acted, I knew management would never allow P.C. inmates to face exposure to those in population.

Ironically, DiLauro had listed this as their first concern when for months he had been writing letters from Block Ten to Butterworth demanding transfer back to population. He, of all people, had nothing to fear there. If anything, those in Population had good reason to fear him.

Peter's actions didn't fool anybody. We knew he relished violent situations. The cause didn't matter. He probably had felt emasculated during his time in Block Ten. Now he could express himself physically and feel powerful again by leading this insurrection. If in the process he could terrify some screws, great. If he killed a couple, tough shit. What could we do to him, return him to Block Ten? He might hate it there, but the thrill of being a "big man" again, if only for a few hours, might be worth the punishment.

The rest of the list was obviously smoke. Complaints about guard brutality, visiting rights, food, recreation periods, and so on. We constantly saw gripes like these from all areas of the prison. They'd continue even if we turned the place into Caesar's Palace.

Randall wisely didn't comment on the list. Instead he called up a demand of his own.

"Peter, before we do anything with this list we want to send a medic in to check on our men's condition."

"What the fuck for? Northrup told you everybody's all right."

"Yeah, with a shank at his back. We want to make sure for ourselves."

"All right, all right. Send a medic. But try any shit and even he won't be able to help these assholes."

Medical Assistant Ken Tuttle showed real courage by agreeing without hesitation to enter Block Nine. DiLauro had guaranteed Tuttle's safety but that didn't particularly reassure us. I feared we had given them a fifth hostage.

After Tuttle disappeared inside we sweated out the next quarter-hour. To our great relief he finally came out, looking a bit pale but none the worse for his experience. We surrounded and congratulated him, delighted to find ourselves back to just four hostages.

Tuttle reported, "Things inside are pretty much what they said. Northrup is okay, considering he's got a broken nose, a deep cut above one eye, and some bruises. The others haven't been harmed."

"What about weapons?"

"I only saw one shank. But you know those guys. They could have anything hidden in there." Tuttle left us there to maintain our vigil.

As the minutes went by my frustration built. All my training and experience told me we should be taking precautions with the rest of the prison. Also we should have been preparing for aggressive action against Block Nine. Instead we stood there doing nothing, just waiting for Butterworth to show up.

Even the arrival of Associate Superintendent Tom McCoy didn't persuade DiLauro to begin negotiating. Peter brushed off McCoy's overtures and insisted he would only talk to Butterworth. He did ramble on that during the past month he'd sent a dozen letters to Butterworth and Larker concerning the proposed transfer to Block Four, and that none of them had been answered.

I didn't believe this but I decided to jump in.

"Peter," I called up to him, "you never sent me any letters. You know how hard I've been fighting to improve safety conditions for the inmates."

In spite of wanting to kill me, DiLauro did respect my fight for improved safety. He also clearly recognized the hostility between management and the union. I hoped that by putting the union's integrity forward I would win enough of his confidence to open a serious dialogue.

To a limited degree my strategy worked. DiLauro began nodding and agreeing that he should have contacted me concerning the proposed transfer to Block Four. I would have drawn out the conversation had not Fred Butterworth made his appearance. This completely stole Peter's attention.

"It's about time, Butterworth," he shouted. "We got four pigs in here and we're gonna kill 'em unless we get what we want."

Back to square one.

I had to give credit to Fred—he was cool. He ignored DiLauro's threats and went directly to Randall and Tinker. They quickly filled him in on the situation and handed him the list of demands. After briefly perusing it he calmly announced, "I'm going in."

In that instant I saw a side of Fred Butterworth I'd never realized existed. Grudgingly, I found myself filled with sudden admiration.

Those of us who'd been talking to DiLauro tried hard to dissuade Butterworth. We saw him as a potential fifth hostage, one whose position would build the inmates' arrogance and make them even harder to deal with.

Fred wouldn't listen. Whether he didn't grasp the situation or was in the grip of some noble notions about his leadership duties, I can't say. At any rate he remained determined to confront DiLauro face to face.

After sixteen years in Walpole, several spent in Block Ten, DiLauro had to hate Butterworth. If Fred didn't handle himself properly I had little doubt that Peter would first kill him, and then the other hostages.

When Butterworth started toward Block Nine I walked beside him. A crazy notion of my own had suddenly taken hold.

"Fred, if you're going in, I'm going in too."

He frowned at me. "No you're not."

"Those are my men in there. If you're going to negotiate their release I want to be there."

"I'm not going in to negotiate. I'm going in to convince them to call this thing off and release everyone."

"You make it sound easy, Fred. Even so, the safety of my men is at stake. As union president I have a right to be there."

He stopped and stared at me, obviously not wanting to turn this into a big scene.

"All right, but no deals."

I made the decision to go in without pondering the possible consequences. If I'd had time to think I'd like to believe I would've been smart enough to stay out.

As we approached the door, Butterworth called out that he wanted them to let him in. I heard footsteps running down the stairs and excited voices calling out, "Fred's coming!"

Then I heard the barricade sliding aside and my stomach started to churn. Fred stepped in front of me. The door opened and he went in. Then WHAM! Without comment the inmates slammed the door in my face.

I stepped back, stunned by the realization that Fred was on his own. Now he would be the only voice speaking for my men and he always gave the highest priority to maintaining his own prerogatives. Even if he did manage to preserve the hostages' lives, what concessions would he make that would increase our problems dealing with inmates in the future?

Everyone outside went still, listening intently, trying to pick up what was going on inside. We could hear chairs being dragged along the floor and inmates commenting optimistically that now the situation could be brought to a favorable conclusion.

During the ensuing discussion we couldn't make out the words, but from the tone of the voices it seemed that cordiality prevailed for about fifteen minutes. Then suddenly, loud angry voices; chairs pushed away; objects banging against walls. One voice dominated, that of Peter DiLauro.

"You think I'm fuckin' around here? I'll kill one of these cocksuckers right now and throw his head out to your pigs in the yard!"

More sounds of scuffling.

"Take it easy, Peter!" we heard another inmate say.

"Lemme go! I want Varney! That little fucker with his big mouth has it coming!"

I held my breath. If we'd had the Tac Team in position to rush the block we might have done something. Now we were helpless. The life of Mel Varney, a friend of mine, hung in the balance because Tinker hadn't had the guts to make the right decision.

Suddenly the scuffling stopped. I stood there agonizing. Had DiLauro carried out his threat?

A moment later he came to the window, looking distraught and confused.

"McLaughlin, I should've known all along that you were the power at Walpole. I can't get anywhere with Fred. Maybe we better talk."

"We'll talk if you can assure me everyone is all right up there."

"They're all right, goddamn it! I'm not tossing out anybody's head, am I?"

I took that as the best assurance I could get from Peter. While I had no intention of striking any deals with him, I figured if I kept him talking he wouldn't be cutting anybody up.

"Let's get to it then," I said. "Where are we?"

Peter proceeded into a long harangue, running down the entire list of demands all over again. He commented that Fred had refused to discuss anything until the hostages were released. I did not tell him that I totally supported that position. Nor did I remind him that I had no official authority to negotiate as long as the Superintendent was present.

When DiLauro finally ended his tirade, Randall asked to see Butterworth. A moment later Fred came to the window, looking haggard.

Randall asked, "Mr. Butterworth, could you come back down to the yard so we can discuss the situation?"

Fred seemed to have trouble finding words. Finally, in a cracked voice, he revealed that our worst fears had become reality. "Ben, they won't let me out."

DiLauro had made the Superintendent the fifth hostage.

All my other emotions gave way to cold determination. I could see we had played around long enough. Butterworth's gamble had failed. As far as I was concerned, he had taken himself out of the decision-making process, leaving us on our own. We should finally deploy the Tac Team and assault the block at once.

I turned to Stanley Tinker. Knowing he'd never take the initiative, I advised, "Stanley, we've got to terminate all visits and secure the rest of the prison."

He looked startled. "You mean penalize every inmate in the prison because of these few in Block Nine? We can't do that."

"Lock them in their blocks and secure the corridors. That will free up most of the officers to help us here."

"We don't need more officers here. We've got this place secured now."

Obviously Stanley had not even considered assault. It would take courage to order such an extreme measure, a commodity he sorely lacked. I didn't want to usurp Stanley's authority, but I saw him allowing our opportunity to slip away.

DiLauro and the others continued to expose themselves at the windows. By preparing carefully, sharpshooters firing from the roof of A-6 could pick off three or four of the conspirators simultaneously. If we broke in immediately afterwards, the remaining inmates would succumb.

On the other hand, if we did nothing they might kill someone at any time for the slightest reason. Even if Tinker preferred not to attack, it only made sense to be ready with as many men as possible should the inmates ultimately force that alternative upon us.

Another important consideration was the potential powderkeg at our backs. Once the rest of the population got wind of the situation here, the most unstable inmates might see this as a great opportunity to riot. Others might want to create a diversion to help the Block Niners. And some might want to initiate a similar action of their own. If we continued allowing them access to the main corridor, we could face a general uprising, with more hostages taken.

Having pointed all this out to Tinker, I refused to tolerate any more of his indecisiveness.

"Stanley, if you don't give the orders, I will."

My words again startled him. "Y-you can't," he stammered. "I'm in charge here."

"Then give the orders. Otherwise, under the provisions of Article Twenty, I'll order my men to do what must be done."

After fumbling for a answer, Tinker finally said, "You'll answer to Mr. Butterworth for this."

"If we keep messing around, Fred won't be here to be answered to."

Tinker looked embarrassed but also relieved. He turned to Randall, "Go ahead, Ben."

Inside Block Nine the inmates suddenly began shouting demands to see an attorney. They wanted Don Roach, who had a big reputation for representing inmate causes.

I opposed this. Every demand we gave in to only fed their feelings of power. We'd soon have our men in position to attack. I wanted to bust in there the instant we were ready.

To my great disappointment, higher management interfered. We learned that Associate Commissioner Mike Fair had arrived some time before and had taken charge of the crisis. Without informing us, he had been communicating directly with DiLauro by phone from Butterworth's office.

Why Fair had not notified those of us outside Block Nine of his arrival, I can't explain. We conceivably could have initiated actions destructive to his negotiations. We also could have advised him regarding the personalities he was dealing with. Fair had never had any personal contact with DiLauro. Perhaps that was why he allowed Peter an outside line to call his mother.

From the yard we could just make out Peter's end of the conversation. He explained the situation and asked his mother to call Roach, interrupting himself once to make a chilling remark to a fellow inmate.

"Hey man, that's not a shank, that's a fuckin' sword." Then he laughed. Peter DiLauro does not have a pleasant laugh.

The sound of metal being scraped on concrete provided a background to his conversation. We knew what the sound meant. They were making more weapons.

And still we waited.

At one point we heard Butterworth ask DiLauro to let those inmates go who had no part in this. Later we learned that two inmates did leave the tier at that time. To their credit, the other three tiers of inmates also refused to join the uprising. In the next few hours we easily identified those allied with DiLauro.

As the afternoon wore on the sky clouded over and the promised rain began to fall. Many officers had to remain posted outside without shelter. This further taxed their patience.

From time to time Peter would come to the window and banter with me. Once he even said, "Hey, McLaughlin, tell you what. I'll trade all the hostages for you."

Without thinking, I replied, "It's a deal."

This brought loud protests from Peter's companions and he withdrew the offer. They knew how adept I was at defusing tense situations and were afraid I'd manipulate Peter to their disadvantage.

Block Nine would remain quiet for awhile, then suddenly reverberate with shouts. The ninety-plus temperature in the block certainly added to the tension. Several outbursts were sprinkled with threats to "kill screws." With self-control so tenuous, anything seemed capable of triggering a violent outburst. Just seeing Officer Zachary walking across the yard set off DiLauro.

He screamed, "There's the motherfucker whose fault it is! You asshole, Zachary, you son of a bitch. In three weeks you wrote forty-two tickets in Block Ten!"

Just what this had to do with the current situation was anyone's guess. But then none of us ever accused Peter of being logical.

When not yelling at us, the inmates yelled at each other. Convinced they stood on the verge of killing someone, my urge to order an immediate assault grew stronger than ever. Instead, I had to satisfy myself by talking to DiLauro through the window, trying to keep him calm and build some credibility for the union.

The situation really made no sense. I continued communicating with Peter through the window while Fair talked to him separately by phone. Neither of us knew what the other was saying. Fair, of course, did have the authority, but I was at the scene. Four of the hostages were my men. I knew these inmates and had a better understanding of their fragile grip on rationality. Fair should have coordinated with me.

Periodically an inmate would escort Butterworth to a window and hurl more threats. Some of my fellow officers claimed they saw a shank held to Fred's throat.

During these incidents Fred surprised me by talking to me either about the weather, or about sailing, an avocation he knew I had recently taken up. He was acting completely out of character. Due to our adversary relationship, in ordinary circumstances he never engaged me in light conversation. His joking now came across as a laudable attempt to appear calm. His cracking voice, however, revealed the great stress he actually felt.

I couldn't fault him for his fear. A lesser man might have crumbled completely. Fred was standing tall in his toughest hour.

Finally attorney Don Roach arrived. Tom McCoy and I went to the administration building to meet him, then escorted him back to Block Nine, where he was immediately admitted. Then we stood by, straining our ears to pick up the conversation through the sounds of rain and water trickling off the roofs.

Again, much of what we gleaned came from the tone of the conversation. The inmates' enthusiasm at the sight of Roach quickly dissipated and they again began ranting and raving. The exchange became so loud I could make out every word of a crazy conversation.

"You still think I'm bluffing?" DiLauro bellowed. "Gimme that fuckin' sword! I'll cut Varney's arm off and throw it out in the yard!"

A scuffle ensued, chairs sliding about, a cell door banging. Voices tried to calm DiLauro. Then I heard Varney.

"Peter, you hate me and I hate you! But we've got one thing in common—we both hate Fred. Cut *his* fuckin' arm off!"

Butterworth responded, his voice barely recognizable in its higher pitch. "Keep quiet, Mel. Remember who you work for."

"Shut the fuck up!" Varney yelled back. "I don't owe you a goddam thing. Peter, give me the sword and I'll cut his fuckin' arm off myself."

A demented, macabre exchange—yet in that overstressed situation, it struck me as darkly humorous. Varney hadn't lost his acid tongue, even with his life hanging in the balance.

And poor Fred. It was bad enough being surrounded by an angry gang teetering on the brink of carving him up. But now he also faced a seemingly berserk guard inciting the inmates against him. Fortunately Varney had infused such absurdity into the scene that even DiLauro found it comical and stopped talking about cutting off arms.

At 7:30 I received another summons to the administration building. Sensing that something official might be coming down, I had Marty Trent, a member of my E-Board, accompany me. Crossing the lawn between blocks, I couldn't help but feel admiration for my fellow officers. Many of them had been on duty for over twelve hours, the last three or four standing tensely on station in the rain.

One of the sharpshooters who'd just come down from the A-6 roof stopped me and asked: "What're we waiting for, Mike? We've had clear shots at them all day. It's going to be dark soon. Give us a signal and we'll blow the bastards away."

"I'd like to," I said, "but I can't as long as they're still talking. Try to take it easy. Fair must have something to tell me. I should have some answers when I come back from administration."

In Butterworth's office, Fair had been joined by a number of familiar, unfriendly faces, including Senator Jack Backman and Assistant DA Jim Auker.

"Mike," Fair said, "I've just finished hammering out an agreement with DiLauro. Mr. Roach has drawn up a document that Superintendent Butterworth has already approved. The only hitch is that DiLauro considers your signature vital."

"Does the document agree to their demands?"

Fair looked sheepish. "Basically, but there's nothing on there so vital that we can't bend a little, at least for the time being. Freeing the hostages is more important than anything else right now."

"I'll be glad to sign anything that will free the hostages," I told them. "But what happens after? Do these bastards get away with this?"

Auker immediately jumped in and said, "You will definitely be signing this document under duress. Legally it's worthless. You can be sure we'll prosecute."

His words sounded authentic, but I still felt fortunate to have another officer with me as witness.

"Okay," I responded, "where does this signing take place?"

"DiLauro wants you to come up to the second tier lobby of Block Nine," Fair said.

"Now wait a minute, that just sounds like a ploy to take me hostage."

"They don't want you. They just want to get this over with. All of it's going to be filmed for TV. Two cameramen are already here."

"You'd allow two civilians to go into Block Nine at a time like this? What happens if DiLauro or any of the others blow their cool while we're in there?"

I stared at him incredulously. "They've been threatening to kill people all day," I went on. "Aren't you concerned that two civilians might lose their lives?"

"I tell you there's no danger. Just you don't do something crazy. Sign the document and it'll all be over."

I had to smile at Fair's smugness. I wondered how he would've felt had the inmates insisted on him meeting DiLauro face to face inside Block Nine.

"There's only one way I'll do it. I want your promise to immediately send the Tac Team against the block if they try to take me hostage."

"If the Tac Team goes in people will be killed."

"If I'm taken hostage I figure I'm as good as dead anyway."

Fair looked troubled and annoyed. "Look, McLaughlin, if there's trouble we'll do what we have to."

"Hey, that's not good enough! I'm the one who's got to face those maniacs."

Fair threw his arms into the air. "All right," he sighed. "I'll try for a neutral site. Some place where they wouldn't dare try to take you hostage."

"You do that."

I turned and walked out of the office. A terrible sense of foreboding had descended upon me. I had little doubt that in the next few hours this whole thing would come down to me against DiLauro. Time and again management had proven its inability to make prudent decisions when dealing with inmates. I might very well be sacrificed, unwittingly by their incompetence, or purposely to be rid of me.

As I stood out in the lobby by myself, foreboding gave way to melancholy. Suddenly I wanted to see Karen. I ordinarily would never have interrupted her beach day to drag her here, of all places. But I really felt the end might be near.

All the years she had quietly supported me came back. I wanted to see her now to tell her how much I appreciated her. When I reached Karen by phone I tried to keep from frightening her by not elaborating about the crisis.

She responded, "You want me to come to Walpole now, in this rain? Michael, something's very wrong."

"We have a little trouble here. Don't ask me to explain. I'd just like you to be nearby."

After a moment of silence, her voice filled with tension. "I'll leave right away."

I didn't have time to reflect on her coming. An officer rushed up to me outside Butterworth's office.

"Mike, they're blowing their tops in Block Nine again. They say if we don't get the news cameramen inside within five minutes they're going to throw somebody's head out."

Once through the trap I raced for Block Nine. As I burst through the gate into the yard I saw two news camera teams standing in the open filming the block.

My anger rose. The TV cameras should have been kept out of sight until an agreement was reached. Now they were inciting the inmates' impatience.

In the midst of this filming another figure entered the block. The door closed behind him before I could see who it was. A moment later I learned that Al Swain had gone inside.

I couldn't believe it. Was Fair going to turn this into a circus? Officially Swain headed Family and Friends of Prisoners, the Boston-based inmates advocacy group.

I saw Swain as simply a loudmouthed ex-con who had caused us all kinds of trouble by backing any and every inmate cause, no matter how outrageous. His presence inside now might briefly calm the inmates, but over the long run it could only feed their sense of power and encourage them to hold out.

Darkness fell and I circulated among my men, doing my best to keep them calm. Finally, near nine o'clock, Fair and his team came into the A-6 visiting room. One of the group informed me that Karen was waiting in the front lobby. Although I wanted to go to her at once, I didn't dare miss the ensuing discussion here in case they still intended making me a sacrificial lamb. A short time later attorney Roach and ex-con Swain emerged from Block Nine and joined us.

"DiLauro's all set with the document," Roach told us. "One of the inmates will let McLaughlin and the camera guys in through the yard door. The three of them can then follow him up the stairs to the second floor where DiLauro will be waiting."

I didn't know whether to be angry or plain disgusted. Fair had heard me refuse that arrangement in Butterworth's office. Now he stood there looking at me expectantly as if I might have changed my mind.

Before he could say anything I spun around and stormed out of A-6, walking over to where the cameramen were filming. They worked for competitive local stations but had agreed to work as a team, one getting the pictures, the other the sound.

"Look you guys, if he hasn't already, Associate Commissioner Fair is going to ask you to enter Block Nine with me."

I gave them the hardest look I could manage. "You don't want to do it. The inmates holding the hostages are armed and extremely dangerous. They've been threatening to kill people all day. If I go in,

I'll do so knowing that I face the distinct possibility of not coming out alive. I certainly can't protect you or guarantee your safety."

They listened, wide-eyed, and nodded. One of them said, "We'd still like to help. It's a helluva story. Isn't there some way to film this thing without putting our heads in a noose?"

"I don't know. Let's go talk to Fair. Whatever you decide, I'm urging you not to take any chances."

Together we reentered the A-6 visiting room and approached Fair. He spoke before we had a chance.

"Look, I don't know what McLaughlin's been telling you guys, but there's no danger. The inmates just want you to film them signing the document. You can understand their position. It has to be done inside so they have some protection. Right now they have no interest in harming anyone."

One camerman said, "I understand this DiLauro is a convicted killer who's taken hostages before—"

Roach jumped in. "That's ancient history. He's got legitimate grievances now. He overreacted taking hostages, yes, but he's tired of this now. He just wants to get this paper signed and end this thing. You've got to go up there and film the signing or this thing's going to drag out and somebody might get seriously hurt."

I shook my head. "DiLauro has recently threatened to kill me. When he sees me up close nobody in this room can promise that he'll be able to control himself."

The two cameramen looked at each other and nodded in agreement. "We'll follow Officer McLaughlin's advice. We're quite willing to film the signing, but we won't go inside to do it."

Roach and Swain cast me angry stares. Fair simply looked defeated. Finally he turned to Roach.

"What about signing in the Block nine weight room?"

I definitely favored this suggestion. The weight room was located between the Block Nine lobby and the main corridor. There, only one door would separate the Tac Team from the signing.

"I don't think they'll buy it," Roach replied, "but I'll pose it to them."

He and Swain again made the long walk to Nine only to reappear a few minutes later with DiLauro's refusal. Our rejection of their proposal seemed to set them off again because suddenly Javery and Palmero appeared at the window and began yelling down.

"You motherfuckers put screws with guns on the Block Nine roof!

You better get em' off quick or we're gonna kill these fuckers in here!"

This time the inmates were mistaken. We had guns all over the A-6 roof opposite Block Nine but, although we would have loved to put sharpshooters atop Block nine itself, we had no access. Randall went out there to try to convince them of that.

In the meantime another officer approached me with more startling news.

"Mike, hold off on sending in the Tac Team. We don't have spare keys to Block Nine yet."

"Don't—? What the hell is going on? We should've had those keys here within minutes of the takeover."

"I know, I know," he shrugged, trying to keep his voice low. "We took care of everything else but somehow we overlooked that item. I guess everybody assumed someone else was getting them."

A cold chill shot through me. How many times that day had I been close to giving the order to attack? Snipers would have blazed away. Tear gas would have been fired through the second tier's windows. Dozens of officers would have hurled themselves toward Block Nine only to find the doors secured against them. What would the surviving inmates have done to Butterworth and the officers then? Especially if DiLauro was still among the living.

Things continued happening fast. We no sooner convinced the inmates that we had no officers on Block Nine when DiLauro came to the window with more startling news.

"We've got a problem here with your screw Northrup. He says he's got chest pains. Thinks it might be a heart attack. I figure he's bullshitting and just wants to make us sorry for him so we'll let him out. But I'm willing to let a medic take a look at him."

I immediately barged into the conversation. "Peter, you send Northrup out at once!"

"Who the fuck do you think you're ordering around. Northrup ain't goin' nowhere."

"Look, Peter, we've bargained with you in good faith up till now. But if Northrup dies in there because you kept him from getting proper medical attention, it's as bad as murder. Maybe the DA won't prosecute, but you can be sure the guards will remember it that way."

Peter left the window, refusing to give me the satisfaction of verbally acceding to my demand. Nevertheless, a few minutes later Northrup wobbled out the yard door and was quickly rushed to a hospital. That put us back down to four hostages.

With things again reasonably calm I returned to the A-6 visiting room to meet with Fair, Roach and Swain.

Fair asked me, "Would you agree to meet with DiLauro in Block Nine's lower lobby, just inside the yard door?"

I thought about it a second. This was not as good a proposal as the weight room, but it had possibilities.

"I'll agree with certain stipulations. I want a desk or table separating me from the inmates. I want the window in the door leading from the weight room into Block Nine uncovered so an officer can observe. And I want the Block Nine yard door to remain open after I enter."

This time Roach and Swain were amenable. As they headed off to Block Nine to try to convince DiLauro, something told me I should go see Karen now.

When I reached the administration building I found it strangely deserted. No one was in the lobby to control visitors. Not an officer was in sight.

After a brief search I found Karen sitting with, of all people, Johnny Regalado in his Avocation Department office. It seemed ironic that it should be Johnny, a convicted killer, who had made the effort to treat her with the respect and consideration the situation warranted.

I thanked him and led her out to a more private area of the lobby. She looked pale and I thought at first it was because of her concern for me. Before she would even embrace me she revealed it was something else.

"Michael, who is that guy?"

"That's Johnny Regalado. He's an inmate here."

"I know his name and that he's an inmate. What's he doing out here acting like he owns the place?"

"It's a long story. He didn't bother you, did he?"

"Actually, he was very nice," Karen said. "When I got here a cordon of State Police stopped me just outside the prison parking lot. Even after I identified myself they still refused to let me through."

"How'd you get in?" I asked, starting to smile.

"I had to drive down the road and call in here on a pay phone. This Johnny person answered and told me to come back, he'd get me in. Sure enough, when I pulled up at the roadblock he came walking out of the prison all the way to the highway, like he's the mayor or something."

"That sounds like Johnny," I said.

Karen gave me a quizzical look and went on. "He told the State

Police, 'She's okay, that's Mike McLaughlin's wife. Let her through.' And they did. No questions, nothing. It was like God had spoken. I thought for sure he was one of Fred Butterworth's top men so I drove him back and accompanied him to his office."

By now I was laughing. Karen's wide-eyed description had given me a precious opportunity to relieve some of my tension.

She wasn't finished. "So this guy has me sit down and offers to get me coffee and a snack from the vending machines. I might never have found out he was an inmate if I hadn't asked him what he thought of capital punishment."

I whistled. "Why'd you say that?"

"I was nervous, Michael. You made it sound like an emergency, and I wanted to make small talk. Anyway, he said, 'I'm not the guy to ask about capital punishment. I'm here because I killed somebody.' I sort of gave a little strangled gasp and just stared at him for what seemed like ten minutes, but it probably wasn't more than ten seconds."

The picture of Karen innocently asking a convicted Mafia murderer for his views on capital punishment almost had me rolling on the floor.

Smiling at the absurdity of the situation, Karen went on, "Then to calm me he said, 'But don't worry, I don't kill women or kids.' I might've run for the door right then except he started talking about you."

"What did he say?"

"That you're going to be facing some madman who has taken hostages and wants to kill you. Is that true?"

Her question doused the good mood brought by my brief surge of tension-breaking gallows humor. Just seeing her fear in that moment of crisis made me feel like breaking down again.

Here I was, this macho, tough guy who's never been able to tolerate being pushed or abused. I'd been forced to stand idly by for hours, knowing the proper things that should have been done, knowing that people who wanted me removed had forged an agreement that called for me to put my head in the lion's mouth. I again thought of DiLauro reaching out for me through the bars in Block Ten. If anything went wrong, he'd probably get his chance to tear me apart with his bare hands, just as he'd promised.

Finally I hugged and kissed Karen, struggling to express my deep feelings without letting them slip out of control. I had to keep up my image, not so much for her, but for those who depended on me in this crisis. Any signs of my cracking would shake the confidence of others. No telling what would happen then.

I fumbled for words and spoke in a soft voice. "Look I, uh, I'm going to have to go in and face this inmate. He's a pretty bad character. Everything is supposed to be set, but something could always go wrong. I just didn't want that to happen without my telling you how much you mean to me."

She nodded, seemingly having as difficult a time finding words as I. Her composure helped keep my own feelings in check. We just sat there in silence, holding each other. We'd known each other intimately so long that words were not needed.

With lives on the line, I had to limit my time with her. After several minutes I had to leave her there.

I returned to the trap leading back into the prison, where I paused to psyche myself up for the ordeal. By the time the men saw me near A-6, I appeared as steely as ever.

When I checked in with Fair he advised, "It's all set. You meet DiLauro in the lower lobby. He'll have the Superintendent with him. As a gesture of good faith Peter has agreed to a second table between you and him. Roach will sit between the tables and pass the document back and forth so you won't have to get within arm's reach of Peter."

"That suits me fine," I commented. "What about the weight room window and yard door?"

"The window will be uncovered, the door open, just like you asked. The cameramen can film the signing from just outside the door in the yard.

I thought a moment to make sure I'd covered all the details, then finally nodded and looked at Roach and Swain. "We ready?"

Andrew Larker had joined Fair and both of them appeared more nervous than ever. I suddenly realized that their anxiety had shifted away from the inmates. Instead, they feared not having control over me. They had no idea of what I might do. In their eyes I was as crazy and unpredictable as Peter DiLauro, maybe more so. And they knew my men stood solidly behind me.

"Mike," Fair said, "play it cool. Don't do anything that'll result in a negative reaction from the inmates, particularly DiLauro. We're almost at the end of this thing. All it takes is to sign a paper."

Throughout my tenure as president of the union they had never understood me or seen the consistency in my thinking and actions. They couldn't begin to conceive that I might have a methodical plan for handling myself in this situation.

"Gentlemen," I responded, "I appreciate your concern. I'll do what's necessary and avoid trouble. All I want is your word that if the inmates try to take me you'll assault the block and get me out."

Both Fair and Larker stood there at a loss for words. I could see they wouldn't make that promise.

"All right," I finally said. "I'll take care of it myself."

I walked out of the A-6 visiting room into the main corridor where a large contingent of the Tac Team had lined up. Fair and Larker followed close behind me. Raising my voice loud enough for all to hear, I said, "All right, you guys, I'm going in now to sign the agreement. If I yell, don't hesitate. Come and get me. I'll hold them off as long as I can."

Mike Gilmore, one of the Team's leaders replied, "Don't worry, Mike, we're behind you all the way. One word and we'll be all over them."

Fair immediately jumped in. "Now listen! I'm the Associate Commissioner here. You'll do what I tell you!"

Gilmore didn't even look at him. "Get the fuck out of here. He's our president. We'll do what he says."

Fair stared at him, too stunned to speak. Then he turned and walked away.

Relief and gratitude swept me. Here was a career corrections officer telling one of the state's top brass to get lost. The solidarity of the union remained firm. I knew then I could totally concentrate on the role I had to play. At the same time I felt outraged that the Department had refused to stand completely behind me in my moment of greatest risk.

As a parting gesture before starting for Block Nine, I stripped off my uniform shirt. Seeing this, Larker turned pale and asked:

"What are you doing, Mike?"

I tossed the shirt aside and pointed at him. "Since the Department refuses to back me all the way, I don't want to be identified with it when I go in. I'll talk to DiLauro as a representative of my union, not the Department!"

Larker turned even whiter. "Mike, be careful. DiLauro wants to kill you. He's just looking for an excuse."

I glared at him, unable to respond. I almost choked, recalling all the times I'd told him that very thing, only to have him say, "Give Peter an out and he won't attack." Larker's latest remark showed how foolishly inconsistent and ambiguous their treatment of Peter Di-

Lauro had been. I didn't bother asking Larker why they had allowed DiLauro into Block Nine where he could instigate this fiasco.

I found Roach, Swain and the two cameramen waiting and together we started across the yard. Apprehension nearly overwhelmed me during that short walk.

It struck me that Block Nine had been designed as Walpole's death house before a change in state law had forbidden executions. As a result, no one had ever been executed there. Would I be put to death in that building? To fend off other morbid thoughts and bolster my courage, I said a silent prayer.

A short distance from the door DiLauro ordered us to stop in our tracks. His voice transformed me like the first hit in a football game. I had entered the situation and could not turn back. Recognizing that, my anxieties dissolved. I still felt a certain amount of raw physical fear, but this now served to heighten my senses.

Foremost in my mind was the need to exercise psychological control of the situation. The inmates always had a keen sense of this. Whoever established control would determine how this encounter turned out. I knew the inmates thought they held it. I had to show them otherwise as soon as possible.

To my chagrin they struck the first blow. DiLauro ordered Swain to shake me down for weapons before they'd let me inside. I was reluctant to allow it, because I knew it would take away any control I did have. And yet I couldn't allow such a little thing to get in the way of resolving the crisis. I had no choice but to stand there and endure the humiliating search.

"He's clean," Swain called out and started again for the door. I allowed him to get several steps ahead so I'd have a few extra moments to recompose myself. I knew I had to convey an image of fearlessness, so I reached deep inside myself and in those final ten or twelve steps felt a surge of energy. I knew I was as ready as I'd ever be.

Just outside the door I turned and whispered to the cameramen, "If anything goes wrong, drop your equipment and run." When I saw they understood that I was talking life and death, I stepped inside the yard door into Block Nine.

My mind had shifted onto a special level of awareness, like a cornered animal ready to do whatever needed to defend itself. It felt like being in a twilight zone of action and reaction. Even with my mind clear, I knew I'd have no time to reason anything out. I had to trust my instincts.

I paused a moment to survey the setup, attuned to every figure in the room and to their slightest movements. The lightbulbs had been tampered with, leaving the lobby only semi-lit, but I could still see reasonably well. Directly to my right the grille door that accessed the lower right tier of cells appeared secured. The entrances to the guard's office, visiting room, and left tier were far enough across the long room that they posed no immediate threat.

The inmates had arranged the furniture as Roach had promised. Two narrow tables sat parallel to each other, separated by just enough space to fit a chair. There sat Roach. On the far side of one table sat DiLauro and Butterworth. Right behind Fred stood an inmate, who held a shank and looked ready to pounce at the slightest hint of trouble.

Inmate Javery stood against the wall further back in the room. Another inmate poked his head in and out of the stairwell, keeping a line of communication open to the second tier where three guards were still being held. Only a few feet away, inmate Palmero leaned against the wall directly to my right, his hands suspiciously hidden behind his back.

I quickly assessed DiLauro's state of mind. He looked surprisingly calm, almost weary. I had seen enough of Peter to know that this could change in an instant if I challenged him or showed weakness. I had to walk a tightrope, both to keep him calm and to maintain my image for any future dealings I might have with these same inmates.

"Have a seat," DiLauro invited, gesturing toward a chair they had set up for me on this side of the near table.

I glanced at the chair and then kicked it off to the side. "There won't be any need for that, Peter. I came here to take care of business, not to get chummy."

I was not about to sit and thus be on their level. By remaining on my feet I exercised more control and retained much greater mobility.

DiLauro's eyes flared and for a second I thought I saw a tinge of craziness returning. Then it subsided. Suddenly Peter was no longer my greatest threat. Instead I saw Palmero edging along the wall, trying to get behind me. This I couldn't tolerate. I glared at him and gestured toward the far side of the tables.

"Get over there," I ordered.

He stood up straight, arms tensing, a shank clenched in one fist. "Who the fuck you think you're ordering around?"

I raised my voice several decibels louder. "Get the fuck over there!"

We stared at each other. Palmero looked ready to leap at me. I stood there defiantly, hands on hips. Tension hung in the air, thick as jello.

Finally DiLauro spoke in a subdued voice. “Do like he says, Warren.”

Although incensed and on edge, Palmero didn’t have the guts to defy DiLauro. He grudgingly moved to the far side of the table.

I then turned my full attention to DiLauro and Butterworth. I felt like a powerhouse, knowing I’d just wrested the dominant position away from Peter. Instead of supporting Palmero, he had responded meekly, bowing to my demand. His response deflated his henchmen.

I had gambled. Palmero could have attacked anyway. If he’d done so I would’ve called for help. Probably before it arrived someone would have struck Fred. The three remaining hostages upstairs might then also have faced a horrible execution. I’d made my decision instinctively, because I had no time for deep thought. Thank God I’d gotten my message across, silently but powerfully: “You may think you’re in control, but be careful. Don’t get me mad. You may have me, but I’m prepared to die. Are you?”

Whether out of personal respect or an urge to play to the cameras, DiLauro acted very polite with me. With all the melodrama he could pump into his words, he proceeded to explain the inmates’ position all over again.

“Hey, we don’t want to hurt anybody. We’re just concerned that you’re gonna stick us in with people who can kill us—” He continued on and on with other lesser complaints.

I stood there, keeping an eye on everyone, hardly listening. Throughout his little speech I kept politely answering, “Yes, Peter,” or “I agree, Peter.” If he wanted to drag this out for effect, fine with me. I felt I had the situation in hand.

Roach, however, quickly tired of the charade. “Peter, let’s get on with it. Sign the agreement.”

DiLauro abruptly shut up. Down deep he now wanted to see this thing end. In order to squeeze out anything more than already contained in the document, they would be forced to kill people and risk being killed themselves. My attitude had made that clear.

The look on Peter’s face told me he no longer felt indifferent to dying. The ordeal had tired him and now he only wanted to save face. So he signed and gave the document to Roach, who slid it across the table to me.

All eyes watched intently, expecting me to simply sign. But I wasn’t quite finished playing out my role. Even though Auker had assured me that we were signing under duress and that prosecutions would follow, I had never seen this document.

By signing it I would appear to commit the union to compliance. If I treated the document carelessly, signing without bothering to read it, the inmates might pick up that the paper didn't signify anything. If they suspected this, they might ask questions I could not answer. This might stir them up into doing something desperate. Regardless of the tension, I knew I should give the appearance of reading the document. I proceeded to do just that.

I hadn't gone more than a few sentences when one of the inmates shouted, "Just sign the fuckin' thing!"

I looked up and went eyeball to eyeball with DiLauro. "I don't sign anything for my union that I don't read first."

With a sick look on his face, DiLauro nodded. "He's right. He's got to read it first."

I read on, not really absorbing the content. Actually I couldn't help enjoying the fact that the delay was making both Butterworth and the inmates sweat. Fred's policies had as much to do with causing this crisis as the inmates. He, of course, had been held at knifepoint for eight hours. Now he had to sit there, knife still jabbing into his back, watching me slowly read the two-page document word for word. He knew I didn't like him and wanted him removed as Superintendent. If I incited the inmates they might do the job for me. He must've been thinking, "We're so close. What's this nut going to do next?"

When I finally finished reading it I said, "I have no objections to this." I leaned over and signed. Roach now passed the document over to Butterworth, who looked nearly comatose. Fred hastily scribbled his signature, not one his bank would recognize, I'm sure. And with that, the crisis ended.

I walked out of Block Nine feeling enormously relieved that we had suffered no loss of life. I felt a little torn, having signed something I had no intention of honoring. That went against my nature, but under the circumstances I'd had no choice.

Admirably, Fred remained inside Block Nine until the other hostages came out. They were physically unharmed.

A short time later I saw Larker, Tinker, Randall, Fair, and Meacham escorting Fred in the corridor. This was the first time I'd seen Meacham since the Block Ten strike. When I offered Fred my hand, he accepted it in a way that made me feel he understood where I had been coming from.

I told him, "Fred, I may want your resignation, but I'd never want to see you hurt like that."

He looked a little taken aback by my remark, but he smiled and replied, "Thanks, Mike."

I turned and walked out to see Karen.

16 Back From the Edge

Tension in Block Nine did not end with the signing of the agreement. As I feared, the inmates, especially DiLauro, saw the signing as encouragement to continue challenging authority at every opportunity.

Since the officers taken hostage were still off from work, a new senior officer was put in charge of Nine. He was expected to reestablish discipline. In trying to do that, he met with verbal abuse, physical resistance, and overt threats on his and the other guards' lives. As DiLauro put it, "You work for us, not those pieces of shit over there. Try to stop me and you'll go down."

The officer could only write reports to Administration asking for guidance. He, like the rest of us, had anticipated that the District Attorney would move against DiLauro and the others at once. But Delahunt's office remained suspiciously quiet, leaving DiLauro to prowl Block Nine, as dangerous as ever.

Ever since the hostage crisis, I'd felt fatigue. In the past several months I had fought so many battles with management, faced so many physical threats from inmates, that I began sensing the signs of burnout. Still, I dared not take a day off as long as tension in the prison ran high.

Officer hostility toward inmates was building as the days went by without any word of prosecutions. At the same time the inmates were angered by the guards spreading rumors that prosecutions were imminent. Tempers were shortened even further by the ever present short-staffing problem that forced us to work double shifts and days off. I myself worked thirty hours overtime each week and went twelve days without time off—plus doing my usual union work.

Then, at lunch hour on August 15th, a startling news report came to my attention. I had been posted to a block in the Max-section that day, and as I sat at my desk I suddenly saw inmates gathering around televisions in various cells. They had hushed to hear the audio, allowing me to hear it as well. The newscaster distinctly mentioned the name Delahunt so my ears perked up. Then, in response to a question I heard Delahunt's voice reply.

"I have reluctantly decided not to pursue the prosecution of eight Walpole inmates who took Superintendent Butterworth and four guards hostage in Cellblock Nine on July 29th. Prison officials signed a document stating that they would not seek prosecutions. I do not wish to put them in a situation where it would appear they had broken their word. However, I want to make one thing clear. Any further taking of hostages by inmates will result in prosecutions regardless of what agreements are signed."

When the brief interview ended, the inmates erupted in cheers. I could hear more coming from other cellblocks down the corridor.

I waited for the block to quiet, then picked up the phone and called Jim Auker in Delahunt's office. "Jim, what the hell's going on? I just heard your boss say on the news that he's not going to prosecute DiLauro and the others."

"That's right. Under the circumstances we can't. The inmates have a signed agreement stating that we won't seek prosecutions. Even your signature is on it."

"Jim, you told me in Butterworth's office that we were all signing under duress. That you would definitely seek out prosecutions later. I would never have signed without that promise."

Brief silence.

"I don't remember making such a promise."

"Jim, don't pull that on me. I have a witness that heard you say it."

"And I have witnesses that will confirm that I didn't."

If he'd been standing there I might've socked him. As it was, the statement made further conversation useless.

After I hung up I asked the senior in the corridor to relieve me. I knew the officers would have received the news almost as rapidly as the inmates, so I began calling them aside singly and in small groups. All were miffed at the development but still open to reason.

"Guys," I told them, "I know how you feel. But for now the best thing we can do is swallow our pride and remain calm. The Department of Corrections is not responsible for this decision. Delahunt is. Our quarrel is with the DA's office, so a job action would not serve any useful purpose. The only way we can get back at Delahunt is to hit at him politically. We can do that by embarrassing him when he runs for reelection."

I spent the rest of the shift conveying that message and the guys listened. Finally, shortly before three o'clock I went outside to the rec-room to meet with the 3–11 shift. Many had already arrived for roll call and I could see that the news had swept their ranks like wildfire. I no sooner stepped into the room when they began tossing complaints.

"Mac, you told us Delahunt was going to prosecute DiLauro and those other bastards."

"That's what I was promised. The DA's office has gone back on its word."

"Yeah? Well we've already talked it over. We're going to walk out."

Murmurs of assent filled the room.

"Now wait a minute," I protested. "I know you're upset; I am too. But I can't defend a walkout under the circumstances. The Department isn't responsible for this; the DA's office is. What would we be striking for that the Department could give us?"

"We can force the Department to push for prosecutions."

"It won't work. Delahunt has already gone public. He's got a signed document to back him up. We don't have a concrete issue to present."

"What do we do then, let them get away with this?"

"I've already discussed this with the dayshift and they're in agreement. We go after Delahunt politically. He'll be running for reelection soon. We'll organize ourselves and demonstrate at every place he gives a speech during his campaign. That's how we can really hurt him, not by striking here, now."

I could see them pondering my idea, some liking it. But then the outspoken Marty Trent, who had accompanied me during the fateful meeting with Auker, stepped forward and faced the group.

"What Mike says may work down the road, but what about now? The inmates in this place have just been given a message that they can take hostages and get away with it. The way I see it, that encourages them to grab someone whenever they feel like it."

His words immediately drew agreement from the others.

"Marty," I countered, "that's not the way it is. Delahunt made it clear he would seek prosecutions against anyone taking hostages in the future."

"You mean after this you still believe him? Well I don't. And I don't think the inmates will take him seriously either."

"I only believe him because he went public with his statement. He'd look like a complete ass if he tried to back away from it."

"Well I don't think his statement will have any effect on the inmates. Right now I don't feel safe going into my cellblock while they're free. I think we ought to teach this prison a lesson about taking hostages, once and for all. I'm for locking up the entire place tonight as a last great act of defiance over Delahunt's decision."

Voices rose in support of his suggestion. It soon became clear that sentiment had swung completely behind Trent. They intended locking up the entire prison, denying inmates all activities and privileges.

I saw this as a serious mistake, so I tried one last time.

"Guys, I don't think we can win this. I don't think I can protect you from suspensions. It's not reasonable to punish the entire prison for the actions of the eight inmates in Block Nine. Everyone else behaved themselves. By doing so they allowed us to concentrate on rescuing the hostages. The dayshift doesn't see it your way. You'll be on your own in this."

"We don't care about the dayshift," Trent retorted.

"Look, you'll be forcing me to defend this to the public. If you must go ahead and do something, make it something that looks remotely reasonable. Lock up Block Nine and leave the rest of the prison alone. At least it'll look like you're trying to punish the inmates who took the hostages."

Their grumbling told me my plea had been ignored. I followed them back into the prison and remained in the corridor as they assumed their posts. A short time later Andrew Larker entered the Max-end and found seven block officers refusing to unlock and enter their blocks. Trent and I walked with him as he, one-by-one, issued the usual ultimatum, "Unlock your block, Mister, or you're suspended."

I dared not speak in front of Larker, but in those few seconds I still tried to convince the officers to follow orders by nodding my head. But they chose instead to heed Trent's verbal urging, "Give him the keys."

All seven officers turned in their keys and were sent home. Already short-handed, the loss of these seven key officers forced Larker to lock up the prison.

The action of my guys discouraged me. After all the trouble we'd faced together, they'd refused to listen to me. I totally disagreed with their action but now they were forcing me to defend it. I had always maintained a sense of inner integrity whenever going public. This time I found it difficult, and I didn't like the feeling. I felt used.

To try to protect them I called a news conference that evening in the prison lobby. I managed to hide my displeasure with them and focus my remarks upon Delahunt. After all, his decision had caused this action.

I told the reporters: "This afternoon seven officers, fearing for their safety, defied an order from Deputy Superintendent Larker and refused to release inmates from their cells.

"This was brought on by District Attorney Delahunt's announcement earlier in the day that inmates responsible for taking hostages on July 29th would not be prosecuted. Management immediately suspended the seven officers.

"I find this entire situation tragic. The District Attorney of Norfolk County has sworn to uphold the laws of this Commonwealth and he's not doing it."

A reporter interrupted. "Excuse me, Mike, but the District Attorney in his news conference stated that he made his decision only after his office interviewed guards and found that they agreed he should not pursue prosecutions."

"I defy you to find guards in this institution who were questioned about the matter or would recommend not prosecuting. Besides, it's a union issue. No one from the DA's office contacted me as spokesman of the union. On behalf of my union I walked in and faced those armed inmates. I signed the document Delahunt refers to. Before doing so, a member of the DA's office told me I was signing 'under duress' and promised that prosecutions would follow. To free the guards and the Superintendent, I would have signed anything."

The interview was aired that evening and hit the newspapers the following day. The controversy it generated prompted Delahunt to agree to a meeting with myself, Sam Frustaci, and the union presidents of the other prisons. We gathered at Council 93 headquarters in Boston.

The hour-long meeting began with a great surge of emotion from Delahunt. He pounded the table and verbally lambasted me for the comments I'd made to the press. He threatened to take me to court to force me to prove them.

Sitting back in my seat and staring him straight in the eye I told him: "I don't care about your threats. Your man Jim Auker promised me there'd be prosecutions. You've backed out on us and we're not forgetting it. You're going to see a lot of us in your next campaign. We'll be working hard for your opponent. Maybe we can't do anything about your bailing out on us now, but in the long run you won't get away with this."

He looked ready to leap across the table at me. But Frustaci quickly intervened to calm the situation.

"Gentlemen, please. Mr. District Attorney, we would like you to explain why you have chosen not to prosecute."

Delahunt repeated the same explanation he had given to the press. Then he became apologetic and assured us, "Future hostage incidents will be prosecuted to the fullest extent of the law. This pertains, as long as I am District Attorney in Norfolk County and no matter what's agreed to in the heat of the moment."

The rest of the meeting was anticlimactic and upon its conclusion the others in attendance persuaded him and me to shake hands and suspend our attacks on each other. I went along, but felt that this truce was another I'd agreed to under duress.

The prison remained locked up for that one shift. The dayshift arrived the next morning fully prepared to operate the prison normally. The inmates, however, had decided to put on their own demonstration after having been "mistreated" the night before. Those in the Minimum Section refused to go to work in protest.

I learned of the inmates' action as I arrived back at the prison just before noon. It didn't particularly alarm me. I'd seen enough of these strikes before. At the moment my big concern was to inform the officers of the results of the meeting with Delahunt.

Vice President Bob Furtado and Secretary Steve Adair accompanied me inside. We entered the main corridor and turned toward the Minimum Section. I had expected the Minimum inmates to be locked up and was therefore surprised to see what looked like all 200 of them casually milling around in the corridor just the other side of the security grille that sealed off the Minimum Section. As usual, the gate remained open. Apparently, although they refused to work, they still intended taking advantage of the dining hall for lunch. I noted this without concern and continued on.

We first stopped at the security gate that sealed off the hospital from the corridor. Officer Vern Warstler stood posted on the opposite side. I stopped paying attention to the inmates and began informing Vern about my meeting. I'd barely gotten out a few words when suddenly I heard the unmistakable voice of Chuck Small shout out above all the inmate chatter.

"There's that fuckin' asshole McLaughlin! Let's kill that motherfucker!"

Turning, I saw Small charge through the open gate. His words had instantaneously turned the previously docile group with him into raving maniacs. All two hundred pushed forward to follow. Only two at a time could squeeze through, giving them the appearance of a swarm of bees exiting a hive.

Seventy-five feet at most separated us from this stampeding, yelling mass of enraged humanity. I could see that nearly all of them were armed. Shanks, pipes, swords and chains—all had appeared as if from nowhere. Most were being brandished menacingly as the wave bore down on us. The angry, distorted faces told me that nothing less than murder would satisfy them.

A thought flashed through my mind that it wasn't fair for Adair and Furtado to be killed because of me. I heard Warstler fumbling with his keys to open the grille that barred entrance into the hospital. He worked fast, but I sensed that all three of us would not have enough time to slip through before the inmates fell upon us. If we didn't make it we'd die.

In those brief seconds I remembered a trick I had been taught in my training at the Academy. Even as Warstler was swinging open the grille I moved aside to allow Bob and Steve to go first. Then I stepped toward the inmates with one foot, pointed at them with a finger, and shouted, "Stop where you are!"

Amazingly, those in front broke stride, causing those behind to crash into them. For a split-second all came to a stop. Then Small, looking confused, waved them forward yelling: "Come on, get that motherfucker!" They surged forward again.

But their brief hesitation allowed me to slip through the opening and Warstler to slam the gate behind me just an instant before Small and the others reached us. We stepped further inside, out of sight but could easily hear the frustrated Small rattling the bars and screaming, "I want that motherfucker! Send him out!"

Warstler replied calmly, "Officer McLaughlin has already left."

Exchanging relieved glances with Bob and Steve, I led them through a side exit into the prison yard away from the mayhem. I'd seen enough in those few seconds and was satisfied to let other officers deal with the disturbance. I later learned that when Small was convinced that I had indeed escaped, he'd given a command and the entire mob abruptly dispersed. When extra officers arrived on the scene they found nothing to put down. Nor, of course, did they find any sign of weapons.

I knew then that I had to get away from the prison for awhile. I had fought mental and physical exhaustion for months, ignoring my doctor's advice to take off a few weeks. Now I was bone tired—too tired to deal with what had just happened.

Two hundred inmates had just tried to kill me! Many would likely try again. I no longer felt confident I could handle them.

I managed to take two weeks away from the facility, but I spent five days of that time transacting union business. Some vacation.

However, the free time did afford me an opportunity to put into perspective what had just happened between me and the union. When I had first assumed the presidency I had committed myself to working for penological reform in Walpole while simultaneously improving the status of the officers. I saw no conflict in those goals.

Unfortunately, on numerous occasions I seemed to be furthering the cause of the officers at the expense of the prison. Administration usually forced me into that position by refusing to bend on even the simplest of issues. Our strikes did inconvenience many innocent inmates, but we had no choice if we were to establish basic safety policies.

Now the action of the 3–11 shift, locking up the prison in defiance of my recommendation, had shaken me. My oath as president obligated me to defend my members. They knew I would not break that oath.

At the same time for months they had seen me demonstrate the power I had gathered. They had now begun entertaining a false sense of their own power as exercised through me. This concerned me. I did not want them forcing me into confrontations with management on issues that did not reflect good correctional practice.

In spite of what the Department of Corrections believed, I did not have as a goal placing Walpole under union management. I wanted a cooperative partnership between the union and the Department.

I did not foresee turning Walpole into an ideal facility as long as we faced a constant fight with a hostile administration. Nor could we achieve positive reform by concentraing on our own goals and ignoring the bigger picture. My objective was to see the old hierarchy in the Department replaced with one which would listen to reason.

The lockup told me that many of my membership did not see things the same way. They had come to enjoy doing battle. They did not appreciate the fact that most of our success had come from my skillfully maneuvering us through negotiations.

I had only been able to do this because I believed strongly in the issues I was presenting. Now they expected me to fight for them on issues I did not embrace. I had done so with the lockup, but I didn't want to do it with future issues.

During those vacation days I began seriously planning to bow out of the presidency and begin organizing my campaign for Sheriff. The only thing holding me back was my intense desire to achieve the goal I had set for myself two years before. I wanted to see Walpole placed on the right track before I resigned.

So far I had achieved several major objectives. I had built the union to where the administration no longer dared to step on the officers. I had seen to Frank Hall's removal as Commissioner. I had led the action that straightened out Block Ten. And on the way I had helped "Dump the Duke."

What remained was the appointment of a new Commissioner, sensitive to the real needs of the prison system, and a new Superintendent at Walpole itself. The programs I had advocated could not be forced down anyone's throat. They would only be implemented and properly administered by managers sympathetic to them.

I decided to stick it out a while longer in spite of knowing I'd face times of inner conflict. My first priority was to save the jobs of those officers who had caused the lockup. The Department had already initiated proceedings that would lead to these officers' termination. So far, as a union, we had managed to delay a decision. But the sword of Damocles still hung above them.

A main reason why the Department had not tried to force through a decision was the turmoil surrounding the sudden resignation of Larry Meacham. Having known from the start that his status was interim, he had obtained the Commissioner of Corrections post in the State of Oklahoma.

As an interesting sidelight to this, shortly after I returned to the prison I received a phone call from a television reporter in Oklahoma. He told me he had heard that I had vigorously opposed Larry Meacham as Commissioner of Corrections in Massachusetts.

He asked, "Would you be willing to do an interview with me if I came to Boston?"

"Of course. Tell me when you're coming and I'll make time for you."

He arrived a few days later with a cameraman and we did a forty-minute interview in which I described Meacham's abilities as Commissioner in very uncomplimentary terms. Knowing the news media, I thought they'd use perhaps one small segment of our discussion, if that much. I didn't know these two individuals represented a large pool of Oklahoma reporters who shared stories.

For the next week my interview showed up all over the Oklahoma news media. It triggered so much static for Meacham that our new Interim Commissioner in Boston received a call from Oklahoma asking him to try to get me to shut up.

Neither he nor Meacham realized that I'd only given the one interview. Meacham held on to his job in Oklahoma and did not trouble me again.

As if my relationship with the inmates wasn't already bad enough, shortly after I returned to work I ran afoul of Johnny Regalado. During the previous three years Johnny and I had maintained a cordial relationship. I seldom had official dealings with him, because he spent nearly all his time in the administration building. He worked and slept there, virtually unsupervised, while my duties always centered inside the prison. Knowing Johnny's privileged position with Administration, I didn't bother trying to enforce any rules upon him.

Johnny did talk to me from time to time concerning my union activities and the safety measures I was attempting to introduce into the prison. Once he became confident that my activities wouldn't interfere with the network he had established at Walpole, he didn't fight me.

He could have been real trouble because in reality he had more power than even Kramer and Mancuso. But he wasn't interested in their petty games. He had long since established himself both on the inside with administration, and the outside with his Mafia connections. He simply didn't want his little feudal fief disrupted.

Unfortunately for Johnny, during this time he somehow got himself entangled in the web of suspicion surrounding a spectacular crime called the Blackfires murders. The incident actually began inside Walpole just a few days after I returned to work.

One morning the officers were shocked to learn that Lanny Dascoli, an extremely violent, dangerous inmate serving 12–20 years for armed robbery, had just been granted parole. This despite his having served but eight years of his sentence and having spent the past several months of it in Block Ten for having attacked officers.

Most men about to gain their freedom would be cooperative. But we knew Dascoli a lot better than the parole board did. Instead of dispatching one officer to bring Dascoli to the administration building for his release, the shift commander sent a team of four bearing both wrist and leg irons. Dascoli had displayed such a hatred of officers that we dared not allow him total freedom around us.

Sure enough, as soon as the officers appeared before his cell, Dascoli lashed out.

"What do you fuckin' assholes want?"

Senior Officer Dick Kline replied, "We've got good news for you, Lanny. Your parole went through. We've come to release you."

It took a moment for the words to sink in. Then Dascoli threw his head back and emitted a chilling laugh. "You mean I won't have to look at you cocksuckers every day? I'm almost disappointed. I've got a number of scores to settle."

"All right, Lanny, why don't you just cool it and make it easy on everybody."

"Fuck you! You pricks have been making it hard on me ever since I got here. If I get a chance I'll bash your fuckin' heads in." He waved a fist at them through the bars.

Kline heaved a deep sigh and looked at his companions. "All right, you know what we've gotta do."

When Dascoli saw the irons he went crazy. He first fought to keep them from opening the door then tried to pummel them with his fists, all the while cursing and spitting on them. After a long struggle they finally secured the irons on both wrists and ankles. Then they dragged him out of his cell and down the corridor amidst a serenade of cheers from the other Block Ten inmates.

He continued striking out at his captors for the benefit of the inmates in the Minimum Section and still had to be restrained while being processed in the administration building. The officers didn't dare remove the irons until they dragged him out on the front steps. Then they quickly backed away and tossed him a small bag containing his possessions.

A car was waiting, but still Dascoli wasn't finished.

"You motherfuckers! If you think you're through with me, you'd better guess again." He pointed at them one by one. "I know all of your fuckin' names! I'm gonna look you cocksuckers up. And when I find you I won't have any fuckin' chains holdin' me back."

Then he turned and jumped into the car.

Three days later Dascoli and an accomplice shotgunned five men to death. We shed no tears over the four who were gangland figures. But the fifth was an innocent reporter.

Within hours Dascoli was captured and locked away elsewhere to await trial on this new outrage. It had only taken him three days to arm himself and carry out the crime—referred to as the Blackfires Murders. What other acts he might have committed had not the police caught him immediately is anybody's guess. I can't help wondering how a parole board could have decided to release him. He showed not one ounce of respect for normal human values.

In any case, Johnny Regalado came under suspicion for having given Dascoli a contract to commit the crime. With an investigation in progress and Johnny in the spotlight, management had no choice but to separate him from his life of relative luxury and bring him and his inmate assistant (who served more like Johnny's servant) back inside the walls. Both were assigned to the Minimum Section.

Suddenly Johnny found himself in my territory and subject to my strict enforcement of regulations. A confrontation was inevitable, because Johnny was not accustomed to being ordered around at Walpole. He was used to the freedom of moving about and having access to the kitchen whenever he wanted.

Johnny's freedom had reached such a ridiculous extent that he ordered his food specially prepared. Then he sent his assistant down to pick up a snack whenever he felt inclined.

On one of Johnny's first days back inside I intercepted his assistant heading for the kitchen several hours after regular meals had been served.

"Where do you think you're going?" I asked, as if I didn't know.

"Johnny sent me down to see what's left over in the kitchen."

"Sorry," I told him, "inmates do not have access to the dining area except at meal times."

"Hey man, it's all right," he smiled. "I'm talking about Johnny Regalado. He's always been a special case. You know that."

"Not anymore he's not. Not with me, anyway. Once he became part of the Minimum Section he became subject to its rules."

I envisioned myself trying to explain to the other Minimum inmates why they too couldn't just wander down to the kitchen whenever their stomach moved them.

Johnny's assistant stared at me in disbelief. "Johnny's not going to like this. He's always been able to get what he wants from the kitchen. You sure you know who you're dealing with?"

"I know exactly who I'm dealing with."

The inmate turned and walked briskly back toward his block. I knew Johnny well enough. He would not take this sitting down. In anticipation of a confrontation, I walked across the corridor to the Deputy's office and there found Stanley Tinker idly shuffling paper. I wanted a credible witness should anything serious develop with Johnny.

"Stanley," I said, "in a few minutes I'm expecting to have trouble with an inmate new to the Minimum Section." I felt it would be better not to identify who it was.

"What's the problem?" Tinker said.

"He wants access to the kitchen. I denied him. I suspect he'll be stopping by any minute to confront me about it. I'd like you to witness what happens."

Stanley immediately perked up. He liked seeing others enforce the little rules.

"Sure, Mike," he eagerly responded. "I'm not doing anything important now anyway. Who does the guy think he is? Inmates aren't allowed access to the kitchen under any circumstances."

Stanley followed me back into the corridor and we stood waiting just outside the office. Sure enough, within seconds a large figure stepped out into the corridor and began plodding in our direction.

Two hundred feet separated him from us, but there was no mistaking that lumbering step. No one in Walpole walked quite like Johnny Regalado.

Suddenly I realized that Tinker had tensed up beside me. He watched Regalado's approach for only a few seconds. Then he said, "Officer McLaughlin, I don't have time for this. I've got other more important things to do." He spun around and started off in the opposite direction into the Max-section. The mystique of Johnny Regalado had struck again.

I remained standing my ground as Johnny walked up to me. "Hey, Mac, what's this shit about you not letting my man into the kitchen?"

"That's the way it is, Johnny. Inmates are not allowed access to the kitchen. They're only allowed into the dining hall, and that only at the designated times."

"Hey, you know I'm not like everyone else. I'm only back inside for a short time until they clear me of this thing."

"As long as you are inside and holding Minimum status, you'll follow the same rules as all Minimum inmates."

He cast me a sour look. "You know, I'm the wrong guy to throw your weight around with. I could have you hit at the top of the hill," he snapped his fingers, "just like that."

Walpole had been constructed on a hill. He meant he could have me killed just outside the prison parking lot.

This threat showed the treacherous natures of men like Regalado. We had never had a confrontation before. He had treated Karen politely during the hostage crisis. Now, over a small matter, he had threatened my life without as much as blinking.

I looked him directly in the eye and said, "You could do that, but you'll still be inside facing three hundred pissed-off officers. If you want a war, Johnny, I can give you a war."

When it struck him that his threat had been returned in kind, he took a few steps back, arms raised in that familiar Walpole pose, as if someone had the drop on him.

"What is this?" he complained. "I just came here to talk. I didn't expect to be threatened."

"What did you just do to me?"

He looked at me sheepishly for a moment. Then he turned and walked back down the corridor. I had the sudden urge to laugh hysterically but managed to control it.

After the Block Ten strike Governor King never talked to me directly concerning my preferences for candidates for Commissioner of Corrections. He did, however, heed my advice about Larry Meacham and also did not try to force someone we didn't like on us. After Meacham he went through three more Interim Commissioners. He knew my feelings about each applicant because any time a name arose, the press would interview me to learn my opinion. I was always happy to make it quite clear.

Finally, in late September, King brought up Bill Hogan's name for the permanent Commissioner's job. Besides being a long time friend of King's, Hogan had significant credentials. He had worked in probation with the Federal system for several years, earning a solid reputation there. He certainly had heavy experience dealing directly with inmates, something I felt was important. And he also had firsthand knowledge of recidivism, a major result of poorly run prison systems. Up until now too many Department managers making important decisions had minimal prior contact with inmates.

Since I didn't have a snowball's chance of blocking the appointment of one of King's long-time friends, I gave Hogan favorable reviews. The Department had gone long enough without a permanent Commissioner. The Interims had sidestepped many important issues that needed solutions. I was willing to gamble that I could work with Hogan.

I waited just a few days after King made the official announcement of the appointment. Then I called Hogan's office to speak to him. I wanted to find out one-on-one what he was like and where he stood on the issues of importance to me. I could then determine how to approach my presidency. Would I be faced with a dogfight, or could I begin backing away and trust the Department to handle the issues?

"Of course I know who you are," Hogan responded, as I introduced myself. "I've been looking forward to talking with you."

The greeting surprised me. "I'm flattered. The reason I'm calling is that I think we should get together and talk over things of concern to both of us."

He agreed and we decided upon meeting after hours at a neutral site where no one would recognize us or know that we had talked.

He picked a quiet restaurant in a suburb of Boston and we finally sat down together around 7:30 that evening. I couldn't help remembering a similar meeting I'd had with Commissioner Hall over two years before. A lot had happened since. I wondered what this one would bring.

It began warmly, with both of us relating a little of our personal backgrounds and how we had come to know the Governor. Never one to dawdle when business matters lay ready for discussion, I soon directed the conversation to corrections issues.

"Commissioner, for over two years I've been fighting your predecessors trying to win some basic reform within the prison system."

"I've heard." He smiled at me.

"Honestly," I continued, "I'd rather not have to fight you as well. But there are issues too important for me to back away from. I'd like to see where you stand on them."

"That's why I came. Also, of course, to see where you stand."

"Fine. Some of these things may sound silly because they're so basic. But nevertheless, your department has resisted us on them.

"First, general maintenance. We haven't been able to get light bulbs replaced, dirty windows cleaned, or broken windows fixed with any consistency. Management has treated these items as if they are of low priority. And yet a simple matter of replacing a broken padlock could have averted the entire Block Nine hostage crisis this past summer."

I briefly explained. By the time I finished he was shaking his head.

"That's absurd. Under me, I assure you, the Department will not penny-pinch on maintenance. My managers will attend to these things promptly."

"What about officers? Ever since I started at Walpole we've been operating twenty per cent understaffed. Right now only one officer per shift supervises each Max-cellblock. Each Minimum block is supposed to be assigned two, but often shortstaffing forces the duties in these blocks on a single officer."

"Run that by me again. You say one officer is responsible for an entire Maximum Security cellblock? How many inmates does he supervise?"

"Forty-five.And he's locked up with them all day."

Another amazed shake of the head.

"That will not continue. Each block definitely needs more supervision, both Maximum and Minimum. I'll try to provide it by filling the officer vacancies. But if that doesn't do it, I'm not against increasing staff."

I could hardly believe my ears. This guy actually sounded attuned to what we needed.

"There's more," I told him. "Officer morale has been low not only because of the dangerous environment, but because of poor job prospects. Qualified officers have been continuously passed over for promotion. No Civil Service exams have been given for years. That puts supervisory positions out of the reach of most officers."

He pondered a moment before replying, "Mike, I want to assure you of something. I've been a career-oriented employee all my adult years. I know what it's like to work my way up through the system. I know what it means to an employee to have the opportunity to advance on merit."

Hogan took a deep breath and leaned forward, his face intent. "I promise you that from here on, officers with solid experience will receive every chance to advance. I'll see that the Civil Service exam program is made available again so that junior officers can gain senior status and eventually become supervisors, based on merit. I can't envision running a system any other way."

Again I found it hard to believe what I was hearing. But instead of celebrating I continued on. "What about the treatment of inmates? At Walpole fifteen per cent of the inmates are real bad apples that continue to spoil the rest of the barrel. Until now, management has tried to coddle them and bribe them into behaving."

He stopped me. "My experience in the probation system has convinced me that such an approach won't work. You've got to separate the bad apples from the good. How do you suggest we do it at Walpole?"

"I've been pushing for two years to isolate the troublemakers in one or two separate cellblocks. I think that would work. But I'd rather go even one step further and begin using the inter-state compact program. We've had the law on the books, but management has refused to implement it."

"Why do you think that is?"

"Because I've strongly recommended it."

He chuckled. "Whether that's true or not, it won't be a problem between us. I'm familiar with the inmate transfer program as administered by the Federal Bureau of Prisons. I've seen it work. I'd certainly be willing to try something similar here."

"I'm sure that would go a long way toward stopping the major violence in the institution. Then we would be left with battling the other major contributor—drugs. I'm convinced the appetite for drugs in Walpole causes 75% of the violence. We could reduce this drastically if we could control the flow from the outside. But again, management refuses to give us the tools. I've asked for stricter searches of visitors, a drug-sniffing dog, an end to contact visits, and prosecutions of visitors bringing in drugs. We've been frustrated on all points."

Again he looked at me, puzzled. "Passing drugs is a crime anywhere. Are you saying that visitors caught doing it at Walpole are not legally pursued?"

"Yes. But even worse, they're not restricted from returning to the institution. They'll be back in a few days, a week, a month, to try again."

"Not under me they won't," Hogan said, a hard glint of determination in his eye. "I intend working closely with the District Attorney's office to press for prosecutions of any visitors committing crimes in our prisons."

"What about my other suggestions for interdicting drug flow? Searches, a dog, contact visits?"

"All of them are certainly worth serious consideration. I'd like some time to look into them before making a commitment to specifics, but they certainly seem reasonable."

The discussion continued for nearly two hours, ranging over the full spectrum of penal philosophy and practices. In no area did we have a major disagreement. Throughout, I tried to measure his sincerity and as the evening wore on I felt more and more confident that he was talking straight.

It suddenly dawned on me that if this was true, the entire posture of my presidency would have to shift. I must take myself from out front and throw my weight behind the Commissioner in his effort to implement the reforms I wanted.

But would my members let me? Would they be willing to stand back and give Hogan a chance to do his thing? Or would they try to retain every ounce of their power and, in the process, fight the Commissioner's reforms? If they did so, they would force me to become an unwilling adversary of Hogan. This wouldn't help anyone, certainly not the cause of prison reform.

Reflecting I saw that if what I'd just heard was genuine, the time had come to step down as president. But how could I be sure Hogan meant what he'd said? Words flow easily. Following through on them often proves to be another matter. I needed to see a significant gesture that would authenticate them.

All along, the issues at Walpole had taken a back seat to the personalities in conflict over them. Now one of my last two major goals—to see a competent commissioner appointed—appeared to have been accomplished. All that remained was for Walpole to receive a new superintendent who would reflect the views of his new boss. Once I saw that happen I could feel satisfied that I'd accomplished everything and move on.

To realize this I sensed I had to move cautiously. I saw a chance to use my presidency as a very important bargaining chip.

"Commissioner," I finally said, "I'm very encouraged by what you've had to say here. The way I see it, you face only two major obstacles to achieving genuine reform in the system. First, Fred Butterworth, and second, me."

His eyebrows rose. "You?"

"As president, I'm obligated to present the majority opinion of my union whether I agree with it or not. I've always taken that responsibility seriously. Now my guys might force me, against my better judgment, to oppose you."

"Isn't there some way to avoid that?"

"There is, but first I want to clear up one other issue. The guys who locked up Block Nine still have suspensions and possible termination pending. I can't argue against some sort of punishment, but under the circumstances I don't think it's fair to go beyond suspensions. It would certainly serve as an olive branch gesture for you to show leniency."

He didn't hesitate. "I promise that the most severe punishment will be a suspension. The length, of course, will depend upon the degree of disobedience. Most likely we'll settle on the standard two weeks. Certainly no longer than a month. No one will lose his job."

"I can accept that." I paused to gather my words. He sat watching me closely. "There's only one way I can see of avoiding becoming a thorn in your side. I would have to resign my presidency. I plan to run for Sheriff of Middlesex County next year and ordinarily would hold on to my presidency until then. But if what you have told me today is genuine, I would prefer not to fight you. Only one thing stands in the way of my resigning."

I could sense him hanging on every word. "What's that?"

"I must see Fred Butterworth replaced at Walpole."

He paused, seemingly having trouble directly addressing my demand. "As president, you see no way we could work together?"

"I think the guys would make it difficult. If you get yourself a new superintendent in harmony with your views, you shouldn't have many problems with the union."

He nodded, still pondering. Finally he said, "I appreciate your trying to be helpful and want you to know that if you do leave the Department and then ever want to return to corrections, either here or on the federal level, I'll be glad to do all I can to try to help you. My door will be open."

"I appreciate that."

"Now I don't want to misunderstand. You're saying that you'll only resign if I replace Fred Butterworth?"

"Yes."

We locked stares.

Then he said, "You first."

* * *

The next day I presented my letter of resignation to my E-Board. At first, all my guys were shocked. The majority didn't want me to leave. They gathered around me at roll call, stopped me in the corridor, all asking why. I couldn't tell them of my discussion with Hogan, so I mentioned my coming campaign for sheriff.

That same day the news media heard of my resignation and came to interview me. I gave them the same reason I'd given the guys. During the interview, however, they asked me directly about the lockup incident.

My conscience had been bothering me ever since the incident had occurred. I hadn't liked twisting words with the press to defend my members. Now, I decided to get the truth off my chest.

"Gentlemen," I responded, "the prison lockup after the Block Nine hostage affair was a mistake. The guys overreacted and did not use sound judgment. I only defended the action to you because it was my responsibility as president."

These comments angered many guards, especially those on the 3–11 shift. They had known my feelings but had expected me to keep them to myself. Now I had placed the union in a bad light with the public.

Within a week after I announced my resignation a quiet announcement circulated through the Department of Correction. Fred Butterworth had been promoted to Associate Commissioner operating directly out of Hogan's office. He no longer would have anything directly to do with Walpole.

Shortly afterward I transferred to the overnight shift to take myself further out of danger and to free up more daytime hours to work on my election campaign. At the same time I divorced myself from the union. I had given it everything I had and left the presidency in the capable hands of Bob Furtado. Now I had new goals to pursue.

Watching from a distant perspective as the months went by I began to see that I had made the right assessment of Hogan. I saw an immediate improvement in maintenance and money spent on capital improvements.

I also saw the interstate compact begin to be used. But most important of all, I sensed a vast improvement in officer morale. When management is in tune with the needs of its employees, a warm glow seems to filter down. It's as if you're covered by a blanket of security.

This became particularly evident at Walpole because we'd gone so long without management's support.

I knew it would take Hogan some time to address all the prison's problems, but having observed his approach I felt confident he would succeed.

As for myself, I had decided upon April as the time when I would leave the prison and campaign full-time. I kept a low profile with the inmates those final weeks but many refused to put aside their hatred of me. On the 11–7 shift one had little direct contact with them so I found myself facing few dangerous situations. I worked towers two or three nights a week; blocks the other nights. I no longer resented towers and I even found the block assignments relaxing since during that shift the inmates were locked in. You simply made rounds of the tiers once an hour, checking with a flashlight to see skin or something that would indicate the inmate was alive and still in his cell. Other than that you could sit at your desk with a book or paperwork, being alert of course, for any strange sounds.

Several times I received Block Two in Max as my assignment. This was still the lair of Connie Mancuso. On one night here I noticed that a new inmate had been moved into a cell halfway down the third tier. Ordinarily I wouldn't have paid much attention because inmates moved about constantly. But in this case I found the young man standing by the bars as I made my first rounds. I noted that he was definitely new to the prison as well as to Block Two.

"Hi," he said, as I walked by.

"Hi," I replied, not stopping.

On my next round an hour later, he was still there.

"How's it goin'?" he asked.

"Good," I replied, glancing at my watch. It read two a.m. "What're you doing up?"

"Can't sleep. This place, prison, I can't get used to it." He looked sad.

"First time inside, huh?"

"Yeah, and I shouldn't be here. They charged me with a robbery I didn't commit. I had a lousy lawyer—"

"Now wait," I stopped him. "I've been here nearly four years now. I've heard just about every tale there is, and not one of them admits to any guilt. You'd think this place is filled with innocent men.

"Even if you are innocent, I can't do anything for you. All you can do is make the best of it. Behave yourself, get yourself out of this block, and start moving through the system."

He nodded, and I moved on to complete my rounds.

During the next few days the fellow seemed to take a liking to me. Once or twice an evening I'd pause by his cell and we'd smoke a cigarette while exchanging pleasantries. I sensed he was a young man who just might straighten himself out. I guess he saw me as a breath of sanity amidst all the animals he lived with.

Then suddenly his attitude changed. One night as I made my rounds I spotted the young man lying on his bunk still awake. I paused and said, "Hi."

He didn't bother to rise, just acknowledged my greeting with a wave.

I shrugged and moved on, figuring he either wasn't feeling well or we would talk later.

He remained in his bunk all that night, not acknowledging me further. The next evening I again found him awake on my first trip, but again received nothing more than a wave. When this happened a third night, I suspected what had happened and asked him outright.

"Did they tell you not to talk to me?"

"Yeah," he replied, shrugging apologetically.

"Don't worry about it," I told him. "I understand."

I didn't want to get him in trouble. Mancuso was making a point, showing me he still had control over this block. So for the next few days I purposely ignored the young man, doing nothing more than exchanging nods.

Then one evening he was waiting at the bars again.

"You got a light?" he asked.

"Sure," I replied, pulling out my lighter.

"Man, I don't like being told who I can talk to."

"One of the realities of this place is that people will try to control you. Be careful and don't take their orders lightly."

"Hey, I'll talk to who I want."

We ended up talking five minutes or so.

I should have known better and moved on after a few words. But I no longer viewed myself as an important person at the prison. The inmates knew I would soon be leaving. I had no power to disrupt their kingdoms. I was serving out my time much like they were serving theirs. But inmates have long memories and short fuses.

I was relaxing at home the next day when I heard a minor news item on the radio. An inmate had been murdered at Walpole. It took me a moment to place the name. Then I realized the victim was the young man I had befriended.

The rest of the day I felt sick. Upon reaching the prison that evening I read the officer's report. It said that the murder had taken place in the gymnasium. The young man was playing basketball with other inmates when suddenly a circle formed around him. Another inmate, this one carrying a broomstick sharpened into a spear, stepped abruptly into the ring. Before officers could intervene, he plunged the spearpoint several times into the young man's abdomen, ripping open a gaping hole that no physician could repair in time to save his life.

The murder was committed by an inmate who had only two weeks left on his sentence. I knew immediately that he had acted upon orders. The young inmate hadn't been around long enough to make serious enemies. Only one man in Block Two could give such orders.

Upon reaching the block I went directly to the cell of Connie Mancuso. When he saw me he came forward to the door.

"Why'd you have that kid killed, Connie?" I accused. "He wasn't bothering anyone by talking to me. How come you can talk to me but nobody else can?"

My verbal onslaught surprised him and he stepped back, raising his hands in that familiar pose.

"Hey, Mac, I had nothing to do with it. I was here in my cell the whole time."

In that, at least, he spoke the truth. He had passed up his gym period that day. But I didn't see that as an alibi, rather as proof of his implication. All inmates, including Mancuso, looked forward to gym privileges. To voluntarily skip a gym period was highly unusual. The most likely reason for him to do so would be to avoid the scene of impending violence. As I've said before, the kingpins stayed clear of the crimes they masterminded.

"Don't give me that, Connie," I replied. "I know you had it done. You disgust me, you know that? Some day you'll get yours the same way as that kid, and I won't feel a bit sorry."

I walked away knowing that I had indeed chosen the right time to leave Walpole. It's not pleasant to realize that a moment's indiscretion has caused another man's death. Had I remained on, the episode could easily have been repeated.

17 Epilogue

Six years later I revisited Walpole for the first time. No, I did not return as a conquering hero, or even as an honored guest. I almost had to sneak in, the inconspicuous member of a tour I had barely managed to arrange for my two co-authors.

Had it not been for this book I might never have visited the prison again. Trying to reenter the field of corrections after losing my bid to be elected sheriff, I found every door securely locked.

Even Hogan, who had promised to aid my effort to return, refused to see me. Since the field of corrections is tightly knit throughout the country, my prospects for a management job anywhere was bleak. And I had promised myself that I would never again work as a guard.

I admit feeling bitter about the situation, especially considering Hogan's promise. But I won't deny that he kept his word in regard to implementing positive changes at Walpole. Whatever kept him from aiding me must have concerned my personality, not my penal philosophy, for he had set in motion virtually every program I had outlined.

Hogan only remained Commissioner for little over a year before being appointed by Governor King as Secretary of Human Services. The Commissioner's job then went to Mike Fair, an appointment that deteriorated my career prospects even further.

Fair, of course, had once been a protege of Frank Hall. Two years later Dukakis recaptured the governorship, obliterating any hope I had of pursuing a corrections career, certainly in Massachusetts.

And so, during those intervening years corrections and Walpole drifted off into the distance. Then the chance came to tell my story.

The morning of our Walpole tour I felt many of the old anxieties returning. A high-ranking law enforcement friend of mine had arranged the tour for us. I suspect he did so without the knowledge of officials within the Department of Corrections. I felt sure that if they got wind of my coming they would either cancel the tour for all three of us, or keep me outside.

At the same time I feared how I might be received by both guards and inmates. I had lost contact with the guards. Some who still worked there resented it when I left. I didn't want any confrontations, either with them or with inmates who knew me.

Naturally I thought back to my final months as a guard and all the inmate hostility directed towards me. No one could guarantee that one sight of me wouldn't trigger an attack or violent demonstration by them. After six years away from the mayhem a sudden paranoia swept me.

The thought of being taken hostage crossed my mind. Before leaving I even warned my second wife, Claudia, to listen to the noon news to see if any disturbance had occurred at Walpole. Mercifully, I didn't inform my co-authors of my fears until later.

After my first few days as an officer I made it a rule never to enter Walpole without my "guard's face" on. Now as I drove, I found myself tempted to initiate the psyching up process again. The familiar rolling rural countryside brought back many memories of other drives up this same road, when matters of life and death had occupied my mind. My anxiety reached full intensity as I rounded the final curve and started ascending "The Hill."

The prison has been renamed Massachusetts Correctional Institute Cedar Junction, a feeble attempt to distance it from its bloody history; people still vividly remember the past and call it Walpole. After turning into the lot and parking my car I instructed my companions as to what they could take inside—that is, nothing. I then led them up the small flight of stairs into the administration building. I paused just inside at the sight of officers standing everywhere.

Fortune had brought us to the prison at the same time a class of officer trainees from the Academy were also to receive a tour. Conspicuous among these uniformed young people were several women, some of relatively small size.

Immediately I recognized the officer at the control room window as an old-timer who had clashed with me several times when he'd served on my initial E-Board. Right then and there I figured attention would be drawn to my presence and our tour would be canceled. I knew our names had already been given to the Superintendent's office. Perhaps the manager in charge had already given instructions to deny us entrance.

To my surprise these anxieties proved groundless. The officer greeted me politely, if not warmly. He allowed us to sign in, took our identification, and then called in for an escort. Even then I still expected that at any moment someone in authority would appear, point at me, and say, "You, out!"

Instead, a few minutes later a petite, attractive young lady, who looked businesslike in her modest pants suit, emerged from the outer trap and introduced herself as our guide. We learned that she served as an inmate counselor. Her relaxed cordiality told me that she had not been told who I was.

Thinking back to my days as an officer when I couldn't guarantee my own safety inside, I felt doubtful about being placed in the care of this vulnerable looking young woman. If the inmates did decide to act up, we grown men would have our hands full defending ourselves. She would be defenseless.

My fears were somewhat allayed when we entered the prison directly behind the Academy group. Inexperienced or not, a group of some thirty uniformed officers presented a formidable sight inside Walpole. Once pat-searched and allowed through the trap, I found that our guide's voice had slipped into the background. My eyes wandered the setting with that same old heightened awareness, watching for potential danger. This intensified as we passed through the inner trap into the main corridor.

What immediately struck me was the cleanliness of the facility and the increased number of officers on duty. We had barely started walking toward the Max-section when I began running into old comrades. All of them greeted me warmly, some even asking enthusiastically if I was coming back. One wore a bandage on his cheek, having just that morning been injured breaking up an inmate fist fight. Some things would never change.

The warm reception gratified me. It had always been hard for me to accept the ill feelings borne by a few officers after my resignation. I'd felt like an outcast from my own family. Now I finally felt vindicated, both by what I saw and by how I was received.

Some of the tension left, but I could never feel totally at ease in Walpole. For forty-five minutes we toured the facility in the wake of the Academy group. Our guide was not allowed to take us into Block Ten, but we were allowed access with the trainees into Block Nine, where I had faced DiLauro.

I learned that Peter was still in Walpole. The years had gradually worn him down to where he'd modified his behavior considerably. Whereas before, everyone had treaded lightly around him, now he often was the victim of officer harassment. Once the newer guards learned of his reputation from the old days, they tended to be tougher on him than on the other inmates.

As I continued the tour, other inmate faces came to mind. Lyle Kramer had gained his freedom just a short time before, after serving an additional year for trying to escape during a retrial that ultimately struck down his second sentence and freed him. Johnny Regalado had spent time out of state as part of the inter-state transfer program. He had now returned to Massachusetts and was assigned to a halfway house in preparation for his release.

Then there was Connie Mancuso. He too had been shipped out of state for an extended period. He'd only recently returned to Walpole to find his kingdom controlled by others. Powerless, his reputation had suddenly become a millstone.

In his case, he had more to fear from fellow inmates than officers. The new kingpins didn't feel comfortable with him around. The young toughs, always looking for ways to build their reputations, saw him as fair game. And older inmates he'd bullied now had the chance to take him on one-on-one.

More than anyone, Mancuso recognized the precarious position he occupied, because he had been one of those who had set the ground rules. Now he had become vulnerable to them. Every moment he had to tread cautiously and watch his back. I didn't feel sorry. I only remembered that if he'd been shipped out of state two years sooner at least one more inmate would still be alive.

Fortunately during the tour we didn't run into anyone who wanted to cause trouble. The Minimum inmates had been at work call; the Max-inmates were not in a position to see me. I did not see everything I would've liked, but enough to convince me that progress had indeed been made.

When we exited out past the visiting room we paused on the sidewalk by the lawn to chat. Today no amorous activities were taking place. Instead, two inmates were working on hands and knees in the bordering flower beds.

I immediately recognized one and I went on full alert. O'Dea, the inmate who had threatened to "kill a screw" after the Block Ten shakedown, was now daintily packing dirt around newly planted shrubs. I had little doubt that six years ago he would have tried to use his garden trowel on me.

O'Dea looked older, tired, out of shape, and probably less inclined to chew glass as he had so often boasted of doing. I'm sure he recognized me, but I quickly saw that he had no desire to cause trouble. Eventually the weight of dreary years passed behind bars broke down the worst of them. Whether it would ever be safe to return them to society is another question.

One cannot get a true picture of a prison during a short tour, but I came away from Walpole that day generally impressed. The place looked cleaner, better maintained, and certainly better manned. I did have doubts concerning the number of women officers working the exclusively men's facility.

I wondered how management could justify female block officers patrolling living quarters and being in a position to observe male inmates undressed or responding to the call of nature. Or how they could expect females to subdue male rioters.

But even these questions weighed little against the improvements I saw. I drove home feeling fulfilled, knowing that, mostly through my efforts, Walpole had finally gotten clean.

Then, three days later I took one of my co-authors to meet with a veteran officer of the prison who had been close at my side during my efforts to gain reform. He told a sobering story of a prison on the slide.

Yes, conditions were much better than they had been at the time I took over the presidency. But they had deteriorated from the even higher level of a few years prior. A permissive policy had again begun to take hold.

A few years back the union had allowed management to abolish the safety committee. The Block Ten agreement had all but been torn up. Ten's inmates again were being allowed extensive personal possessions. Even the screens that had remained in place to separate inmates from visitors in the Block Ten visiting rooms had been taken down. Now, once again, no physical obstacles existed to prevent the contact visits that brought so many drugs inside.

The officer claimed conditions in Block Ten approached those that had put us on strike seven years before. The only thing preventing numerous injuries was the increased number of officers working the block.

One new major problem had sprung up since I'd worked at the prison. Officers always faced being spit on, bit, scratched, and hit with urine and feces. Now they faced the additional anxiety of knowing that a large number of inmates are AIDS-infected. Any wound inflicted by these inmates could eventually prove fatal. Any body fluids accidentally entering open wounds carried the same threat.

My friend emphasized that today the serious problems existing inside are effectively hidden from the public. The administration strictly enforces the gag order that threatens officers with suspension and/or termination should they talk to the press about what occurs inside. The union no longer has a president willing to defy administration's threats and report everything to the news media.

Barely six weeks after our discussion, a state police officer chased a new Corvette at high speed for several miles down the busy Route 93 Interstate. When he finally pulled it over, he found two men inside, babysitting an uncut kilogram of cocaine. Subsequent investigation triggered a series of arrests connected to a $1 million-a-year drug ring centered inside of Walpole Prison! The ring involved the financing of rental cars and apartments, not to mention paid salaries, to outside accomplices masterminded from inside the prison.

District Attorney Delahunt and Walpole Superintendent Mike Maloney then held their news conference to praise their investigation and claim that the million-dollar-a-day drug ring had been busted.

The media event made a big splash in the papers at the time, but, two years later, the public had still heard nothing of the progress in the case. Were indictments handed down? Did inmates face more time added to their sentences? Were the outsiders punished? Prosecuted? Sentenced?

On April 14, 1988 the public finally learned about the deteriorating conditions in Walpole (Cedar Junction). A violent uprising on Block Ten forced Commissioner Mike Fair to send the prison tactical team inside to restore order. When reporters were given access to Ten, the inmates barraged them with claims of being beaten and gassed. Fair counter-charged that for months inmates in Ten had been uncontrollable, starting fires with toilet paper, acting "aggressively" toward officers and beating up on each other. Finally, he'd had enough.

"I will not tolerate inmates throwing urine and feces on officers in the block," he told the press.

I wish I'd heard that when I worked there.

For three days, officers used tear gas to restore order. They shook down the cells and found guns, knives and other weapons, hidden containers of urine and feces, and other contraband. My friend's description of what was really going on at Walpole had been authenticated.

I applaud Commissioner Fair for his quick action in putting down the disturbance. But how could he allow Block Ten—his personal responsibility—to slip back so badly? What happened to the Block Ten agreement we had hammered out with him and his superiors in 1979? Had it been strictly adhered to, the inmates would not have had access to materials from which to make so many weapons. The conditions leading to the disturbance and crackdown would never have occurred. We proved that in 1979–80.

What does all this tell us? The fact that Walpole had cleaned up its act during the early 1980's indicates that the proper tools did indeed exist all along. The problems were not insurmountable. The measures necessary were not complicated or prohibitively expensive.

It was not necessary to "tear the place down" as some had suggested. The problems at Walpole occurred because of laissez-faire philosophy, headstrong attitudes, lack of dedication, and the absence of managerial skill. They flourished under certain individuals, disappeared under others, and now again begin to rear their ugly heads.

We as citizens have a right to demand more out of our prisons. We should not face violence spilling out upon us from inside. Neither should we ask those who work inside to tolerate their violence. "What do you expect, this is the Big House?" does not qualify as a reasonable excuse for what occurs under lax administgration.

If we are to feel reasonably safe from those we incarcerate then we must be careful whom we elect, monitor whom they appoint, and demand an accounting of what goes on inside the walls.

We can't just say, "Lock them up and throw away the key." All but two percent of those we put away eventually return to walk among us. If we don't take more interest in seeing them dealt with constructively on the inside, we will pay for our indifference when they get out. Far too often that payment will be made by a check signed in our blood.